Crossing Borders,
Writing Texts,
Being Evaluated

NEW PERSPECTIVES ON LANGUAGE AND EDUCATION

Founding Editor: Viv Edwards, *University of Reading, UK*
Series Editors: Phan Le Ha, *University of Hawaii at Manoa, USA* and Joel Windle, *Monash University, Australia.*

Two decades of research and development in language and literacy education have yielded a broad, multidisciplinary focus. Yet education systems face constant economic and technological change, with attendant issues of identity and power, community and culture. What are the implications for language education of new 'semiotic economies' and communications technologies? Of complex blendings of cultural and linguistic diversity in communities and institutions? Of new cultural, regional and national identities and practices? The New Perspectives on Language and Education series will feature critical and interpretive, disciplinary and multidisciplinary perspectives on teaching and learning, language and literacy in new times. New proposals, particularly for edited volumes, are expected to acknowledge and include perspectives from the Global South. Contributions from scholars from the Global South will be particularly sought out and welcomed, as well as those from marginalized communities within the Global North.

All books in this series are externally peer-reviewed.

Full details of all the books in this series and of all our other publications can be found on http://www.multilingual-matters.com, or by writing to Multilingual Matters, St Nicholas House, 31-34 High Street, Bristol BS1 2AW, UK.

NEW PERSPECTIVES ON LANGUAGE AND EDUCATION: 97

Crossing Borders, Writing Texts, Being Evaluated

Cultural and Disciplinary Norms in Academic Writing

Edited by
Anne Golden, Lars Anders Kulbrandstad and Lawrence Jun Zhang

MULTILINGUAL MATTERS
Bristol • Jackson

DOI https://doi.org/10.21832/GOLDEN8564
Library of Congress Cataloging in Publication Data
A catalog record for this book is available from the Library of Congress.
Names: Golden, Anne, editor. | Kulbrandstad, Lars Anders, editor. | Zhang,
  Lawrence Jun, editor. | Sociolinguistics Symposium (22th: 2018:
  Auckland, New Zealand)
Title: Crossing Borders, Writing Texts, Being Evaluated: Cultural and
  Disciplinary Norms in Academic Writing/Edited by Anne Golden, Lars
  Anders Kulbrandstad and Lawrence Jun Zhang.
Description: Bristol; Blue Ridge Summit: Multilingual Matters, [2021] |
  Series: New Perspectives on Language and Education: 97 | Four of the
  chapters were presented as papers at the 22nd Sociolinguistics Symposium
  in June 2018 hosted at The University of Auckland, New Zealand. |
  Includes bibliographical references and index. | Summary: 'This book
  examines both writing norms and assessment, and proficiency development,
  and suggests that scholars need to critically examine testing regimes
  and develop research-based perspectives on tests and testing practices,
  so that educational institutions can prepare learners with differing
  cultural experiences for tests and assessments' – Provided by publisher.
  Identifiers: LCCN 2021039788 (print) | LCCN 2021039789 (ebook) | ISBN
  9781788928557 (paperback) | ISBN 9781788928564 (hardback) | ISBN
  9781788928571 (pdf) | ISBN 9781788928588 (epub)
Subjects: LCSH: Academic writing – Study and teaching – Congresses. | English
  language – Rhetoric – Study and teaching – Foreign speakers – Congresses. |
  LCGFT: Essays. | Conference papers and proceedings.
Classification: LCC P301.5.A27 C77 2022 (print) | LCC P301.5.A27 (ebook)
  | DDC 808.06/6378 – dc23/eng/20211104
LC record available at https://lccn.loc.gov/2021039788
LC ebook record available at https://lccn.loc.gov/2021039789

British Library Cataloguing in Publication Data
A catalogue entry for this book is available from the British Library.

ISBN-13: 978-1-78892-856-4 (hbk)
ISBN-13: 978-1-78892-855-7 (pbk)

Multilingual Matters
UK: St Nicholas House, 31-34 High Street, Bristol BS1 2AW, UK.
USA: Ingram, Jackson, TN, USA.

Website: www.multilingual-matters.com
Twitter: Multi_Ling_Mat
Facebook: https://www.facebook.com/multilingualmatters
Blog: www.channelviewpublications.wordpress.com

The policy of Multilingual Matters/Channel View Publications is to use papers that are
natural, renewable and recyclable products, made from wood grown in sustainable forests.
In the manufacturing process of our books, and to further support our policy, preference
is given to printers that have FSC and PEFC Chain of Custody certification. The FSC and/
or PEFC logos will appear on those books where full certification has been granted to the
printer concerned.

Typeset by Riverside Publishing Solutions.

Contents

Acknowledgements   vii

Contributors   ix

Preface   xiii

1 Crossing Borders   1
   Anne Golden and Lars Anders Kulbrandstad

2 When Errors Are Corrected   18
   Anne Golden and Lars Anders Kulbrandstad

3 Writing Academically in English as a Second Language:
   The Case of Syntactic Constructions   38
   Rosmawati

4 Writing in School Science for EAL Students: Linguistic
   Challenges and Pedagogical Response   64
   Zhihui Fang and Guofang Li

5 Supporting EAL Writing Development in the Early Stages of
   the Doctorate: Candidates from the East Writing in the West   84
   Morena Botelho de Magalhães

6 Agency in L2 Academic Literacies: Immigrant Students' Lived
   Experiences in Focus   107
   Kirsi Leskinen

7 Constructing Persuasion: A Cross-cultural Comparison of
   Chinese and English Student Writings   131
   Jihua Dong

8 Crossing Literacy Borders through Writing:
   Transformational Apprenticeship and Repositioning
   of EAL Learners   147
   Lawrence Jun Zhang

Index   165

Acknowledgements

The editors and publishers are indebted to the anonymous reviewers who have spent time in reviewing the book proposal and the whole completed book manuscript. The editors are particularly grateful to the 16 scholars who reviewed the individual manuscripts submitted for consideration for inclusion in this collection. Their reviews have helped the authors to improve the quality of the chapters.

Contributors

Anne Golden is Professor Emeritus of Norwegian as a Second Language at MultiLing, University of Oslo and was the research leader for theme *Multilingual competence* 2013–19. Her research focuses on various aspects of literacy in a second language, with an emphasis on vocabulary, in particular metaphors. She has been studying learners' comprehension and practice, and has used corpus methods for studying cross-linguistic influences in learners' texts. Identity negotiations among migrants are also part of her research with narratives and metaphors as research tools. Most recently, she has co-edited and contributed to *Reconceptualizing Connections between Language, Literacy and Learning* (2019) and *Crosslinguistic Influence and Distinctive Patterns of Language Learning: Findings and Insights from a Learner Corpus* (2017).

Lars Anders Kulbrandstad is Professor Emeritus of Norwegian Language from a Didactic Perspective at Inland Norway University of Applied Sciences and Senior Professor of Swedish as a Second Language at Karlstad University, Sweden. His main research interests are multilingualism, second language acquisition and language attitudes both in Norwegian and English and he has published a number of articles and books on these topics. Most recently, he has co-edited and contributed to the two volumes, *Norwegian Perspectives on Education and Cultural Diversity* (2018) and *Learning Spaces for Inclusion and Social Justice* (2018). Professor Kulbrandstad has been leader or co-leader of several national or Nordic research projects.

Lawrence Jun Zhang, PhD, is Professor of Linguistics-in-Education and Associate Dean, Faculty of Education and Social Work, University of Auckland, New Zealand. His major interests and 100-plus publications are on learner metacognition, language-teacher education, and L2 reading-writing development, which appear in various journals, including *Applied Linguistics*, *MLJ*, *TESOL Quarterly*, *JEAP*, *Discourse Processes*, *Reading and Writing*, *Language Teaching Research*. He is co-editor for *System* and serves on the editorial boards for *Applied Linguistics Review*, *Australian Review of Applied Linguistics*, *Journal of Second Language Writing*, *Metacognition and Learning* and *RELC*

Journal. He was honoured by TESOL International Association in 2016 with the award of '50@50', acknowledging '50 Outstanding Leaders' and was officially installed as a newly elected member of the Board of Directors of the Association in 2017.

Jihua Dong (PhD, University of Auckland) is Professor, 'Qilu Young Scholar', and 'Taishan Young Scholar' in the School of Foreign Languages and Literature at Shandong University, China. Her research interests include corpus linguistics, corpus-based teaching, academic writing, and discourse analysis. She has previously published in *English for Specific Purposes*, *International Journal of Corpus Linguistics*, *Journal of English for Academic Purposes* and *System*, among others.

Zhihui Fang (PhD Purdue University) is currently the Irving & Rose Fien Endowed Professor of Education in the School of Teaching and Learning at the University of Florida, USA. He has published widely in the areas of language and literacy education, English teacher education, and functional linguistics in education. His latest books include *Demystifying Academic Writing: Genres, Moves, Skills, and Strategies* (2021) and *Using Functional Grammar in English Literacy Teaching and Learning* (2021).

Guofang Li, PhD, is a Professor and Tier 1 Canada Research Chair in Transnational/Global Perspectives of Language and Literacy Education of Children and Youth in the Department of Language and Literacy Education, University of British Columbia, Canada. Her program of research focuses on bilingualism and biliteracy development, pre- and in-service TESOL teacher education, and current language and educational policies and practices in globalized contexts. Her recent books include *Superdiversity and Teacher Education* (2021), *Languages, Identities, Power and Cross-Cultural Pedagogies in Transnational Literacy Education* (2019) and *Educating Chinese-heritage Students in the Global-Local Nexus: Identities, Challenges, and Opportunities* (2017). Li is co-editor of *Journal of Literacy Research* and serves as an editorial board member and reviewer of many key SSCI language and literacy journals.

Kirsi Leskinen is a doctoral researcher in the Department of Language and Communication Studies at the University of Jyväskylä, Finland. Her doctoral study focuses on academic literacies and Finnish language development of immigrant students. She is also a teacher of Finnish as a second language and she has taught Finnish in vocational education and in university language classes in Finland and Minnesota, USA. Leskinen is a member of the research team *Building Blocks: Developing second language resources for working life.*

Morena Botelho de Magalhães, PhD, manages the Diagnostic English Language Needs Assessment (DELNA) programme at the University of Auckland, New Zealand, having previously taught ESOL in Brazil and in New Zealand. Botelho de Magalhães' PhD research focused on the language learning and identity experiences of a group of EAL doctoral candidates. Her co-authored article on identity, voice and agency in EAL doctoral writing was recently published in the *Journal of Second Language Writing*. She currently serves on the executive committee of the Association for Language Testing and Assessment of Australia and New Zealand (ALTAANZ) as its Co-President.

Rosmawati is a postdoctoral researcher at the University of Sydney, Australia. Her main research areas include the application of Complex Dynamic Systems Theory (CDST) in second language acquisition and development, academic writing in English, and teaching English to speakers of other languages (TESOL). Her most recent research focuses on the construct of syntactic complexity in academic writing and she has recently contributed to an edited volume on *CDST and L2 Writing Development* (2020).

Preface

Time really flies, as the saying goes! We did not realise that it was around three years ago that a group of scholars met in a colloquium organised by Professors Anne Golden and Lars Anders Kulbrandstad from Norway for the 22nd Sociolinguistics Symposium (SS22) hosted in June 2018 at the University of Auckland, New Zealand. It was during this colloquium that like-minded people presented their work and started a conversation. I was fortunate to be the commentator or discussant. The original colloquium was titled 'Crossing Borders, Writing Texts, Being Evaluated: Students with Text Norms from the East and South Writing in the West and North'. In fact, the first encounters happened at the 14th Symposium on Second Language Writing (SSLW 2015) in Auckland 2015, when Professor Anne Golden met Dr Jihua Dong. They were both interested in L2 writing. Then, at the 2017 meeting of the American Association for Applied Linguistics (AAAL 2017) in Portland, USA, they met again. Professor Lars Anders Kulbrandstad was also present. The two Norwegian professors had collaborated for several years and they came up with the idea of organising a colloquium for SS22, which readily materialised. Five papers were presented in this colloquium in 2018 and the presenters were invited after the colloquium to contribute full chapters to this volume. A call for chapters was also distributed to many e-serv lists or contacts soon afterwards. Upon selection by the three editors, seven chapters survived the reviews, four of which were from the participants in the SS22 colloquium, with the other three contributions coming from colleagues who were not part of the original colloquium.

Readers with sharp eyes will see that the theme of the colloquium is maintained in this volume. They will also find a noticeable feature: namely, that the seven chapters are from contributors situated around the world, showing a good geographical representation, which serves the purpose of our book well – *Crossing Borders, Writing Texts, Being Evaluated*. The purpose of such a conceptualisation is to highlight the significance of writing and its evaluation in academic settings (Golden *et al.*, 2017), which includes, but not exclusively, crossing literacy borders from the global East to the global West, or across Europe.

In this volume, we are very happy to have, in alphabetical order, Dr Morena Botelho de Magalhães (University of Auckland, New Zealand),

Professor Jihua Dong (Shandong University, China), Professor Zhihui Fang (University of Florida, USA), Professor Anne Golden (University of Oslo, Norway), Professor Lars Anders Kulbrandstad (Inland Norway University of Applied Sciences, Norway), doctoral researcher Kirsi Leskinen (University of Jyväskylä, Finland), Professor Guofang Li (University of British Columbia, Canada), Dr Rosmawati (University of Sydney, Australia), and Professor Lawrence Jun Zhang (University of Auckland, New Zealand). Our open call for chapters did not produce anything from Africa, unfortunately, and we feel it a pity that there is a lack of representation of the African continent in our book. This needs to be made clear here.

Given that writing in another language, especially in an academic genre, is daunting, a fact that is well acknowledged by many scholars in the field (Fang, 2021; Hyland, 2000; Xu & Zhang, 2019), and that the learning to write and writing to learn processes are inseparable from each other (Golden et al., 2017; Zhang, 2013), it is our hope that the key issues in relation to crossing literacy borders in disciplinary writing, or any closely allied field, have been addressed in our book relatively successfully. Of necessity, crossing literacy borders from the global East to the global West, or even from the global South to the global North, poses challenges to many students and to the teachers who teach them as their daily routinised tasks (Zhang, 2016). To say the least, even the use of hedging and boosting devices distinguishes one group of writers from another (see, for example, Chen & Zhang, 2017; Hyland, 2018); therefore, our attempt to put together these chapters in a single volume has really been an attempt to create and strengthen linkages between/among different languages and literacy traditions in academic writing. As Qi and Zhang's (2015) review shows, traditional contrastive rhetoric and its latest development in the field – cross-cultural rhetoric – point to the value of taking stock of learners' funds of knowledge for a common good: to enhance their performance in academic writing by resorting to their knowledge base (Wei et al., 2020). Part of our effort is to bring this focus to the fore so that readers will be well anchored to go deeper into the chapters as a literacy adventure in itself so that those issues that we have not been able to give any systematic treatment to can be further explored in future studies or in another volume of this kind. Together with Professors Anne Golden and Lars Anders Kulbrandstad, I sincerely hope that our readers will be as candid as we have been and share their experiences with us when they read these chapters presented in this volume.

Lawrence Jun Zhang
University of Auckland, New Zealand

References

Chen, C. and Zhang, L.J. (2017) An intercultural analysis of the use of hedging by Chinese and Anglophone academic English writers. *Applied Linguistics Review* 8 (1), 1–34.

Fang, Z.H. (2021) *Demystifying Academic Writing: Genres, Moves, Skills, and Strategies.* Abingdon: Routledge.

Golden, A., Jarvis, S. and Tenfjord, K. (eds) (2017) *Crosslinguistic Influence and Distinctive Patterns of Language Learning: Findings and Insights from a Learner Corpus.* Bristol: Multilingual Matters.

Hyland, K. (2000) *Disciplinary Discourses: Social Interactions in Academic Writing.* London: Longman.

Hyland, K. (2018) *Metadiscourse: Exploring Interaction in Writing.* London: Bloomsbury Publishing.

Qi, F. and Zhang, L.J. (2015) A critical review of 40 years of contrastive rhetoric studies into L2 learners' written discourse overseas and in China. *Foreign Languages in China* 12 (6), 48–57.

Wei, X., Zhang, L.J. and Zhang, W.X. (2020) Associations of L1-to-L2 rhetorical transfer with L2 writers' perception of L2 writing difficulty and L2 writing proficiency. *Journal of English for Academic Purposes* 41 (100907), 1–14.

Xu, L.L. and Zhang, L.J. (2019) L2 doctoral students' experiences in thesis writing in an English-medium university in New Zealand. *Journal of English for Academic Purposes* 41 (100779), 1–13.

Zhang, L.J. (2013) Second language writing *as* and *for* second language learning. *Journal of Second Language Writing* 22 (4), 446–447.

Zhang, L.J. (2016) Reflections on the pedagogical imports of western practices for professionalizing ESL/EFL writing and writing-teacher education. *Australian Review of Applied Linguistics* 39 (3), 203–232.

1 Crossing Borders

Anne Golden
MultiLing, University of Oslo, Norway

Lars Anders Kulbrandstad
Inland Norway University of Applied Sciences and Karlstad University, Sweden

Gatekeeping

Crossing borders between countries is no longer an experience for the few. An ever-increasing number of people not only traverse borders but also have to engage in literacy activities in a new culture and in a new setting. They may be applicants trying to be accepted to an educational program, students passing exams to get their degrees, or refugees trying to settle in a new country with the possibility of working and participating in the new community and maybe obtaining residence or citizenship. The extent of testing is paramount and the requirements might seem overwhelming for some. In some cases, the real function of the tests seems to be to serve as tools for stifling immigration or upholding privileges for the majority population and not primarily to assess language skills (Khan, 2020; Tracy, 2017).

In European countries, language testing is mainly based on the Common European Framework of Reference for Languages (CEFR) in the official language of the country and there are often requirements for English as well. In English-speaking countries, the requirements in English are usually a certain score on the Test of English as a Foreign Language (TOEFL) or the International English Language Testing System (IELTS), or proficiency has to be proven in other ways depending on the specific institution. Even if these tests are mainly developed by national or international bodies (like the Council of Europe for CEFR) or by private non-profit organizations (like Educational Testing Service ATS for TOEFL), there are fees to be paid and often practical obstacles to overcome and, hence, accessibility is unevenly distributed around the world. In addition, not everybody who *is* able to take a test succeeds. Different levels are required for different purposes, and although the levels are intended to be more or less universal, they have been strongly criticized (e.g. Alderson, 2007) and accused of being biased and unfit for certain groups and certain purposes – for example, admitting citizenship (Bhambra, 2015; Fortier, 2018; McNamara & Ryan, 2011). Test takers have diverse backgrounds and varying life experiences, so giving the same test and using an equal grading system for all, as with standardized tests, does not guarantee fairness. Some of the tests have been found to be Eurocentric, presupposing a Western way of life and having a monolingual bias (Mirhosseini & De Costa, 2020). For students who want to enter university, there are particular obstacles with testing. They might be inexperienced with the specific academic context asked for in the test or not be acquainted with the writing conventions of the new discipline they are entering. Hence, both inside and outside academia, the tests serve as gatekeepers (Shohamy, 1998) to a new life. For some, the failure seems to stem from some additional boundaries, e.g. special writing norms in the new community or settings that are not always easy to detect or explain. Meeting these norms often implies greater difficulties for some groups of students than others and this is not least connected to differences in social, cultural and educational background (Olshtain *et al.*, 1990; Zawacki & Cox, 2014). Teachers and raters often lack awareness of the effects of such differences.

Scholarly work needs to address this situation on two fronts. On one front, scholars should critically examine testing regimes and raise public awareness about the hidden agendas and social injustice implicit in language tests. On the other front, scholars should also develop research-based knowledge about tests and testing practices, including concealed or unconscious norms as well as raters' bias, so that institutions of adult education, schools and universities can better prepare learners for the tests they are required to take.

Cultures: Different Categorizations and Definitions

In anthropology, sociology and other research areas, a series of labels has been used to categorize societies and cultures based on observed differences in areas like technological development, modes of communication, belief systems and interpersonal relationships. Often the epithets form dichotomous pairs, such as Traditional versus Modern, Non-complex versus Complex, Closed versus Open, Oral versus Literate (see, for example, Deliège, 2001; Freeman & Winch, 1957; Hvitfeldt, 1986). In the present volume, we have employed the categorization South/East versus North/West, which in spite of the geographical terminology is meant to mark significant differences in educational experience, as writing is the object of the investigations reported in this book. Our point of departure is inspired by the extended notion of cross-linguistic influence (Jarvis, 2017), experientialism in the cognitive framework (Lakoff, 1993; Lakoff & Johnson, 1980) and the labels Global South/Global North in post-colonial studies (e.g. Kerfoot & Hyltenstam, 2017; Pennycook & Makoni, 2019).

There is a plethora of definitions of the concept 'culture'. One of the simplest attempts to pinpoint the essence of the phenomenon has been circulating in the academic literature for some time, and in our view it is a fitting attempt to the present context. It reads as follows: culture is the way we are doing things around here (e.g. Grissinger, 2014; Martin, 2006; Schulz, 2001; Van Lier, 2004).[1] Here, culture is identified with the way in which it is spelt out in practice, in the common habitual manner in which people go about carrying out their doings. Some of these procedures are openly talked about and described; most of them are, however, only enacted upon, and thus not made explicit. For persons who need to learn how to master a new culture – both the overt and the implied ways of doing things – this endeavor might be challenging, and the tacit ones are most often the hardest to acquire (Hinkel, 2011).

The concept 'national culture' is much debated, one of the main arguments being that the purported cultural uniformity within the nation is essentialist and flawed. Nonetheless, the concept is frequently used in areas like cultural studies (see, for example, Easthorpe, 1999; Hartley, 2002) and intercultural communication (Baldwin *et al.*, 2014; Bjørge, 2007; Mehra, 2014). Geert Hofstede (1991, 2001; Hofstede *et al.*, 2005) has developed a 6-dimensional model of national cultures, which, for instance, includes an Individualism vs. Collectivism dimension and an Uncertainty or Avoidance dimension. The model has met considerable criticism, i.e. for neglecting the international variety in cultural values and for holding a deterministic view of culture (McSweeney, 2002; Taras & Steel, 2009). Nonetheless, it is extensively applied in empirical research, as well as in studies of cultural differences in language teaching and assessment (Breton, 2021; Fang *et al.*, 2013; Zhang *et al.*, 2015). Although the model may offer some insight into relevant aspects of the cultural background of second language learners, there is clearly a danger that characterizations based on tendencies found in broad national surveys will be used to explain the behavior of individual second language learners.

Contrastive and Intercultural Rhetoric

There is a rather long tradition of research, under the name of 'contrastive rhetoric', into the cultural differences in how academic texts are written (Connor, 1996; Connor & Kaplan, 1987; Hinkel, 2002; Kaplan, 1966). In a study of paragraph structure in 600 L2 English essays, Kaplan (1966) identified different types of paragraph development, e.g. coordinate, digressive and circular, and linked each type to a specific linguistic and cultural background of the writer and the preferred rhetorical conventions in the culture. In the same vein, researchers have found L1 influence on argumentative patterns (Connor, 1987), indirectness devices (Hinkel, 1997), and rhetorical appeals and reasoning strategies (Kamimura & Oi, 1998). Some subsequent studies have confirmed the transfer of such rhetorical organization (e.g. González *et al.*, 2001; Wu, 2003; Yin, 1999). However, findings in other studies indicate either no significant differences in rhetorical profile between L1 and L2 writers (e.g. Hirose, 2003), or factors other than appropriate compositions practices in L1 behind such deviances. e.g. proficiency level in L2 (Kubota, 1998). Leki (1997) notes, for instance, that many of the rhetorical and stylistic patterns that are claimed to be typical of Chinese, Japanese and Thai writing also appear in English in certain contexts. Lillis (2014: 67–68) characterizes Kaplan's typology of paragraph development as '(in)famous "doodles"' and maintains that claims about rhetorical features of text (and culture and language) are 'based on assumptions about contentions and expectations that do not in fact map onto descriptions of actual usage and practice'. Similar critical views on traditional contrastive rhetoric are found in Kubota and Lehner (2004), claiming:

> [a] fixed view of cultural difference that legitimates an invisible norm of the rhetoric of power in an idealized and apolitical way while debasing others does not help to cultivate a profound understanding of how culture is implicated in ever-shifting power relations, constructing and transforming the ways we engage in communication. (2004: 23)

As for rhetorical differences in academic writing, Fløttum *et al.* (2006) used a corpus-based approach in a study of person manifestation in research articles in English, French and Norwegian within the disciplines of economics, linguistics and medicine. The authors found differences between French on the one hand and English and Norwegian on the other hand, which they see as a possible effect of differences in the cultures, namely

> [...] the contrast between the Anglo-American and Scandinavian cultures relying on explicit transformation of information, and the French culture, where more implicit information coded in the context would appear to be the norm. (Fløttum *et al.*, 2006: 266)

Thus, research in contrastive rhetoric has addressed possible differences in writing norms not only between the Global East and West, and Global North and South but also within the Western world.

Writing in Different Disciplines

For students with a different L1, there are several literary borders that need to be crossed. The challenges they face are not just those of operating in a new language, but also within specific registers of that language. In academic language, there are different disciplinary field-specific writing styles, genres, and the like. As Bourdieu *et al.* (1995: 4) point out, 'academic language is [...] no one's mother tongue' and neither is the special register required in the different subjects. Hence, this is something to be acquired, or socialized into, also for students who have the specific language as their first language. The norms and expectations have to be spelled out in these areas or disciplines, which are part of what Holliday (1999) calls 'small cultures'. Several researchers, like Hyland (2002: 252), have claimed that disciplines have 'different views of knowledge, different research practices, and different ways of seeing the world'. We find these differences in a variety of ways in which the writers in the disciplines compose their text, in the ways they form their arguments and expressions (Hyland, 2000; Johns, 1997), the presence of the author, the use of certain linguistics features like nominalizations and passive, etc. So, when students enter a new field, they need to know, as Currie (1994) asks in the title of a book chapter on learning and teaching genre, 'What counts as good writing?' in order to use conventions appropriate to expectations and to be evaluated as a good student. Not only do novice scholars (cf. Chapter 5 by Botelho de Magalhães in this volume), but also younger students in schools face the problem of not knowing how or when they have to write an assignment or compose a text in the expected style, and more so in some subjects than others.

Hyland (2015) discusses the notion of genre and aligns with Swales (1990, 1998), who connects genres to the communities in which they are used or rather to 'the practices and discourses routinely used by a particular group' (Hyland, 2015: 4). The academic context is such a community and Hyland sees this as an arena where the various disciplines – with their genres – meet with the different identities of the members of the group. For an individual to become part of this community they need to find a fit between the community's rhetorical conventions or 'the ways things are done' and the persona they wish to project. To enter an academic community is hence to 'learn to communicate and to interpret each other's talk, gradually acquiring the specialized discourse competencies to participate as members' (Hyland, 2015: 33). It is also a place where 'we craft our identities, cement relationships and achieve recognition, where we find the tools and resources to live out our professional lives'. Therefore, disciplines can be seen as language-using communities that make it possible to bring writers, texts and readers together. When students start their academic careers and encounter academia with the different specialties, they first have to understand the norms that will give them access to the specific disciplines. Then they have to learn an accepted way to position themselves, to stand out as good students or researchers, and, by that, enable themselves to challenge these norms if this is called for (see, for examle, Canagarajah, 2021).

There are numerous studies of text and writing related to subjects, genres and registers with different foci (see Canagarajah, 2013; Deane & O'Neill, 2011; Hardy & Clughen, 2012, among others). In the last decade, there has also been an increase in studies in the Nordic countries, and here the spotlight has been turned to practices in primary and secondary school. After a flurry of studies examining language learners' *understanding* of different text types and genres in different school subjects, research interest has extended to students' *writing* of academic texts in school. These text studies have provided insight into the special challenges faced by language learners in various disciplines at different levels of the educational system. Many of the text studies related to subjects, genres and registers also include analyses of the vocabulary used in a school context, i.e. in textbooks, in exam papers and in student writing. These vocabulary analyses are based on previous research on the differences in vocabulary types in various subjects or disciplines, not only the technical vocabulary but also the mezzanine words, i.e. words that are not considered subject specific but have a much higher frequency in some subjects compared to others, where they are almost absent (Golden, 2018; Golden & Hvenekilde, 1983). In other contexts, however, these words belong to a more general vocabulary of a middle-to-low frequency and are often familiar to most L1 children (Lindberg, 2009). Hence, research on writing requirements in primary and secondary school has revealed the need not only for academic writing in general but also for an awareness of the writing cultures that exist in the different subjects or disciplines and the diversity of the vocabulary in these fields throughout the educational path. As Hyland (2004: 3) claims, disciplines are defined by their writing, and what distinguishes them 'is how they write rather than simply what they write [and this] makes the crucial difference between them'.

Several of the Swedish studies investigating language in different subject are based on the framework of Systemic Functional Linguistics (SFL) with the theoretical assumption that there is a strong connection between language and learning and that language development occurs in interaction (Halliday, 1993; Martin, 1999; Rothery, 1996). One example is Judy Ribeck (2015), who studied the development of texts at different levels in the educational process that forms the basis of the student learning. She compared what she calls natural science subjects (i.e. biology, physics and chemistry) with social science subjects (i.e. geography, history and social science) from two different levels, *ungdomsskolen* (i.e. junior high school) and *gymnasiet* (i.e. high school), as well as texts from the university level (humanities and social sciences) and novels (for children, youth and adults). She found that the difference between the subjects is large, both in relation to the number of technical words and to the size of the gap that appears from one level to the next in the different subjects. In the natural science subjects especially, the difference between the texts the students meet at the various levels of education is remarkable and the volume of technical vocabulary huge.

Persson (2016) has examined scientific language in different subjects by analysing grade 8 science items from TIMSS 2011 (Trends in International Mathematics and Science Study) where he used the four characteristic meaning dimensions of scientific language – *Packing*, *Precision* and *Presentation* of information, and the level of *Personification* in a text. These features have turned out to characterize science texts in earlier research as they are seen to make the information more packed and precise, with downgraded personal relationships and with information presented in more complex ways. Persson correlated the results with test performances of various student groups. He found differences in the different subjects and therefore postulated that there is *not one single* scientific language: biology shows higher Packing and lower Precision, while physics shows the opposite pattern and physics also uses more words. The science items are generally low in Personification; however, physics has higher levels, earth science lower. Chemistry often presents information in more complex ways. In addition, the students' performance is evaluated differently in the various subjects – for example, Higher Packing is positively correlated with students' results in earth science, negatively correlated in physics, and has no significant correlations in biology or chemistry. In addition, the vocabulary types differ, e.g. nominalizations are more common in biology and rare in chemistry. Persson therefore offers Swedish evidence for Hyland's claim that there is no single academic literacy but rather a variety of practices relevant to, and appropriate for, particular disciplines and purposes (Hyland, 2002: 357).

Rater Variability

Border-crossers' mastery of writing conventions in the new language is subject to both informal and formal forms of evaluation. In the latter case, their abilities are judged by raters who place the performance at a level on a given scale, in principle based upon criteria in scoring instructions. However, research clearly demonstrates that there is much variation in how the criteria are interpreted and applied by the raters (see Golden & Kulbrandstad, Chapter 2 of this volume).

In language testing there has been an increasing interest in rater bias, which Engelhard (1994: 98) defines as 'the tendency on the part of raters to consistently provide ratings that are lower or higher than is warranted by students' performances' (e.g. Brown, 1995; Lumley & McNamara, 1995; Wigglesworth, 1993). Of particular concern has been bias stemming from raters' attitudes towards emerging varieties of English (World Englishes) and English spoken and written by second language learners (Ahn, 2019; Hamp-Lyons & Xia, 2001; Heng Hartse & Kubota, 2014; Hsu, 2015, 2019; Kobayashi, 1992). There are two main stances on what norms should guide the assessment of English L2 language production (see, for example, Hamp-Lyons & Davis, 2008). The International English (IE) view recognizes only one norm, that of an educated native speaker of English. The opposing World English (WE) view holds that imposing IE on non-native speakers of English is discriminatory and, hence, maintains that 'the English language belongs to all those who use it'. Shohamy (2006) argues that not recognizing non-native varieties of English is to deny the sociolinguistic reality of English and to create a linguistic hierarchy in which test-takers' Englishes are seen as lacking legitimacy.

In an article on linguistic creativity, Rimmer (2009) points to the asymmetrical relationship between first and second language users and creativity. While native-speaker innovation is viewed as resourceful, learner innovation is considered deviant. Similar arguments are found for other languages, too (Ahlgren *et al.*, 2021). Rimmer suggests that 'the changing demography of English is both licensing and encouraging creativity in a second language context' (2009: 176).

Research findings so far indicate that the International English stance and a deficit view of second language innovation still dominate. One example is Gu and So's (2015) survey on what properties a global academic English test should include, with respondents from different groups of stakeholders: test-takers, English teachers, score users and language test professionals. The results show a general willingness to embrace diversity but reservations about accommodating differences. A majority of respondents favor the inclusion of different oral and written varieties of Standard English, but they are less positive to accents and written traits of non-Standard forms of English. The English teachers, who have rating as a routine part of their job, are open to diversifying the spoken language in the test input but tend to be opposed to incorporating non-Standard written language in the test and signal that the test-takers' performance should be assessed according to the conventions of Standard English only.

One aspect of second language academic writing that has attracted much attention has to do with textual appropriation, i.e. the incorporation of outside texts in one's own writing (Polio & Shi, 2012; Jølbo, 2015). This is an essential academic skill but at the same time a challenging one, even for experienced writers. It is often a complex task to determine 'what and who to cite, why to cite, how to cite' (Polio & Shi, 2012: 95) and the line between legitimate textual borrowing and plagiarism is not always easy to draw. There are both individual, cultural and disciplinary differences at play here. Instructors or raters may have diverging opinions as to what counts as acceptable reuse of formulations from other authors, Western cultural traditions view authorship and ownership of texts differently from, for example, traditional East Asian conceptions (Pennycook, 1996), and science and the humanities differ in the weight they put on verbal originality.

Actions to Be Taken

Over the past couple of decades, strategies for writing pedagogy in increasingly multicultural and multilingual societies have been the object of intense debate between scholars. Some criticize the traditional monolingual approach and call for a translingual reorientation; others are also critical of monolingual ideology, but still have their primary focus on ways to help learners gain writing proficiency in a second language that is required of them (Frost *et al.*, 2020; Silva & Wang, 2021). At times there seem to be irreconcilable differences between the two groups. Although this book chiefly deals with issues concerning target language writing, in our view good writing pedagogy needs to incorporate perspectives from both camps.

Among the questions we address are the following: What may be done to help more people succeed? How can we make students more accustomed to the specific academic context or feel more at ease with the writing conventions of the new discipline they are entering? How do we make test-takers produce a text that is accepted by raters in high-stakes exams and how do we raise the raters' attentions and prepare them to see value in texts written in 'an other way' than that which the raters are used to? What are the bridges that need to be built to support all learners across all the borders, and to enable teachers and raters to notice qualities that need an extra bit of attention?

First, there is a need for an awareness – like many researchers have claimed before and are claiming in this book – of *the ways things are done*, not only *here*, but also *there*, and hence, what the challenges are. This implies a need to spell out the different norms that often are hidden, and to focus on and discuss the different styles, genres etc., that are expected in different 'small cultures' (Holliday, 1999).

Paltridge reminds us that 'there is no such thing as the one-size-fits-all academic essay that can be written in all areas of study' (2004: 90). However, there are certain common characteristics that distinguish highly academic from less academic or more conversational language and that make academic language – even well-written, carefully constructed, and professionally edited academic language – difficult to comprehend and hard to produce (Snow, 2010). The teachers are the ones to model these differences. Nonetheless, it is important for the students to see that 'learning to write at university is not a process of "fixing up" language weaknesses, but of coming to use discipline specific conventions appropriately' (Hyland, 2002: 357). And for adults without much schooling who are writing a text for a test that is needed to get a much-desired job, it is important that they learn *how* to write it, and that the raters learn *how* to evaluate their writings in order not to disqualify well-qualified applicants.

Most research points to the important part played by teachers in demonstrating *the ways things are done* in different cultures and contexts and in revealing the hidden norms. But teachers have to be informed not only about differences between *here* and *there*: they also have to be aware of the ideologies behinds such decisions.

Golden and Kulbrandstad ask teachers and raters to be aware of cultural transfer. Teachers must help newcomers master the new language and the new text norms that might be different from those they are used to in their prior educational experiences. Raters must realize such differences when they assess second language writing and reflect critically upon their frequent function as gatekeepers for the host society.

Rosmawati sees the need for the L2-students to be made aware of the syntactic characteristics of academic writing in English and also advocates explicit teaching of the differences between their two languages. Her example is the syntactic constructions that should be given more consideration to help students be aware of, and gradually develop familiarity with, the norms of writing academically in English.

Fang and Li have a younger group of learners in mind and advocate a genre-based approach to teaching adolescent English as Additional Language (EAL) learners writing, as this promotes content learning and literacy development simultaneously. They also ask for collaboration between content area (e.g. science) teachers and EAL specialists.

Botelho de Magalhães sends a message to institutions and supervisors regarding doctoral candidates with English as an Additional Language: they need to expand the opportunities for the doctoral candidates to participate in various academic practices that can afford more occasions for writing development. This will contribute to their growth as writers, which in turn will enable (more) participation in disciplinary conversations amongst members of the international academic community and therefore the realization of a desired academic identity.

Leskinen reminds us that academic writing always takes place inside power hierarchies. In designing the entrance criteria mainly intended for first language speakers, therefore, more sensitivity is needed towards highly skilled immigrants' earlier experiences as well as their capacities and potential. For immigrant students, gaining agency with academic literacies is also about gaining access to the academic community.

Dong points to the appropriate linguistic devices for argumentative writing in English, in particular with regard to being able to construct conventionalized persuasion expressed in a suitable tone. This enables authors to project a tone of confidence in their argument.

Zhang asks for a total facelift among English teaching professionals as many classroom teachers seem to consider the difference between native and non-native English speakers a difference between good writers and some who do not write well.

More About the Chapters in the Book

Anne Golden and Lars Anders Kulbrandstad's chapter, 'When Errors Are Corrected', reports from a study where experienced raters have evaluated two different versions of texts written by adult learners with a Spanish or Vietnamese background to document their proficiency in Norwegian. One version is the original text produced as part of the official language test in Norwegian for immigrants and later evaluated according to the levels in the Common European Framework of Reference for Languages (CEFR). The other is a version where all orthographic, morphological and syntactic errors have been corrected as well as the wrong use of words and expressions. These texts were evaluated as 'good', 'medium' and 'weak' by a new group of raters, who also gave short comments to their ratings. Golden and Kulbrandstad analyse the comments to some texts that were considered *good* or *weak* and present the aspects that were negatively and positively viewed by the raters. In addition, they discuss the difference between the two language groups as to how the two versions of the texts were evaluated and to what extent there seem to be norms in Norwegian academic writing culture that operate as borders for writers with a different educational and cultural background.

Rosmawati's chapter, 'Writing Academically in English as a Second Language: The Case of Syntactic Constructions', contributes to enriching the description of L2 learners' academic writing. She follows three L2 student writers – postgraduate students of non-Anglophone backgrounds in Australia – in developing their academic writing. Rosmawati explores the different types of syntactic constructions used in the students' academic writing, with a special focus on complex nominal construction – one of the most representative traits of academic prose. One of the findings is the overuse of clausal elaboration in the participants' writing, indicating low awareness of the concise phrasal discourse style of academic prose. These findings have direct pedagogical implications and the author points to a need to improve academic literacy even for students with high proficiency.

The chapter by Zhihui Fang and Guofang Li, 'Writing in School Science for EAL Students: Linguistic Challenges and Pedagogical Response', discusses the stylistic features of academic writing in English in secondary schools. This style is highly valued in the academic community and widely used as a barometer of competence and a key measure of success in academic communication. The features discussed include technicality, density, abstraction, formality, objectivity, and rigor. It exemplifies the challenges these features present to multilingual learners in secondary schooling in the North American context by examining writing samples of diverse learners and listening to learners' perspectives on cross-cultural writing. An SFL-informed genre-based pedagogy is also developed for helping multilingual leaners improve linguistic resources for realizing and instantiating these features in cross-cultural contexts.

'Supporting EAL Writing Development in the Early Stages of the Doctorate: Candidates from the East Writing in the West' is the title of Morena Botelho de Magalhães' chapter. She describes the writing experiences of four Chinese doctoral researchers in the first year of their candidature at a large multicultural university in New Zealand and draws on narrative data collected for a larger study. The four candidates accessed generic support (e.g. grammar and writing workshops) during their first year and were assisted, as well as assessed, by their supervisors in the completion of their writing projects. This chapter focuses on the language recommendations the participants received after a diagnostic language assessment for doctoral candidates at the university. The linguistic issues they encountered while developing a research proposal is also discussed.

Kirsi Leskinen's chapter, 'Agency in L2 Academic Literacies: Immigrant Students' Lived Experiences in Focus', focuses on Finnish academic literacies and literacy practices as perceived and experienced by students with prior university studies who are settling down in Finland and speak Finnish as their L2. Based on a detailed qualitative analysis of students' narratives about working with academic texts, Leskinen's chapter examines learners' beliefs and agency in appropriating literacy practices in L2. The students had migrated from African and Asian countries in recent years, and they took part in a pioneering training program, which integrated language, civic and working life skills studies, and content studies in different academic disciplines, with the aim of supporting the students' access to higher education and academic jobs in Finland. Leskinen discusses the relationship between the students' perceptions and their previous experiences with literacy practices in culturally different settings.

In 'Constructing Persuasion: A Cross-cultural Comparison of Chinese and English Student Writings', Jihua Dong examines the linguistic devices that convey persuasiveness in L1 and L2 students' argumentative texts. Two written corpora are used, one based on Chinese Learners of English, the other based on academic English written by British university students with English as their L1. Dong found statistically significant differences in the use of formulations with persuasive functions between the two groups of writers. The Chinese learner corpus displayed greater usage of the pathos strategy (i.e. appeals to emotion), while greater use of the logos strategy occurred in the L1-corpus. Dong explains this difference as partly a result of different academic writing conventions in the two educational contexts, but also the result of Chinese students' insufficient genre awareness. Their lack of exposure to alternative persuasive linguistic resources in English is also likely to be a contributing factor.

In 'Crossing Literacy Borders through Writing: Transformational Apprenticeship and Repositioning of EAL Learners', Lawrence Jun Zhang explores the big challenge that students with English as a second, foreign, or additional language face in order to pursue various academic qualifications in English as the medium instruction in institutions of higher learning. He brings to the fore the real challenges that researchers and teachers alike need to be aware of if they are keen to show an understanding of these students and are interested in offering the much needed help. Developing academic writing skills in English as an additional language (EAL), and in particular English for academic purposes (EAP), and meeting the expected norms is no easy task, irrespective of being native or non-native speakers. For students crossing geographical borders, in particular from the East to the West, the task is even more demanding. Nonetheless, how each student goes through the learning process, and how teachers conduct their teaching, varies.

Note

(1)   This definition seems to originally stem from Schein (2010).

Acknowledgements

This work is partly supported by the Research Council of Norway through its Centres of Excellence funding scheme, project number 223265.

References

Ahlgren, K., Golden, A. and Magnusson, U. (2021) Introduction. Metaphor in education: A multilingual and Scandinavian perspective. *Metaphor and the Social World* 11 (2), 196–211.

Ahn, H. (2019) *Attitudes to World Englishes: Implications for Teaching English in South Korea*. London & New Yourk: Routledge.

Alderson, J.C. (2007) The CEFR and the need for more research. *The Modern Language Journal* 91 (4), 659–663.

Baldwin, J.R., Coleman, R.R.M., Shenoy-Packer, S. and González, A. (2014) *Intercultural Communication for Everyday Life*. Hoboken, NJ: John Wiley & Sons.

Bhambra, G.K. (2015) Citizens and others: The constitution of citizenship through exclusion. *Alternatives* 40 (2), 102–114.

Bjørge, A.K. (2007) Power distance in English lingua franca email communication. *International Journal of Applied Linguistics* 17 (1), 60–80.

Bourdieu, P., Passeron, J.-C. and De Saint Martin, M. (1995) *Academic Discourse. Linguistic Misunderstanding and Professorial Power*. Paris: Polity Press.

Breton, T.R. (2021) The role of national culture in student acquisition of mathematics and reading skills. *Compare: A Journal of Comparative and International Education*, 1–17.

Brown, A. (1995) The effect of rater variables in the development of an occupation-specific language performance test. *Language Testing* 12 (1), 1–15.

Canagarajah, A.S. (2013) *Critical Academic Writing and Multilingual Students*. Ann Arbor, MI: University of Michigan Press.

Canagarajah, A.S. (2021) Addressing language statuses in the writing on multilingual students. In T. Silva and Z. Wang (eds) *Reconciling Translingualism and Second Language Writing* (pp. 41–54). New York & Abingdon: Routledge.

Connor, U. (1987) Argumentative patterns in student essays: Cross-cultural differences. In U. Connor and R.B. Kaplan (eds) *Writing Across Languages: Analysis of L2 Text* (pp. 57–71). Reading, MA: Addison-Wesley.

Connor, U. (1996) *Contrastive Rhetoric: Cross-Cultural Aspects of Second Language Writing*. Cambridge: Cambridge University Press.

Connor, U. and Kaplan, R.B. (eds) (1987) *Writing Across languages: Analysis of L2 Text*. Reading, MA: Addison-Wesley.

Currie, P. (1994) What counts as good writing? Enculturation and writing assessment. In A. Freedman and P. Medway (eds) *Learning and Teaching Genre* (pp. 63–79). Portsmouth, NH: Boynton/Cook-Heinemann.

Deane, M. and O'Neill, P. (2011) *Writing in the Disciplines*. New York: Palgrave.

Deliège, R. (2001) Types of societies. In J.D. Wright (eds) *International Encyclopedia of the Social and Behavioral Sciences* (pp. 14530–14536). Amsterdam: Elsevier.

Easthorpe, A. (1999) *Englishness and National Culture*. London: Routledge.

Engelhard, G.J. (1994) Examining rater errors in the assessment of written composition with a many-faceted Rasch model. *Journal of Educational Measurement* 31 (2), 93–112.

Fang, Z., Grant, L.W., Xu, X., Stronge, J.H. and Ward, T.J. (2013) An international comparison investigating the relationship between national culture and student achievement. *Educational Assessment, Evaluation, and Accountability* 3 (3), 159–177.

Fløttum, K., Dahl, T. and Kinn, T. (2006) *Academic Voices: Across Languages and Disciplines*. Amsterdam: John Benjamins.

Fortier, A.-M. (2018) On (Not) speaking English: Colonial legacies in language requirements for British citizenship. *Sociology* 52 (6), 1254–1269.

Freeman, L.C. and Winch, R.F. (1957) Societal complexity: An empirical test of a typology of societies *American Journal of Sociology* 62 (5), 461–466.

Frost, A., Kiernan, J. and Blum, S.M. (2020) *Translingual Dispositions: Globalized Approaches to the Teaching of Writing*. Fort Collins, CO: WAC Clearinghouse.

Golden, A. (2018) Utvikling av ordforrådet på et andrespråk [Development of vocabulary in a second language]. In A.-K. H. Gujord and G.T. Randen (eds) *Norsk som andrespråk – perspektiver på læring og utvikling*. (pp. 190–213). Oslo: Cappelen Damm Akademisk.

Golden, A. and Hvenekilde, A. (1983) *Rapport fra prosjektet Lærebokspråk*. [Report from the project Textbook Language]. Oslo: Universitetet.

González, V., Chen, C.-Y. and Sanchez, C. (2001) Cultural thinking and discourse organizational patterns influencing writing skills in a Chinese English-as-a-Foreign-Language (EFL) learner. *Bilingual Research Journal* 25 (4), 627–652.

Grissinger, M. (2014) That's the way we do things around here!: Your actions speak louder than words when it comes to patient safety. *P & T: A Peer-reviewed Journal for Formulary Management* 39 (5), 308–344.

Gu, L. and So, Y. (2015) Voices from stakeholders: What makes an academic English test 'international'? *Journal of English for Academic Purposes* 18, 9–24.

Halliday, M.A.K. (1993) Towards a language-based theory of learning. *Linguistics and Education* 5 (2), 93–116.

Hamp-Lyons, L. and Xia, B.Z.W. (2001) World Englishes: Issues in and from academic writing assessment. In M. Peacock and J. Flowerdew (eds) *English for Academic Purposes: Research Perspectives* (pp. 101–116). Cambridge: Cambridge University Press.

Hamp-Lyons, L. and Davis, A. (2008) The Englishes of English tests: Bias revisited. *World Englishes* 27 (1), 26–39.

Hardy, C. and Clughen, L. (eds) (2012) *Writing in the Disciplines: Building Supportive Cultures for Student Writing*. Bingley: Emerald.

Hartley, J. (2002) *A Short History of Cultural Studies*. London: Sage.

Heng Hartse, J. and Kubota, R. (2014) Pluralizing English? Variation in high-stakes academic texts and challenges of copyediting. *Journal of Second Language Writing* 24, 71–82.

Hinkel, E. (1997) Indirectness in L1 and L2 academic writing. *Journal of Pragmatics* 27, 381–386.

Hinkel, E. (2002) *Second Language Writers' Text: Linguistic and Rhetorical Features.* Mahwah, NJ: Lawrence Erlbaum Associates.

Hinkel, E. (2011) *Culture in Second Language Learning.* In N. Seel (ed.) *Encyclopedia of the Sciences of Learning,* DOI 10.1007/978-1-4419-1428-6. Berlin: Springer.

Hirose, K. (2003) Comparing L1 and L2 organizational patterns in the argumentative writing of Japanese EFL students. *Journal of Second Language Writing* 12, 181–209.

Hofstede, G. (1991) *Cultures and Organizations: Software of the Mind* (1st edn). Maidenhead: McGraw-Hill.

Hofstede, G. (2001) *Culture's Consequences: Comparing Values, Behaviors, Institutions and Organizations Across Nations* (2nd edn). Thousand Oaks, CA: Sage.

Hofstede, G., Hofstede, G.J. and Minkov, M. (2005) *Cultures and Organizations: Software of the Mind* (2nd edn). New York: Mcgraw-Hill.

Holliday, A. (1999) Small cultures. *Applied Linguistics* 20 (2), 237–264.

Hsu, T. (2015) Removing bias towards World Englishes: The development of a Rater Attitude Instrument using Indian English as a stimulus. *Language Testing* 33 (3), 367–389.

Hsu, T. (2019) Rater attitude towards emerging varieties of English: A new rater effect? *Language Testing in Asia* 9 (1), 1–21.

Hvitfeldt, C. (1986) Traditional culture, perceptual style, and learning: The classroom behavior of Hmong adults. *Adult Education Quarterly* 36 (2), 65–77.

Hyland, K. (2000) *Disciplinary Discourses: Social Interactions in Academic Writing.* London: Longman.

Hyland, K. (2002) *Teaching and Researching Writing.* London: Longman.

Hyland, K. (2004) *Genre and Second Language Writing.* Ann Arbor, MI: University of Michigan Press.

Hyland, K. (2015) Genre, discipline and identity. *Journal of English for Academic Purposes* 19, 32–43.

Jarvis, S. (2017) Transfer: An overview with an expanded scope. In A. Golden, S. Jarvis and K. Tenfjord (eds) *Crosslinguistic Influence and Distinctive Patterns of Language Learning* (pp. 12–28). Bristol: Multilingual Matters.

Johns, A. (1997) *Text, Role and Context.* Cambridge: Cambridge University Press.

Jølbo, I. (2015) Å finne sin stemme. Plagiering og polyfoni i andrespråkstekster [Finding your voice. Plagiarism and polyphoni in second language texts]. In A. Golden and E. Selj (eds) *Skriving på norsk som andrespråk. Vurdering, opplæring og elevenes stemmer.* (pp. 127–141). Oslo: Cappelen Damm Akademisk.

Kamimura, T. and Oi, K. (1998) Argumentative strategies in American and Japanese English. *World Englishes* 17 (3), 307–323.

Kaplan, R.B. (1966) Cultural thought patterns in inter-cultural education. *Language Learning* 16 (1), 1–20.

Kerfoot, C. and Hyltenstam, K. (2017) Introduction: Entanglement and order of visibility. In C. Kerfoot and K. Hyltenstam (eds) *Entangled Discourses: South–North Orders of Visibility* (pp. 1–15). New York & Abingdon: Routledge.

Khan, K. (2020) Raciolinguistic border-making and the elasticity of assessment and believeability in the UK citizenship process. *Ethnicities* 21 (2), 333–351.

Kobayashi, T. (1992) Native and nonnative reactions to ESL compositions. *TESOL Quarterly* 26 (1), 81–112.

Kubota, R. (1998) An investigation of L1-L2 transfer in writing among Japanese university students: Implications for contrastive rhetoric. *Journal of Second Language Writing* 7 (1), 69–100.

Kubota, R. and Lehner, A. (2004) Toward critical contrastive rhetoric. *Journal of Second Language Writing* 13 (1), 7–27.

Lakoff, G. (1993) The contemporary theory of metaphor. In A. Ortony (ed.) *Metaphor and Thought* (2nd edn, pp. 202–251). Cambridge: Cambridge University Press.

Lakoff, G. and Johnson, M. (1980) *Metaphors We Live By.* Chicago, IL: University of Chicago Press.

Leki, I. (1997) Cross-talk: ESL issues and contrastive rhetoric. In C. Severino, J.C. Guerra and S.E. Butler (eds) *Writing in Multicultural* Settings (pp. 234–244). New York: Modern Language Association of America.

Lillis, T. (2014) *Sociolinguistics of Writing*. Edinburgh: Edinburgh University Press.

Lindberg, I. (2009) Conceptualizing school-related, academic language: Theoretical and empirical approaches In P.I. Juvonen (ed.) *Språk och lärande. Rapport från ASLAs høstsymposium 2008* [Language and Learning. Report from ASLA's fall symposium 2008] (pp. 27–42). Stockholm: Association suédoise de linguistique sppliquée (ASLA)/ Svenska föreningen för tillämpad språkvetenskap.

Lumley, T. and McNamara, T.F. (1995) Rater characteristics and rater bias: Implications for training. *Language Testing,* 12 (1), 54–71.

Martin, J. (1999) Mentoring semogenesis: 'Genre-based' literacy pedagogy. In F. Christie (ed.) *Pedagogy and the Shaping of Consciousness. Linguistic and Social Processes* (pp. 123–155). London: Cassell.

Martin, M.J. (2006) 'That's the way we do things around here': An overview of organizational culture. *Electronic Journal of Academic and Special Librarianship* 7 (1), 1–8.

McNamara, T. and Ryan, K. (2011) Fairness versus justice in language testing: The place of English literacy in the Australian Citizenship Test. *Language Assessment Quarterly* 8 (2), 161–178.

McSweeney, B. (2002) Hofstede's model of national cultural differences and the consequences: A triumph of faith – a failure of analysis. *Human Relations* 25, 89–118.

Mehra, P. (2014) *Communication Beyond Boundaries*. New York: Business Expert Press.

Mirhosseini, S.-A. and De Costa, P.I. (eds) (2020) *What May Be Done to Help More People Succeed?* London & New York: Bloomsbury Academic.

Olshtain, E., Shohamy, E., Kernp, J. and Chatow, R. (1990) Factors predicting success in EFL among culturally different learners. *Language Learning* 40 (1), 23–44.

Paltridge, B. (2004) Academic writing. *Language Teaching* 37 (2), 87–105.

Pennycook, A. (1996) Borrowing others' words: Text, ownership, memory, and plagiarism. *TESOL Quarterly* 32 (2), 201–230.

Pennycook, A. and Makoni, S. (2019) *Innovations and Challenges in Applied Linguistics from the Global South*. Abingdon: Routledge.

Persson, T. (2016) *De naturvetenskapliga språken. De naturvetenskapliga uppgifterna i och elevers resultat från TIMSS 2011 år 8*. [The natural science languages. The natural science tasks in and the students' results from TIMSS 2011, year 8]. Uppsala: Acta Universitatis Upsaliensis.

Polio, C. and Shi, L. (2012) Perceptions and beliefs about textual appropriation and source use in second language writing. *Journal of Second Language Writing* 21 (2), 95–101.

Ribeck, J. (2015) *Steg för steg. Naturvetenskapligt ämnesspråk som räknas* [Step by step. Science discipline language that counts]. Göteborg: Språkbanken, Department of Swedish, University of Gothenburg.

Rimmer, W. (2009) Operationalising linguistic creativity. In L. Taylor and C.J. Weir (eds) *Language Testing Matters. Investigating the Wider Social and Educational Impact of Assessment. Proceedings of the ALTE Cambridge Conference, April 2008* (pp. 176–189). Cambridge: Cambridge University Press.

Rothery, J. (1996) Making changes. Developing an educational linguistics. In R. Hasan and G. Williams (eds) *Literacy in Society* (pp. 86–123). London: Longman.

Schein, E.H. (2010) *Organizational Culture and Leadership* (4th edn). San Fransciso, CA: Wiley.

Schulz, J.W. (2001) Tapping the best that is within: Why corporate culture matters. *Mangement Quarterly* 42 (1), 29–35.

Shohamy, E. (1998) Critical language testing and beyond. *Studies in Educational Evaluation* 24 (4), 331–345.

Shohamy, E. (2006) *Language Policy: Hidden Agendas and New Approaches*. London: Routledge.

Silva, T. and Wang, Z. (eds) (2021) *Reconciling Translingualism and Second Language Writing*. New York & Abingdon: Routledge.

Snow, C.E. (2010) Academic language and the challenge of reading for learning about science. *Science* 328 (5977), 450–452.

Swales, J. (1990) *Genre Analysis: English in Academic and Research Settings*. Cambridge: Cambridge University Press.

Swales, J. (1998) *Other Floors Other Voices: A Textography of a Small University Building*. Mahwah, NJ: Lawrence Erlbaum.

Taras, V. and Steel, P. (2009) Beyond Hofstede: Challenging the ten testaments of cross-cultural research. In C. Nakata (ed.) *Beyond Hofstede: Culture frameworks for Global Marketing and Management* (pp. 40–61). Chicago, IL: Macmillan/Palgrave.

Tracy, R. (2017) Language testing in the context of migration. In J.-C. Beacco, H.-J. Krumm, D. Little and P. Thalgott (eds) *The Linguistic Integration of Adult Migrants. Some Lessons from Research* (pp. 45–58). Berlin: de Gruyter.

Van Lier, L. (2004) *The Ecology and Semiotics of Language Learning: A Sociocultural Perspective*. Boston, MA: Kluwer Academic.

Wigglesworth, G. (1993) Exploring bias analysis as a tool for improving rater consistency in assessing oral interaction. *Language Testing* 10 (3), 305–335.

Wu, J. (2003) Investigation of features of textual organization in argumentative writings by Chinese college students. The use of thematic sentence and topic sentence. *Foreign Language Teaching Abroad* 2, 35–42.

Yin, G. (1999) Comparative analysis of Chinese and English writings by Chinese college students. *Foreign Language Teaching* 3, 22–27.

Zawacki , T.M. and Cox, M. (eds) (2014) *WAC and Second Language Writers: Research Towards Linguistically and Culturally Inclusive Programs and Practices*. Fort Collins, CO: Parlor Press and WAC Clearinghouse.

Zhang, L., Khan, G. and Tahirsylaj, A. (2015) Student performance, school differentiation, and world cultures: Evidence from PISA 2009. *International Journal of Educational Development* 42, 43–53.

2 When Errors Are Corrected

Anne Golden
MultiLing, University of Oslo, Norway

Lars Anders Kulbrandstad
Inland Norway University of Applied Sciences and Karlstad University, Sweden

Introduction

As written texts play an increasingly greater role in every society, the pressure for passing written exams has likewise increased in many areas. This also applies to people who have moved to a country where – for them – a new language is the official language. As critical sociolinguistic research has demonstrated, fluency in this language is by no means a guarantee of participation in the new society (Flores & Rosa, 2015; Rosa & Flores, 2017; Van der Bracht *et al.*, 2015). Nonetheless access to education, work and public life most often requires that written language skills are documented by performance in language achievement tests. To contribute to social justice, test constructors and test administrators should strive to make the assessment of the test-taker's performance as fair and consistent as possible. This means, for instance, that biases linked to ethnicity, gender and cultural background are to be avoided. A given oral or written performance ought to be evaluated equally by different raters; the personal background and personal qualities of the rater should not play any role. Inversely, each rater should evaluate similar performances in the same way regardless of the personal background and personal qualities of the test-takers (Ross, 2012). This is not always the case, as language-testing research convincingly shows (Isbell, 2017; Pollitt & Murray, 1996; Schaefer, 2008). One way to try to reduce rater bias is to define carefully the criteria according to which the candidates' performances are to be assessed. However, this is a demanding task, and an even harder one to stick to in practice.

In Norway, mastery of the written standard is mainly checked through official tests, and, as with the rest of Europe, this is predominantly done by using the scales and descriptors of the Common

European Framework of Reference for Languages (CEFR) (Council of Europe, 2001; Utdanningsdirektoratet & Council of Europe, 2011). These descriptors have more or less assumed the role of gatekeeper to success in the European countries, as the tests are 'high stakes' for the candidates. The use of CEFR has been the subject of severe critique both from within and outside the community of language-testing researchers (see, for example, Barni, 2015; Deygers *et al.*, 2018). Other grievances are the monolingual orientation of the 2001 version (Shohamy, 2011), the foundation in Western educational traditions (Van Huy & Hamid, 2015) and the narrow view of academic writing (McNamara *et al.*, 2018).

Earlier studies of assessment of texts written in a second language have revealed that the number of errors or forms deviating from the norms plays an important part in the evaluation (see below). This includes violation of orthographic, morphological and syntactic norms as well as the use of wrong words or writing in an unidiomatic way. However, other factors than accuracy do play a part in the assessment. Complexity and fluency have frequently been studied along with accuracy, forming the CAF-triad (Housen *et al.*, 2012) as these aspects are often claimed to be the principal components of second language proficiency. But these notions – fluency and complexity – are harder to define than accuracy; in fact 'they are not monolithic constructs, but rather multidimensional, multifaceted and multi-layered that defy straightforward one-line definitions' (Housen *et al.*, 2012: 300). In other words, norms are less clear for these text features. Our main aim in this study is, therefore, to identify which qualities other than accuracy are favoured by raters when assessing texts written by language learners for high-stakes exams, and by that contribute to an understanding of how language-testing works in practice. The reason for this interest is our previous research on the assessment of texts written by adult learners with Spanish and Vietnamese as their first language on an official Norwegian test. When reassessed according to the CEFR scales, the texts written by the Vietnamese as a group were rated lower despite the fact that they produced slightly fewer errors than the Hispanophone writers (Golden *et al.*, 2017).[1] As it is hard to measure aspects of texts other than accuracy directly, we decided to let a group of experienced raters evaluate a selection of the texts from the previous study but this time used versions of the texts where all the errors in orthography, morphology, syntax and lexicon had been corrected. An additional question in this research is therefore: What differences (if any) are there between the evaluation of the corrected texts written by the Vietnamese and the Spanish test-takers and how may the potential differences be explained?

In the following, we will first present our earlier study and then review relevant research on rater behaviour, with a focus on studies of how raters vary in the weight they give to different text aspects when they evaluate texts written in language-testing situations. Thereafter we will describe our data in more detail and give an account of the methodology we have applied. The next section presents the main findings of the study and these are discussed in the final part of the chapter.

Previous Research

In an earlier study (Golden *et al.*, 2017), we studied 200 texts written by adult learners of Norwegian with Spanish and Vietnamese as their first language that were written at an official test in Norway and later assessed according to the CEFR scales.[2] These texts were part of the ASK-corpus, a learner corpus composed of texts written by adult learners of Norwegian with ten different L1's at two different test levels in an official test situation (Tenfjord *et al.*, 2006b). We analysed all the texts written by these language groups at the lower level (approximately B1), in order to see if any recognizable differences could be detected since, when reassessed, 55% of the texts written by the Vietnamese were assigned to the A2 level, compared to 39% in the Spanish group.[3] Our research question was: How important was prior experience *both* for the writing and for the assessment? We assumed that the candidates would be influenced by *their* previous experience with text writing and test taking and that the raters would be influenced by *their* level of competence in the language being tested, *their* rating experiences and *their* view on the importance of a written norm. 'The writings, and the assessments, may thus be seen as social practices, as two literacy events: the writing of the learners and the reading of the raters' (Golden *et al.*, 2017: 231). In some cases, we claimed that 'it is possible that these other aspects are language and/or culture dependent and therefore will affect the learners with different L1s in different ways' (2017: 231–232). However, the specified criteria given in the CEFR do not draw attention either to the content or to the rhetoric of the texts even if there are reasons to believe that such aspects might influence the raters in conjunction with linguistic and functional qualities. We performed what Jarvis and Crossley (2012) call a detection-based approach to transfer research, and examined a wide array of variables, comprising global text features, fluency features, accuracy features and complexity features as well as the self-presentations of the writers. Using a linear discriminant analysis (see, for example, Balakrishnama & Ganapathiraju, 1998), we found that a combination of five variables, mainly error variables – i.e. morphological errors, wrong word, miscellaneous errors, syntactic errors – and the number of lemmas, correctly identified these texts to different levels of the CEFR in 80% of the cases. However, there remained 20% of the texts that were not recognized through these variables, and we assumed that factors other than accuracy were at play.

For the present study, prior investigations of rater behaviour are relevant, particularly studies of how texts written in the authors' second language are being assessed. In general test research, there is abundant evidence of considerable variability among raters. This has in part to do with the requirement for authenticity in the test situation: the language performance triggered by the test should mirror language use in real life, and the more this requirement is met, the more difficult it is to achieve rater-homogeneity (Ross, 2012: 231). Even if the authenticity ideal is somewhat played down in order to secure consistency in the assessment, variability can still arise because of differences between the raters as to the importance they attach to various assessment criteria, often, but not always, given explicitly in scoring guidelines. This has been explored in a number of studies, including works on the rating of L2 texts. Although there seems to be no study that has addressed potential differences in rater behaviour when L2 texts written in some languages by L1 Spanish and L1 Vietnamese writers are being assessed, several works raise questions that are pertinent for the present study.

An early work is Vaughan (1991), where nine experienced raters produced a think-aloud protocol while re-evaluating six essays written by university students in English as their L2. The most frequent negative comment found in the transcribed protocols was 'content unclear or weak', the next being 'handwriting hard to read'. These two types made up more than half of all comments. However, there was considerable variation among the raters both as to the grade they awarded each of the texts and the criteria on which they based their evaluation. This was the case even if the raters had received similar training. Vaughan concludes that her data show 'that raters are not a tabula rasa, and do not, like computers, internalize a predetermined grid that they apply uniformly to every essay' (1991: 120).

Milanovic *et al.* (1996) supplied the think-aloud protocols with written retrospective reports from raters when they studied raters assessing test essays. The researchers identified the following 11 text traits that the judges had addressed: length, legibility, grammar, structure, communicative effectiveness, tone, vocabulary, spelling, content, task realization, and punctuation. For most of these traits, the raters differed considerably in the weight they gave to a particular trait.

With Sakyi (2000) the notion of raters' reading styles was introduced, based on a study of six experienced raters' assessments of 12 essays written in English by first-year college students. The raters assigned a holistic score to each text based on a scale called PROFAC and commented on the scoring in the form of think-aloud verbal protocols. In these comments, Sakyi observed four distinct reading styles, each characterized by a focus on either (a) errors in the text; (b) essay topic and presentation of ideas; (c) the rater's personal reaction to the text; and (d) the scoring guide. Although the raters appeared to differ in their perception of essay qualities, the analysis of the protocols revealed some features that were typically associated with essays that received

Table 2.1 Main characteristics that determined raters' judgement of the quality of written compositions in Sakyi (2000)

Characteristics	Positive comments	Negative comments
1 Content and organization	well developed & original (logical, intelligent or persuasive)	poorly developed & organized/not relevant
2 Grammatical & mechanical errors	very little	many/persistent
3 Sentence structure & vocabulary	correct & sophisticated/complex	incorrect & simplistic

high grades and some features that were typically associated with low grades. Among the positive features were 'clearly addresses the topic', 'good organization (use of transitions/coherence', 'good/sophisticated vocabulary', and 'complex/correct sentence structure'. Examples of negative features were 'poor development', 'poor organization' and 'poor content – inappropriate/inadequate/no support/examples'. Sakyi combined and summarized the positive and negative comments into three main characteristics that seemed to be decisive for how the raters judged the quality of the essays. These are shown in Table 2.1.

Sakyi grouped the factors that influenced the raters' final decision on grading in two categories: content-related factors and language-related factors. Content factors were, for instance, 'assumptions about task demands/degree to which content addresses task', 'presentations of ideas (development, organization)', 'support', and 'length of essay'. It is worth noticing that the last factor was considered to be of importance only when an essay was exceptionally short. The central language factor was the presence or absence of grammatical errors. Other language-related factors were the scope and complexity of vocabulary and sentence structure, and the style or format used by the writer. Interestingly enough, the order in which the essays were assessed also seemed to have some effect on the assessment for some raters.

The rater typology was further developed in Eckes (2008). Sixty-five raters actively involved in scoring the writing performance of exams in English candidates were asked to indicate how important they found each of nine frequently used rating criteria. The results showed that there was 'a significant degree of rater variability in the importance rating data' (2008: 177). From a two-mode clustering analysis, six rater types stood out, each with a distinct scoring profile. Four of these were characterized by criteria that the raters found particularly important: 'the Syntax Type', 'the Correctness Type', 'the Structure Type', and 'the Fluency Type'. The remaining two types were defined negatively ('the Non-fluency Type' and 'the Non-argumentation Type'), both defined by criteria that the raters considered to be of very little importance.

In a later study of rater bias, Eckes (2012) distinguished between a typology of raters based on what importance they attached to different scoring criteria when asked to indicate this and a typology based on how they seem to apply the different criteria in the rating process. The first typology is said to be about cognitive rater types (CRT), the second about operational rater types (ORT) (Eckes, 2012: 275). Thus, CRT is about what criteria the raters state as being important and what criteria they think are unimportant, whilst the ORT is about what criteria the raters actually treat as important or unimportant when they conduct their rating. While the types that Eckes described in his 2008 article belong to the first category, Schaefer (2008) was concerned with the second category in his study of how 40 inexperienced native English-speaking raters assessed essays written by 40 Japanese students with English a foreign language. Here Schaefer found that raters who rated content and organization severely tended to rate language use and/or mechanics, i.e. capitalization, punctuation and spelling, rather leniently, and vice versa. Eckes (2012) therefore asked whether there is a link between the CRTs and the ORTs and what the precise nature of the link could be. The results suggest that the raters' perceptions of the importance of scoring criteria have an effect on how they use the criteria in actual scoring sessions, i.e. theory and practice tend to go hand in hand.

Friginal *et al*. (2014) is an exploratory study of texts written in English by non-native students and native students who had been given the highest possible score by raters. Some 23 different linguistic features were included in a cluster analysis that resulted in six different clusters, and these were 'interpreted as representing different functional profiles' (2014: 6). Interesting differences were found between the two groups of students, but for both of them the following was clear: texts written by good writers could have quite different linguistic characteristics.

This review shows that research on rater variability has long been concerned with the raters' dissimilar views of how important different text features are for the evaluation of the overall quality of the texts. Of particular interest is the relative importance of features connected to the content, structure and style of the texts on the one hand and accuracy-related features on the other hand. With texts written in the authors' second language, it is often found that language errors have a strong effect on how the texts are rated (see e.g. Golden *et al*., 2017). The impact can be so great that it overshadows other text qualities. Thus, it is interesting to study how raters evaluate second language writing when errors are corrected. To the best of our knowledge, no such study has been conducted so far.

Data and Method

Forty texts were extracted from the 200 texts written by the test-takers with Spanish[4] and Vietnamese backgrounds in the former study. As we were mainly interested in the texts that did not pass the B1 level, we chose 30 of them from the group below B1 level and 10 from above B1 level according to the CEFR scale (for the reassessment, see endnote 3). The 40 texts were selected at random but fulfilled the goal of 50% from each language group (Spanish and Vietnamese). As all the texts in the ASK-corpus are annotated and corrected, there exists a parallel corrected version of all the texts in the corpus ready for use. The corrections had been made manually while compiling the corpus according to two basic principles: (a) the principle of pragmatic probability; and (b) the principle of minimal modification. The first principle asked for the interpretation *most probable* from a pragmatic point of view, taking into account the interpretation of the entire text and the broader context in which the text was produced. The latter principle aimed for a reconstruction that deviated the least dramatically from the original: i.e. the reconstruction that involved *minimal alteration* of the original text was opted for (see Tenfjord *et al.*, 2006a, 2006b) for an in-depth discussion regarding this procedure as well as for more details about the compilation of the ASK-corpus).

These 40 corrected texts were presented to 12 experienced raters – three men and nine women – who were asked to evaluate them and write a short comment giving the rationale for their decisions. The raters were multilingual with Norwegian as their first language and came from different educational institutions (universities and adult education centres) where they were teaching Norwegian to students and adult migrants. They were all experienced teachers and accustomed to assessing exams using the CEFR scale. Inspired by earlier studies (see above) where the concepts 'content', 'texts structure' and 'style' were mentioned in the results, these well-established terms were used in our study, and we gave the raters the following instruction for their work: '[It is] the content, text structure and style that should be evaluated, and this should be done on a three level scale: *good – medium – weak*.'[5] By this we wanted to explore to what extent the raters had a common understanding of the notions behind these terms. The evaluation should be briefly justified through a specific form. Hence, we asked for what Fulcher calls 'a global, holistic judgement of performance, so there is no counting or "tallying"' of particular features or errors' (Fulcher, 2012: 378). It is important to notice that the national, ethnic or linguistic background of the writers was not made known to the raters.

Findings

One of the most striking results in the study is the rater variability. This is observed repeatedly in research on rater behaviour and it characterizes the raters who evaluated the corrected versions of the 40 L2 texts. Figure 2.1 shows the number of times each of the 12 raters used the grades *good*, *medium* and *weak*.

As we can see, rater 1 for instance is seldom satisfied and uses good only five times and frequently opts for medium (17 times) and weak (18 times), while rater 9 is of a very lenient disposition, applying good on

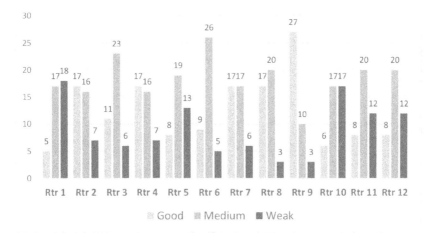

Figure 2.1 The raters' use of the grades

27 occasions and weak only in three instances. Rater 6 falls in between these two, preferring medium almost twice as often as the other alternatives counted together (26 times vs. 14 times). Hence, there was not a unanimous evaluation of any of the 40 texts, but, in two cases, 11 of the 12 raters agreed on the evaluation, and in 11 cases, nine or more of the raters agreed. For 31 texts, that is 77.5% of the total number of texts, more than half – that is seven or more raters – were in agreement. But this left us with nine texts where the discrepancy was rather great. The final categorization of the texts that we use later in the study (called the average grade) is based on the average evaluation calculated in this way: When a text was assessed by a rater as good, it got 3 points, medium was given 2 points and weak was given 1 point, and the total sum was divided into three equal intervals. Hence, to belong to the category good, the points had to be 2.35 or higher, and to be categorized as weak, the average points had to be lower than 1.65. Texts with an average from 1.65 to 2.34 were considered medium.

We were also interested in *why* so many of the texts written by the Vietnamese were assessed at the A level when they originally were assessed according to the CEFR scale. Therefore, we first compared the assessments of the original version with errors and the evaluation of the corrected version without errors. The results are shown in Table 2.2.

As we can see, of the 30 A texts that originally had been assessed as A on the CEFR scale, 8 were now evaluated without errors as good (average grade), 18 as medium and 4 as weak. The 10 texts assessed as B break down as follows: 5 good, 2 medium and 3 weak. Thus, several texts assessed as A in the original version were considered good (average grade) by the raters who evaluated the corrected versions. At the same time, some texts assessed as B in their original version were considered weak (on average) by the raters who evaluated the same texts without errors,

Table 2.2 Comparison of the number of texts originally assessed according to the CEFR scale as A or B and the evaluation of these texts without errors (average grade among 12 raters)

Corrected version (without errors) evaluated as	Original (with errors) assessed as A	Original (with errors) assessed as B	Total
Good	8	5	13
Medium	18	2	20
Weak	4	3	7
Total	30	10	40

i.e. the texts changed position, so to speak. The question is whether the proportion changing position is the same for the two language groups.

In Table 2.3, the same distribution is displayed but now with the texts grouped according to the candidates' language background. Even if the numbers are now small, it is remarkable that almost half the 15 texts written by Spanish-speaking test-takers that had been assessed as A are considered to be good but only one of the Vietnamese-speaking candidates: all the other texts from the Vietnamese group are still considered to be medium or weak even after the errors have been removed.

These results *could* be interpreted as follows. Many of the Spanish speakers' texts that originally were assessed as A on the CEFR scale had qualities that could be appreciated by raters, but these qualities were, so to speak, hidden behind the errors. Once the errors were removed, the qualities stood out and paid off in the evaluation of the corrected version. This was actually the case for 5 of the 7 texts (see Table 2.4). Many Vietnamese speakers' A texts might have lacked such qualities, so they did not profit from the errors being removed. As for the B level texts, two of the texts written by Hispanophones *might have* earned the B because they had few errors; however, it turned out to be the case for only one text. We have checked this by categorizing the A texts into five groups according to the average error frequencies (22.9% errors) of the texts written by

Table 2.3 Comparison of the number of texts originally assessed as A or B according to the CEFR scale and the evaluation of these texts without errors (average grade) according to the L1 of the writers

Corrected version (without errors) evaluated as	Spanish			Vietnamese		
	Original (with errors) assessed as A	Original (with errors) assessed as B	Total	Original (with errors) assessed as A	Original (with errors) assessed as B	Total
Good	7	2	9	1	3	4
Medium	6	1	7	12	1	13
Weak	2	2	4	2	1	3
Total	15	5	20	15	5	20

Table 2.4 Results from evaluation of corrected versions of 12 texts from the two language groups according to five levels of error frequency in the original versions

Error frequency	A texts				B texts			
	Sp A > good	Sp A > weak	Viet A> good	Viet A> weak	Sp B > good	Sp B > weak	Viet B> good	Viet B > weak
Very high	5				1			1
High								
Average			1	1				
Low	2							2
Very low		2		1	1	2	1	

these two language groups in the ASK-corpus. *Very high error frequency* means 20% or more above this average (e.g. more than 27.5% errors); *high frequency* 10% above average (e.g. more than 25.2% errors); *average frequency* (between 20.6% and 25.2% errors); *low frequency* 10% below average (e.g. less than 20.6% errors); and *very low frequency* (e.g. less than 18.3% errors) below average. Table 2.4 displays the number of texts on each of these error-frequency levels written by Spanish and Vietnamese speakers, and sorted into texts that were evaluated as good or weak (average grade) when the errors were removed.

As for A texts, we see that the two Vietnamese speakers' texts that were evaluated as weak originally had an average or lower error frequency. We also see that many of the Spanish speakers' texts that were evaluated as good did have a very high error frequency (more than 20% above average). Even if the numbers are small here, this is in line with the results obtained in the former study (Golden *et al.*, 2017) where the Spanish A texts had a particularly high error frequency of 28.99% compared to the Vietnamese A texts with 24.56% per 100 words.

We also checked what role the spelling errors play in this (see Table 2.5). The same procedure was followed here regarding the categorization of errors: very high error frequency pointed to more than 20% above average; high frequency was above 10% of the average; low frequency was below 10% of average; and very low frequency was below

Table 2.5 Results from evaluation of the corrected versions of 12 texts from the two language groups according to five levels of spelling error frequency in the original versions

Error-frequency	Sp A > good	Sp A > weak	Viet A> good	Viet A> weak	Sp B > good	SP B > weak	Viet B> good	Viet B weak
Very high	4				1			1
High								
Average	1				1			
Low				1				
Very low	2	2	1	1		2	2	2

20% of the average. The average frequency (2.89 per 100 words) was calculated from the texts written by these two language groups in the ASK-corpus.

The average frequency for the spelling errors type is 2.89%. As we can see, four out of the 12 Spanish A texts had a very high frequency of orthographic errors, whereas the Vietnamese A texts all had low or very low frequency. All but one of the Vietnamese B texts also had remarkably few errors, so this might have been the reason for the good grade. However, seven out of the 40 texts were assessed as A even if they contained few spelling errors (low or extra low frequency). Such results triggered us to look for other qualities that might have pleased the raters.

As mentioned above, the raters were asked to give a short justification of their evaluations (see Table A.1 in the Appendix for an example of a completed form for one of the texts). They were asked to comment on content, text structure and style, but other aspects were included as well as finer categorization of these features. The categories addressed in these comments are:

- Answer to the prompt
- Overall content
- Argumentation
- Logic
- Examples
- Elaborations
- Overall structure
- Overall style
- Coherence of the text as a whole and within paragraph
- Introduction and/or conclusion
- Text-binding
- Quality of language (precision, vocabulary, syntax)
- Variation
- Creativity

In our further analysis of the comments, we have been particularly interested in the comments to the texts assessed as A in their original version and later assessed as *good* (average grade, see above) compared to those evaluated as weak (on average) when the errors were removed. Certain explanations reoccurred, and the four categories that dominated when commenting on these texts were: 'Answer to the prompt'; 'Overall content'; 'Overall structure and coherence'; 'Quality of language'. The A texts evaluated as weak were generally said to lack an answer to the prompt or to give an inadequate answer and to have a poorly developed content. The organization of the text was found to be unclear or chaotic, they lacked coherence in the text as a whole and/or within paragraphs, the language lacked clarity, and a limited vocabulary and many unidiomatic expressions were used.

As mentioned earlier, the raters often disagreed, so when we present the data underpinning these generalizations, for each text that was evaluated as good (average grade) we have included only the comments from raters who evaluated the same text as good. We have discarded the comments from raters evaluating the text otherwise (i.e. the comments from the raters who had evaluated the same text as weak or medium). Likewise, for each text that was evaluated as weak (average grade) we have included only the comments from raters who evaluated the same text as weak. Here, too, we have discarded the comments from raters evaluating the text otherwise (i.e. good or medium). The maximum number of comments given to the eight texts rated good would have been 60 if every rater had provided a comment to all the four categories mentioned above for each text they rated as good. However, they did not comment that often. The same goes for the four texts evaluated as weak: the maximum number of comments given to the weak texts might have been 34. Therefore, for each good and weak text respectively, we have summarized all comments to the different categories, and checked how many of these were positive for the good texts and negative for the weak texts. These are displayed in Table 2.6.

Giving one point for each positive comment for the good texts and 0.5 points if the comment was half positive and half negative (e.g. 'ok vocabulary and expressions, but some discrepancies, simple, but inadequate cohesion markers'), we see from Table 2.6 that 33 out of 60 potential comments referring to 'Answer to the prompt' are positive for A texts. Inversely, for the weak texts, 26 out of the potential 34 comments citing these aspects of the texts are negative. For 'content' and 'structure and coherence', the figures are 37 and 36 respectively out of the potential 60 comments for the good texts, and 17 and 15 comments for the weak texts. For quality of language, we see that 33.5 out of the potential 60 comments on the good texts are positive, and 24 out of 34 comments on the weak texts are negative.

Some interpretations of these figures are that good texts tend to attract about the same number of positive comments for all four selected categories (with an average between 55% and 61.7% for each theme). For the weak texts, however, most comments concern 'Answer

Table 2.6 The four main categories in raters' justifications for the 8 A texts considered to be good in their corrected version and the 4 A texts considered to be weak

	Answer to the prompt	Content	Structure and coherence	Quality of language
A texts > good	Adequate answer (33 out of 60 potential comments = 55%)	Well-developed content (37 out of 60 potential comments = 61.7%)	Clear overall structure and coherence in the text as a whole and/or within paragraphs (36 out of 60 potential comments = 60.0%)	Easy to follow, rich vocabulary, varied and nuanced expressions, varied sentence structure (33.5 out of 60 potential comments = 55.8%)
A texts > weak	Lacking or inadequate answer (26 out of 34 potential comments = 76.5%)	Poorly developed content (17 out of 34 potential comments = 50%)	Unclear or chaotic organization of the text, lacking coherence in the text as a whole and/or within paragraphs (15 out of 34 potential comments = 44.0%)	Lack of clarity, limited vocabulary, unidiomatic expressions, (24 out of 34 potential comments = 70.6%)

to the prompt' and 'Quality of language', with more than 70% of the potential 34 comments being negative, while the categories 'Content' and 'Structure and coherence' have fewer comments (50% and below).

Given that so few of the A texts written by Vietnamese speakers were evaluated as good (on average) after the errors were removed, the reason seems to be that more Vietnamese-speaking writers did not answer the prompt and produced texts that were unstructured and lacked global and/or local coherence and had a lower quality of language. Our tentative explanation for this is that these candidates have been more concerned with avoiding errors at the word and sentence level than to write about the topic required by the prompt and to create a clearly structured and coherent text. As we have seen, this was in fact reflected in the error frequency: the Vietnamese speaking writers *did* make fewer errors than the Spanish-speaking writers.

In summary, albeit that we found disagreement among the raters who assessed the corrected versions of the selected 40 texts written in L2 Norwegian, in 31 of them more than half of the raters agreed. Furthermore, we saw traces of a pattern when we discarded the texts considered as medium and analysed the rest, 12 of them, in more detail. Some of the texts written by the Spanish-speaking test-takers were evaluated higher than those written by the Vietnamese-speaking test-takers when the errors were removed: the texts 'jumped', so to speak, to a better evaluation. When we checked the number of errors in the original versions of these texts, we found that most of these texts originally had more errors – also orthographic errors. In addition, we found that in all the texts, the comments centred on four categories: 'Answer to the prompt'; 'Content'; 'Structure and coherence'; 'Quality of language'. The examples that the raters presented to justify their evaluations showed agreement on the meaning of these terms, even if the raters differed in the importance they attached to each category. The comments were positive for the good texts and negative for the weak texts. In particular, the *lack* of answer to the prompt and the *poor* quality of language were most often referred to as justification for evaluating a text as weak.

Discussion

As mentioned earlier, rater variability is next to omnipresent in findings from studies of rater behaviour (Ross, 2012). Even among experienced raters who have received extensive training in the use of rating scales for a particular test, there tends to be both inter-rater variability, i.e. variation between different raters, and intra-rater variability, i.e. inconsistency in the individual rater's rating practice. Some raters are just more lenient than others are, raters may interpret the rating scale differently, and raters often disagree as to which features of the text are most important for the assessment of the texts. In our study, all 12 raters had long experience of assessing essays written in L2 Norwegian by adults. Now they were supposed to assess L2 texts with errors corrected, and asked to look at content, structure and style and to ascribe a grade to each text on the scale good, medium and weak based on their overall impression. This was a new kind of rating task: the raters had not been trained specifically for this, and it is reasonable to suggest that these two circumstances have contributed to the variations in their rating. At the same time, it should be noted that a high degree of disagreement among our raters only concerned a limited number of texts, so all in all the raters were quite consensual in their rating practice.

As in Sakyi's (2000) study we found certain differences in the raters' 'reading style', e.g. some seemed to stick closer to the scoring instructions than others, but there was a common tendency to focus on 'Answer to the prompt' and 'Content'. In the raters' comments on the grades, they mention a wide array of assessment criteria, many of which coincide with findings from research on rater behaviour – for instance, Milanovic *et al.* (1996), Sakyi (2000) and Schaefer (2008). In our study, we were particularly interested in texts that had received an A in their original version with errors but that were considered as either good or weak by the raters who evaluated the corrected version. The rating criteria implicit in the raters' comments are as close as we can come to these raters' operational criteria, i.e. the criteria that actually guided their holistic judgement of the texts (cf. Eckes, 2012: Operational Rater Types, ORT). For A texts that were evaluated as good, all four categories were mentioned, but well-developed 'Content' and qualities of 'Structure and coherence' were referred to somewhat more often than 'Quality of language' and 'Answer to the prompt'. For A texts found to be weak, the most often commented on was 'Answer to the prompt' – it was lacking or inadequate – and the 'Quality of language' was not appropriate. Next came comments on the development of the 'Content', which was seen as insufficient, and comments on 'Structure and coherence', where the raters found weaknesses. Hence, we interpret these findings as an answer to the first research question: Which qualities other than accuracy are favoured by raters when assessing texts written by language learners for high-stakes exams? These raters seem to align with Eckes' (2008) 'Correctness Type' of rater in that they value accuracy but still attach importance to the prompt be answered.

The second research question we formulated had to do with how texts written by Vietnamese-speaking test-takers fared when the corrected versions were evaluated compared with texts authored by Hispanophone candidates. As we have seen in the presentation of the findings, the distribution of the texts previously assessed as A texts and now evaluated as good, medium or weak were different for the two language groups. The texts with Spanish-speaking authors 'jumped' more easily to a better evaluation than the texts written by Vietnamese-speaking candidates. We interpreted this as the texts authored by L1 Spanish test-takers having had qualities that are seen as desirable by Norwegian raters, but these were masked by errors in the original assessment of level A. The Vietnamese speakers' texts, however, lacked these preferred qualities. Our tentative explanation to this was that the Vietnamese-speaking writers were more concerned with avoiding errors at the word and sentence level than to write about the topic required by the prompt, to create a clearly structured and coherent text and to use a rich and varied language. This was supported by our error analysis, in particular the orthographic errors, but we have to keep in mind that we only had three texts in this category.

In our earlier article (Golden *et al.*, 2017) we asked how important earlier experience was for the writers as well as the raters. As for the Vietnamese-speaking writers, who were adult when they took the test and thus went to school in Vietnam around 1980 at the latest, our findings might be seen as a reflection of the importance of formal correctness in the school culture that these test-takers have probably experienced. According to Lê (2011: 12) Vietnam lies towards the conservative end of attitudes to the knowledge continuum in the way that 'students are expected to obey their teachers and work hard to obtain correctness in their work rather than challenging and criticising their teachers'. Lê (2011: 23) notes: 'Students' emphasis on memorisation of grammatical rules, grammatical accuracy, mechanical drills, and repetition has been justified further by many researchers (e.g., Bernat, 2004; Tomlinson & Dat, 2004; Oanh & Hien, 2006; Hiep, 2007).' Ngoc and Iwashita (2012) compared teachers' and students' attitudes towards communicative language teaching at two universities in Vietnam and found that most students viewed errors negatively and expected them to be corrected by the teachers. The authors note that these findings are in line with Lewis and McCook's (2002) observation that verbal perfection has traditionally been valued across many Asian cultures and, as 'a result of the desire for perfection', the students in Ngoc and Iwashita's study 'felt more secure holding on to the traditional view of errors as something bad that should always be corrected' (Ngoc & Iwashita, 2012: 36).

The research we have just referred to gives us reason to believe that the Vietnamese- speaking candidates whose texts got an A in the original assessment and were considered to be weak when the corrected version was rated, consciously or unconsciously used a safety strategy when they wrote the texts, a strategy transferred from their earlier education. The products of their writing *did* contain relatively few errors, but this came at the price of text features that were favoured by the raters evaluating the corrected version. The removal of the errors did not change the raters' impressions of the texts.

We have not been able to find research on where the educational systems in the Spanish-speaking world could be placed on the continuum of attitudes to knowledge. More specifically, we lack information on how formal correctness is weighted compared to other text qualities in writing education in both Latin America and Spain, where the Spanish L1 writers in our study have their background. But from an overview of alphabetization theories that have been most influential in Latin-America between 1980 and 2010 (Castedo & Torres, 2012), it is evident that there has been little focus on correction of errors in the teaching of basic writing skills in this part of the world in recent decades. According to a group of Spanish language experts participating at a seminar in Madrid on language ideologies in February 2020, there is a focus on content in the teaching of Spanish as a first language at all levels in education.[6] This situation is mentioned to be quite different from the one in France where spelling and language structure are drilled throughout the school experience. As the French education system has also been influential in Vietnamese schooling (DeFrancis, 1977; Van, 2016), it is likely to have had an impact on the Vietnamese writers in this study.

As we have seen, candidates with the two language backgrounds that we have been studying here seem to have different *borders to cross* in their effort to master the norms for writing text that are prevalent in Norway. The borders have to do with strategical and pedagogical issues and in the last instance with cultural traditions in their school system. To a greater or lesser degree, the candidates' texts contain traces of norms they have absorbed from their home country's writing culture and these do not always coincide with the norms held by the Norwegian raters. In other words, we might be dealing with cultural transfer (Kubota, 1998; Rass, 2011; Uysal, 2008). This phenomenon deserves attention both from teachers whose task it is to help newcomers master other language and text norms than those they are used to from their country of origin and for raters who, through the assessment of the newcomers' written performance, play the role of gatekeeper for the host society. For all parties involved, a heightened awareness of both overt and covert factors of language-testing is called for.

Appendix

Table A.1 A completed evaluation form for one of the 40 texts

Sensor Rater	Karakter Grade	Karakterbegrunnelse Grade justification	English translation of grade justification
1	God (Middels) Good (medium)	Innhold: Svarer hovedsakelig på oppgaven. Struktur: Teksten er organisert i avsnitt. Avsnittene har en klar struktur: Fra nåtidig problem til framtidig løsning. Skaper sammenheng. Noe redundans på ordnivå. Stil: Enkel med relativt god variasjon.	Content: Overall answer to the prompt. Structure: The text is organized in paragraphs. The paragraphs have a clear structure: From present problem to future solution. Creates coherence. Some redundancy on word level. Style: Simple with relatively good variation.
2	God Good	Svært godt innhold og språk. Stort vokabular. Variasjon i setningstyper og utstrakt bruk av komplekse setninger. God idiomatikk. («Mange vil nok sette økonomi på førsteplass... »)	Very good content and language. Great vocabulary. Variation in sentence types and frequent use of complex sentences. Good use of idioms ('Many will probably put economy in the first place')
3	Middels Medium	Bra introduksjon og avslutning. Presiserer og eksemplifiserer sine drømmer. Er reflektert og beskriver det. Litt naiv i språkformen.	Good introduction and conclusion. Specifies and exemplifies his or her dreams. Is reflexive and describes it. Somewhat naive in language use.
4	God (minus) Good (minus)	Tekstoppbyggingen er veldig god Språket er variert og teksten henger fint sammen. Uttrykker egne meninger og tanker på en god måte. Litt å utsette på setningsstrukturen i enkelte setninger som gjør at flyten ikke blir så god – dette trekker noe ned	The text structure is very good. The language is varied and the text is coherent. Expresses own meanings and thoughts in a good way. The structure of some of the sentences can be criticized. Because of this the fluency is not always that good – this leads to a somewhat weaker impression
5	God Good	God argumentasjon; konsistens.	Good reasoning; consistency.
6	Middels Medium	Teksten har fin innledning og avslutning. Komplekst initialt adverbialt ledd etter subjunksjon trekker ned sammen med tilfeller av krøkkete plassering av setningsadverbial.	The text has a fine introduction and conclusion. Complex initial adverbial after subjunction leads to a weaker impression, together with instances of clumsy placement of sentence adverbial.
7	Middels + Medium +	Kandidaten gir en klar framstilling av sin oppfatning. Holder seg til samme tema, og det fungerer godt. Noen steder blir setningene ufullstendige («.., ikke noe godt.»; «Skilsmissene øker,...» Pragmatiske detaljer: Kan kutte «hele» i «alle land i hele verden» (2. avsnitt). Trenger artikkel («En drøm ..» i siste avsnitt.)	The candidate presents his or her views in a clear way. Sticks to the same topic, and this functions well. In some places the sentences are incomplete ('..., nothing good'; 'Divorces increase, ...'. Pragmatic details: Could drop 'whole' in 'all countries in the whole world' (2. paragraph). Needs article ('A dream ...' in the last paragraph.)
8	Svak Weak	Tja. God start. Uklar avslutning. To fyldige avsnitt der det første er relevant for innholdet. Det andre har mer uklart og kategorisk innhold. Noe uklar sammenheng. Løsrevet avslutning. Relativt enkle setninger, ok vokabular.	Well. Good start. Unclear conclusion. Two substantial paragraphs one of which is relevant for the content. The other one has a more unclear and categorical content. Somewhat unclear coherence. Isolated conclusion. Relatively simple sentences, ok vocabulary.

(Continued)

Table A.1 A completed evaluation form for one of the 40 texts (Continued)

Sensor *Rater*	Karakter *Grade*	Karakterbegrunnelse *Grade justification*	*English translation of grade* *justification*
9	God *Good*	Oppgaven er godt besvart. Teksten er variert selv om det er det ikke er så mange eksempler. Innledning og avslutning er gode.	*The prompt is well answered. The text is varied even if there are not that many examples. Introduction and conclusion are good.*
10	God *Good*	Relevant besvart om «framtiden». God tekstoppbygging. God sammenheng i teksten med variert tekstbinding. Meget godt og bredt vokabular i en tilpasset, saklig og noen steder mot slutten også ekspressiv stil med gode beskrivelser.	*Relevant answer about 'the future'. Good text structure. Good coherence in the text with varied text cohesion. Very good and broad vocabulary in a well-adapted, factual and in some places towards the end also expressive style with good descriptions*
11	Middels *Medium*	Kanskje gode tanker, men ikke overbevisende uttrykt. Umotivert skifte fra ett tema til et annet. Godt retorisk grep å gripe til begynnelsen som avslutning. Holder teksten sammen.	*Perhaps good thoughts, but not convincingly expressed. Unmotivated change of one topic to another. Good rhetorical move to go back to the beginning in the conclusion. Keeps the text together.*
12	God *Good*	Kandidaten er innenfor både formidlingskriterier og tekstoppbygging på nivå B1.	*The candidate satisfies the requirements to both communication and text structure at level B1.*

Notes

(1) The difference was, however, not significant.
(2) There are three main reference levels for language proficiency in the CEFR scale: A = 'basic level', B = 'independent level' and C = 'advanced level'. Each of them is divided into two sub-levels, with a number combination: A1 and A2, B1 and B2, and C1 and C2 (Council of Europe, 2001).
(3) The reassessments were done by 10 experienced raters and, according to Carlsen (2010), with high inter-rater reliability. For the procedure see Carlsen (2010).
(4) The Spanish writers originated both from mainland Spain as well as from South America.
(5) In Norwegian: [Vi vil] gjerne få noen røynde sensorer på feltet til å evaluere 40 tekster fra det såkalte korrigerte parallellkorpuset i ASK, altså korpuset der alle feil er rettet opp. Nå er det altså innhold, tekststruktur og stil som skal vurderes, og det etter en tredelt skala: god – middels – dårlig. Og evalueringen skal kort begrunnes.
(6) Katrin Ahlgren, personal communication 20.02.20.

References

Balakrishnama, S. and Ganapathiraju, A. (1998) Linear discriminant analysis: A brief tutorial. Institute for Signal and information Processing, Department of Electrical and Computer Engineering, Missisippi State University.

Barni, M. (2015) In the name of CEFR: Individuals and standards. In B. Spolsky, O. Inbar-Lourie and M. Tannenbaum (eds) *Challenges for Language Education and Policy: Making Space for People* (pp. 40–51). New York: Routledge.

Bernat, E. (2004) Investigating Vietnamese ESL learners' beliefs about language learning. *English Australia Journal* 21 (2), 40–54.

Castedo, M. and Torres, M. (2012) Un panorama de las teorías de la alfabetización en América Latina durante las últimas décadas (1980–2010). In H.R. Cucuzza and R.P. Spregelburd (eds) *Historia de la lectura en Argentina. Del catecismo colonial en las netbooks estatales* (pp. 615–668). Buenos Aires: Editoras del Calderon.

Council of Europe (2001) *Common European Framework of Reference for Languages: Learning, Teaching, Assessment*. Cambridge: Cambridge University Press.

DeFrancis, J. (1977) *Colonialism and Language Policy in Viet Nam*. The Hague: Mouton.

Deygers, B., Zeidler, B., Vilcu, D. and Carlsen, C.H. (2018) One framework to unite them all? Use of the CEFR in European university entrance policies. *Language Assessment Quarterly* 15 (1), 3–15.

Eckes, T. (2008) Rater types in writing performance assessments: A classification approach to rater variability. *Language Testing* 25 (2), 155–185.

Eckes, T. (2012) Operational rater types in writing assessment: Linking rater cognition to rater behavior. *Language Assessment Quarterly* 9 (3), 270–292.

Flores, N. and Rosa, J. (2015) Undoing appropriateness: Raciolinguistic ideologies and language diversity in education. *Harvard Educational Review* 85 (2), 149–171.

Friginal, E., Li, M. and Weigle, S.C. (2014) Revisiting multiple profiles of learner compositions: A comparison of highly rated NS and NNS essays. *Journal of Second Language Writing* 23, 1–16.

Fulcher, G. (2012) Scoring performance tests. In G. Fulcher and F. Davidson (eds) *The Routledge Handbook of Language Testing* (pp. 378–392). Abingdon: Routledge.

Golden, A., Kulbrandstad, L.A. and Tenfjord, K. (2017) Evaluation of texts in tests, or: Where is the dog buried? In A. Golden, S. Jarvis and K. Tenfjord (eds) *Crosslinguistic Influence and Distinctive Patterns of Language Learning: Findings and Insights from a Learner Corpus* (pp. 231–271). Bristol: Multilingual Matters.

Hiep, P.H. (2007) Communicative language teaching: Unity within diversity. *ELT Journal* 61 (3), 193–201.

Housen, A., Kuiken, F. and Vedder, I. (2012) *Dimensions of L2 Performance and Proficiency: Complexity, Accuracy and Fluency in SLA*. Amsterdam: John Benjamins.

Isbell, D.R. (2017) Assessing C2 writing ability on the Certificate of English Language Proficiency: Rater and examinee age effects. *Assessing Writing* 34, 37–49.

Jarvis, S. and Crossley, S.A. (2012) *Approaching Language Transfer through Text Classification Explorations in the Detection-based Approach*. Bristol: Multilingual Matters.

Kubota, R. (1998) An investigation of L1–L2 transfer in writing among Japanese university students: Implications for contrastive rhetoric. *Journal of Second Language Writing* 7 (1), 69–100.

Lê, V.C. (2011) Form-focused instruction: A case study of Vietnamese teachers' beliefs and practices. PhD thesis, University of Waikato, New Zealand.

Lewis, M. and McCook, F. (2002) Cultures of teaching: Voices from Vietnam. *ELT Journal* 56 (2), 146–152.

McNamara, T., Morton, J., Storch, N. and Thompson, C. (2018) Students' accounts of their first-year undergraduate academic writing experience: Implications for the use of the CEFR. *Language Assessment Quarterly* 15 (1), 16–28.

Milanovic, M., Saville, N. and Shuhong, S. (1996) A study of the decision-making behaviour of composition markers. In M. Milanovic and N. Saville (eds) *Performance Testing, Cognition and Assessment: Selected Papers from the 15th Language Testing Research Colloquium* (pp. 92–114). Cambridge: Cambridge University Press.

Ngnoc, K.M. and Iwashita, N. (2012) A comparison of learners' and teachers' attitudes toward communicative language teaching at two universities in Vietnam. *University of Sydney Papers in TESOL* 7, 45–49.

Oanh, D.T.H. and Hien, N.T. (2006) Memorization and EFL students' strategies at university level in Vietnam. *TESL–EJ* 10 (2), 1–21.

Pollitt, A. and Murray, N.L. (1996) What raters really pay attention to. *Studies in Language Testing* 3, 74–91.

Rass, R.A. (2011) Cultural transfer as an obstacle for writing well in English: The Case of Arabic speakers writing in English. *English Language Teaching* 4 (2), 206–212.

Rosa, J. and Flores, N. (2017) Unsettling race and language: Toward a raciolinguistic perspective. *Language in Society* 46 (5), 621–647.

Ross, S.J. (2012) Claims, evidence, and inference in performance assessment. In G. Fulcher and F. Davidson (eds) *The Routledge Handbook of Language Testing* (pp. 223–233). Abingdon: Routlegde.

Sakyi, A.A. (2000) Validation of holistic scoring for ESL writing assessment: How raters evaluate compositions. In A.J. Kunnan (eds) *Fairness and Validation in Language Assessment* (pp. 129–152). Cambridge: University of Cambridge Press.

Schaefer, E. (2008) Rater bias patterns in an EFL writing assessment. *Language Testing* 25 (4), 465–493.

Shohamy, E. (2011) Assessing multilingual competencies: Adopting construct valid assessment policies. *The Modern Language Journal* 95 (3), 418–429.

Tenfjord, K., Hagen, J.E. and Johansen, H. (2006a) The hows and whys of coding categories in a learner corpus (Or 'How and why an error-tagged learner corpus is not ipso facto one big comparative fallacy'). *Rivista di psicolinguistica applicata (RIPLA)* 6 (3), 93–108.

Tenfjord, K., Meurer, P. and Hofland, K. (2006b) The ASK Corpus: A language learner Corpus of Norwegian as a second language. Proceedings of the Fifth International Conference on Language Resources and Evaluation (LREC'06). Luxembourg & Paris: European Language Resources Association (ELRA) http://hnk.ffzg.hr/bibl/lrec2006/pdf/573_pdf.pdf.

Tomlinson, B. and Dat, B. (2002) Contributions of Vietnamese learners of English to EFL methodology. *Language Teaching Research* 8 (2), 79–105.

Utdanningsdirektoratet and Council of Europe (2011) *Det felles europeiske rammeverket for språk : læring, undervisning, vurdering* [Common European framework of reference for languages : learning, teaching, assessment]. Oslo: Utdanningsdirektoratet.

Uysal, H.H. (2008) Tracing the culture behind writing: Rhetorical patterns and bidirectional transfer in L1 and L2 essays of Turkish writers in relation to educational context. *Journal of Second Language Writing* 17 (3), 181–207.

Van, T.H. (2016) L'Université indochinoise et l'œuvre culturelle de la France au Vietnam. In H.H. Aubert-Nguyen and M. Espagne (eds) *Le Vietnam. Une histoire de transferts culturels* (pp. 151–167). Paris: Demopolis.

Van der Bracht, K., Coenen, A. and Van de Putte, B. (2015) The not-in-my-property syndrome: The occurrence of ethnic discrimination in the rental housing market in Belgium. *Journal of Ethnic and Migration Studies* 41 (1), 158–175.

Van Huy, N. and Hamid, M.O. (2015) Educational policy borrowing in a globalized world: A case study of Common European Framework of Reference for languages in a Vietnamese university. *English Teaching: Practice and Critique* 14 (1), 60–74.

Vaughan, C. (1991) Holistic assessment: What goes on in the rater's mind? In L. Hamp-Lyons (ed.) *Assessing Second Language Writing in Academic Contexts* (pp. 111–125). Norwood, NJ: Ablex.

3 Writing Academically in English as a Second Language: The Case of Syntactic Constructions

Rosmawati
University of Sydney, Australia

Introduction

Ongoing globalisation has pushed education beyond geographical boundaries and resulted in a significant increase in the number of international students in many parts of the world. It has also boosted the growing dominance of English as the world's lingua franca and the language of scientific dissemination (Manchón, 2015). Looking back, both the colonial expansion of English, which has led to the formation of two large English-speaking regions outside Britain – i.e. the Anglophone northen hemisphere settlements (e.g. North America and Canada) and the Anglophone southern hemisphere settlements (e.g. Australia and New Zealand) – and the postcolonial expansion, which eventually resulted in the rise of World Englishes, have paved the way for English's linguistic imperialism, as reflected in many aspects of life, including education. (See Hickey (2020) and Phan (2017) for more discussion on the expansion of English.) Given this background, English emerged as the world's lingua france and the preferred language for scientific dissemination following the collapse of German as the best potential candidate for this purpose after the First World War. Now, with the powerful wave of global mobility and education, the need for fluency in English, the world's lingua franca, has become unavoidable for many. For international students, this translates into an inevitable need for high literacy in academic English in order to successfully engage with academic prose in English in their study. Such engagement with academic prose usually, if not always, includes active production of academic work, which in most cases requires the skills of academic writing.

There are many approaches to studying the challenges that L2 learners face in developing their academic writing and one of them is through exploring the texts they produce (Hyland, 2011). Text exploration can be one of the initial steps in shedding light on the challenges of academic writing, as texts provide a window that enables a glimpse into the learners' internal language systems. Through exploring learners' texts, and building linguistic profiles of their academic writing, it is possible to arrive at an understanding of the manifestation of, for example, syntactic complexity in their writing. With such understanding, it is then possible to attempt to look for the causes of such manifestation and the challenges the learners face that lead to such manifestation.

This chapter constitutes an initial step in this text exploration approach and aims at building linguistic profiles of academic writing produced by advanced learners of English. Three cases are presented in this chapter, each of them being an advanced learner with Japanese, Korean, and Chinese backgrounds respectively. The academic texts they produced are analysed using a combination of textual coding (with 19 measures of syntactic complexity at the sentential, clausal, and phrasal levels) and a multilevel synchrony mapping method to arrive at their linguistic profiles, which are then compared with the characteristics of academic writing in English in terms of syntactic constructions. The findings are interpreted and discussed from the perspective of Complex Dynamic Systems Theory (CDST[1]).

Academic Writing in English

Unanimously considered as the most difficult skill to acquire (even in the L1 context), writing has always been a challenge for many. It is even more difficult having to write, academically, in a second language. Academic writing in English as a second language is therefore one of the major hurdles for students of non-Anglophone backgrounds and a prominent research area for interested researchers (e.g. Fogal, 2020; Leki, 2011; Paltridge, 2017). The challenges can come from various aspects, including from discipline conventions as well as from the language structures. At the language structure level, writing academically in English as a second language presents a major obstacle for L2 student writers. The challenge comes from, among other things,[2] a lack of awareness of the syntactic characteristics of written expressions in academic English that could be very different from those of the spoken register. English academic writing is, for example, characterised by concise language with dense information packaging through heavy nominalisation at the phrasal level (Biber & Gray, 2016), which is distinguishable from the spoken register where clausal subordination is more dominant. In other words, academic English has the characteristic of a compact language with idea elaboration mainly at the lexical and phrasal levels. L2 student writers need to be aware of, and familiar with, these syntactic characteristics in order to produce essays that align better with the conventions of academic writing in English.

However, developing familiarity with the syntactic constructions that characterise academic writing in English is not easy, especially when there is no explicit instruction or training. The ability to use them takes even longer time to develop. Norris and Ortega (2009) pointed out that learners of English generally go through three stages of development in terms of elaboration – learners move from coordination to subordination and then to phrasal complexification as their proficiency grows. Such progress from coordination to subordination and finally to phrasal complexification, along with the growth in proficiency level, has been documented in many studies (e.g. Lu, 2011; Verspoor *et al.*, 2012; Verspoor *et al.*, 2017). Findings from these studies suggest that proficiency in L2 is a main component that plays a substantial role in the learners' ability to develop academic writing skills. In other words, L2 learners need to have reached a relatively high proficiency level in English before they can learn to develop the skill of phrasal elaboration, which is the syntactic construction that is almost exclusive to academic writing, especially in English. As such, it is frequently challenging for L2 learners to write academically in English as their proficiency might have not reached the appropriate level for developing the skill of phrasal elaboration.

Particularly challenging in phrasal elaboration are the complex nominal constructions, which are identified as a typical characteristic of academic writing in English. These complex nominals include (1) noun phrases that are modified with adjectives, other nouns, participles, appositives, preposi-tions, relative clauses, or non-defining clauses; (2) nominal clauses in the subject or object positions; and (3) gerunds and infinitives in the subject or object positions. The difficulty in understanding and mastering these structures stems from many aspects of these complex nominal structures. Biber and Gray (2016) argued that nominalised structures 'entail reduced explicitness' (2016: 221) because they omit (many) points of reference (for example, tense, time, aspect, agent, etc.). The lack of explicitness can be particularly challenging for L2 learners as they might need those references to make sense of the grammatical structures in the L2. Moreover, heightened formality (and consequently, reduction in interpersonal involvement) in the complex nominal structures adds to the challenges, resulting in a significant difference between the use of these structures in non-native speakers' and native speakers' writing (Larsson & Kaatari, 2020; also see Wu *et al.*, 2020).

From a cross-linguistic perspective, the differences between the grammatical structures in L1 and L2 can also present as a cause of this challenge, especially when the grammatical structures of the L1 are vastly different from those of the L2. Chinese, for example, has only one type of modification when forming nominal phrases (i.e. pre-modification) while English has both pre- and post-modification. In Chinese, a head noun can be modified only through the addition of modifiers in front of, and not after, the head noun itself. For example, a head noun 电脑 (*dian*4 *nao*3, computer) can be modified by adding modifiers such as adjectives (新的电脑, *xin*1 *de*1 *dian*4 *nao*3, new computer), nouns (大卫的电脑, *da*4 *wei*4 *de*1 *dian*4 *nao*3, David's computer), or a clause (我刚买的电脑, *wo*3 *gang*1 *mai*3 *de*1 *dian*4 *nao*3, a computer I just bought) in front of the head noun. In other words, the head nouns always occupy the last slot in any noun phrases and hence any modifiers can only be placed in front of them. In Chinese, only pre-modifications, and not post-modifications, are possible. In English, on the other hand, a head noun can be modified through the addition of modifiers in front of as well as after the head noun itself. For example, in the phrase 'a new computer', the modifier (in this case an adjective) 'new' is placed in front of the head noun 'computer', whilst in the phrase 'a computer I just bought' the modifier (in this case a clause) 'I just bought' appears after the head noun. Both pre-modifications and post-modifications are possible in English. Also, compared to English, Chinese has fewer elements that can be used as modifiers (i.e. adjectives, nouns, and some verbal groups only) (Sum & Cong, 2005). Such differences might pose challenges in terms of sentence structures, grammar, lexical choice as well as rhetorical strategies, even when the learners have already reached a relatively high level of proficiency in the non-academic register of the L2 (e.g. Wang & Chen, 2013).

In this chapter, academic texts written by three advanced learners of English during their postgraduate study in Australia are analysed in terms of their syntactic complexity profiles in order to better understand the language-structure related challenges these learners from the East faced when writing in the Western academic context. As syntactic constructions are generally studied through the construct of syntactic complexity, the following section will discuss this construct and the measures that are currently available and employed in measuring syntactic constructions in English.

Measures of Syntactic Complexity in Written English

Research on the construct of complexity, particularly syntactic complexity, is rather popular in L2 writing research through the work of many prominent researchers, such as Biber and his colleagues (e.g. Biber & Gray, 2016; Biber *et al.*, 2011; Biber *et al.*, 2020), Lu and his colleagues (e.g. Lu, 2011; Lu & Ai, 2015; Yin *et al.*, 2021) and Housen and his colleagues (e.g. Bulté & Housen, 2012, 2014, 2019). Despite its prevalence in research, there is no single definition of this construct. Bulté and Housen (2012) argued that complexity is a multidimensional construct, and they proposed a taxonomy to explain the highly complex dimensions of this construct. The construct of complexity in most L2 writing research belongs to the dimension of linguistic complexity in this taxonomy. Within this dimension, complexity has been broadly defined as the degree of elaborateness, diversity and sophistication

(Ellis, 2003; Housen & Kuiken, 2009) in L2 writing research. One of the constructs of linguistic complexity is syntactic complexity and, in many studies of L2 writing, the term 'syntactic complexity' frequently refers to complexity at the clausal level (e.g. Godfrey *et al.*, 2014; Penris & Verspoor, 2017). Many measures have been developed and used extensively in gauging syntactic complexity at the clausal level, which include frequency counts, ratios and mean lengths (Norris & Ortega, 2009; Wolfe-Quintero *et al.*, 1998). All these three categories of measures rely heavily on length-based constructions, like T-units, clauses, and sentences. The simplest of the three is perhaps the frequency-count type. Measures of this type, as the name suggests, count the frequency of occurrences of the target constructs. These measures simply sum the total occurrences of the target subconstructs and present the tallied score. Consequently, these measures are hugely sensitive to text length and are not very informative nor easily comparable due to the absence of a point of reference, for example, text length.

This drawback is, to a certain extent, addressed by ratio measures, which gauge the proportion of subconstructs of syntactic complexity through a comparison with another construct in which the subconstruct is nested (for a discussion on the concept of nestedness, see Rosmawati, 2020). A good example of these ratio measures is the T-unit complexity ratio, which measures the ratio of clauses to T-units in the learners' language. At the core of operationalisation of these ratio measures is an arithmetic operation of division and the result is a numerical value that indicates the proportion of a certain subconstruct in comparison to another subconstruct.

Another type of measure for clausal complexity that also involves such an arithmetic operation is the mean length type of measure. Measures of this type calculate the average length of a certain subconstruct by tallying up the number of words and dividing it by the number of the target subconstructs. An example of this type of measures is the Mean Length Clause (MLC) measure, which is operationalised as the number of words divided by the number of clauses. MLC has been shown to be the most important measure of syntactic complexity in predicting and modelling L2 writing score/quality (Kim & Crossley, 2018; Yang *et al.*, 2015).

A brief overview of these measures is given in Table 3.1, although the list is not in any way exhaustive. The proliferation of available measures sometimes leads to redundancy, as many of them are overlapping (Norris & Ortega, 2009). Lu (2011), who examined 14 different complexity measures through a large-scale corpus study, therefore recommended using measures that did not positively correlate with one another in future studies in order to minimise the possibility of self-confirmatory findings as well as to tap into this construct sufficiently in a more holistic way. This recommendation is in line with

Table 3.1 Examples of syntactic complexity measures

Measure	Code	Definition/Calculation
Dependent clauses	DC	The number of dependent clauses
Independent clauses	IC	The number of independent clauses
T-unit complexity ratio	C/T	The number of clauses per T-unit
Mean length of T-units	W/T	The number of words per T-unit
Sentence complexity ratio	C/S	The number of clauses per sentence
Mean length of sentences (MLS)	W/S	The number of words per sentence
Dependent phrases	DP	The number of dependent phrases
Coordinate phrases	CP	The number of coordinate phrases
Finite verbs	FV	The number of finite verbs
Non-finite verbs	NFV	The number of non-finite verbs
Clausal complexity	FV/S	The number of finite verbs per sentence
Mean length of clauses (MLC)	W/C	The number of words per clauses

the findings of studies on the multidimensional feature of syntactic complexity in L2 writing (e.g. Biber & Gray, 2016). These studies have revealed that syntactic complexity is a multidimensional construct that manifests itself at many levels that are nested in one another. While clausal complexity has been the most commonly explored dimension, recent studies on L2 writing development have shown the importance of integrating at least one other dimension, i.e. phrasal complexity, which has been pointed out as a distinctive feature of academic writing and of L2 writing at the advanced level (e.g. Biber *et al.*, 2011; Penris & Verspoor, 2017). Such studies have noted the progression from clausal complexification (via coordination and subordination) to phrasal complexification as learners develop their proficiency levels (Neary-Sundquist, 2016; Norris & Ortega, 2009). While beginner learners depend more on coordination strategies to make their writing more complex, they progressively learn, and hence use, more subordination strategies as they progress to the intermediate level of proficiency. Both strategies either decrease or reach a ceiling effect once the learners reach the advanced end of the proficiency spectrum. Studies of L2 writing at the advanced level pinpointed phrasal complexification as a distinctive feature of writing at this level and as a good predictor of writing quality scores (Lu & Ai, 2015; Yoon, 2017). As such, the current recommendation for choice of measures to be employed in studies venturing into the realm of syntactic complexity in L2 writing is an efficient combination of judiciously selected non-overlapping measures that correspond to at least three subconstructs of complexity – i.e. coordination, subordination, and phrasal complexification – as complexity may have different manifestations at different proficiency levels.

Complex Dynamic Systems Theory and Syntactic Complexity in L2 Writing

With the recent wider acceptance of Complex Dynamic Systems Theory (CDST) in the field of applied linguistics as well as second language acquisition, language (system, learning and development) is being reconsidered more holistically as a dynamic system. Language is a complex dynamic system in which components are interconnected and which changes over time (Verspoor & Behrens, 2011). Closely connected components tend to cluster together to form a subsystem, which is nested in a larger subsystem that is also interconnected with other subsystems nested within the complex dynamic system of a language. For example, the plural marker /-s/ is made up of a subsystem at the orthographic level which includes its allomorphs /-s/, /-es/, /-ies/, and another closely related subsystem at the phonological level which includes the phonemes /-s/, /-z/, /-iz/ (Rosmawati, 2014). As all these components change over time, changes in one component are very likely to have (ripple) effects on other components and to cause changes in other subsystem(s) that the changing subconstruct is nested in. Changes in any components in such complex connections are very likely to bring about 'differences' in the outward behaviour of the system. In other words, the components of language have the feature of nestedness – therefore, changes in any components can cause ripple effects in any subsystems they are nested in and this leads to variability in the output of a learner as well as to variation between the outputs of different learners (Lowie & Verspoor, 2015).

Syntactic constructions, as components of a language system, also display the feature of nestedness. However, currently available measures of syntactic complexity do not integrate this feature – perhaps because this feature was not included in considerations when those measures were conceived. As a result, while the currently available syntactic complexity measures are able to give a numerical representation of syntactic complexity at their corresponding levels, these numerical values cannot offer insights into the structures that underpin and/or constitute such representations (Rosmawati, 2020). For example, while MLS can tell the average length of sentences in a learner's writing, it does not offer insights into the way(s) in which the sentences are complex. Even when used in combination with other fine-grained measures, these quantified measures can only tell that the learners have used such strategies, and for how many times they have used them, and in what proportion they have used them. They cannot reveal *what* underpins the manifestation of complexity as reflected in those numerical values and, most importantly, they do not offer insights into the underpinning changes that drive the different manifestations at the textual level. Therefore, it is an inherent drawback of these measures that they do not offer adequate insights into the underpinning structures whose manifestations in the learners' text are captured in the numerical values these measures present.

Rosmawati (2020) proposed the use of a multilevel synchrony method to address this concern. Multilevel synchrony is a method of mapping the components of a sentence onto their syntactic property and function at the word, phrasal, clausal, and sentential levels simultaneously. Through this method, each word in a sentence is mapped onto its syntactic property. Such mapping is at the word level. At the same time as the word level mapping, these words are also mapped onto their functions at the phrasal level and are clustered together into the phrasal constructions they are nested in. Such mapping is at the phrasal level. These phrases are then mapped onto the clausal construction they are a part of, and this mapping is at the clausal level. Eventually, the clauses are mapped onto the sentence they are nested in and this is mapping at the sentential level. Rosmawati (2020) termed these concurrent mapping processes the 'multilevel synchrony method' and the product of such mappings is a visual representation of the underpinning structures of the learner's text, which also captures both (intra-individual) variability and (inter-individual) variation in the output of the learners. This method is adopted in this chapter to map the data in each of the cases presented here.

The Three Cases

This study explores the texts produced by three L2 student writers, who were postgraduate students within the same program in an Australian higher education institution and were of higher intermediate/ lower advanced levels of proficiency in English. The purpose of the study was to map the developmental profiles of syntactic complexity in their academic writing (see Table 3.2 for a description of the participants). In this chapter, the different types of syntactic constructions these student writers used in their academic writing are explored and special focus is given to complex nominal construction, which is one of the most representative traits of academic prose (Biber *et al.*, 2011; Ortega, 2015). This chapter maps out the different types of complex nominalisation

Table 3.2 Description of the participants

	Case 1	Case 2	Case 3
Pseudonym	Machiko	Jaeri	Yingying
L1	Japanese	Korean	Chinese
Gender	Female	Female	Female
Age	Early 30s	Late 20s	Mid 20s
L2 proficiency level*	B2/C1	B2/C1	B2/C1

*CEFR equivalent

strategies these three student writers used in their essays and how each strategy changed/developed over the course of one academic year. The aim is to build profiles of syntactic complexity in L2 academic writing at the advanced level in order to identify the alignment (or the gap) between the syntactic constructions these student writers used in their writing and those typical of academic writing in English.

The data were the academic essays written by these three participants. Ten essays were collected from each participant per semester, totalling 20 essays per participant over the two academic semesters during which they completed a master's degree coursework program in an Australian higher education institution. These essays were of a critical argumentative/descriptive nature and written as responses to tasks/prompts such as 'Write a critical review of an article in the TESOL field', 'Write a critical analysis of an issue in TESOL', 'Argue for the rationale for a methodological/pedagogical choice in TESOL', etc. In this study, a purposive sampling procedure (approximately 10% of the original text) was applied to the dataset to filter out paragraphs with dense paraphrases and quotations, as these might give a false impression of the learner's performance. The resulting sub-dataset of approximately 12,000 words was then manually coded and are analysed in this chapter.

The discussion in this chapter is underpinned by Complex Dynamic Systems Theory (de Bot, 2017; Larsen-Freeman, 1997, 2017; Verspoor, 2017) and places the spotlight on the feature of nestedness between components of syntactic complexity. Texts from each participant are mapped with the multilevel synchrony method in order to integrate the feature of nestedness into data exploration. Measures used in the three case studies in this chapter are listed in Table 3.3.

Results

The overall complexity measures (FVTR) fluctuated much in the essays produced by the three participants over the two semesters. As can be seen in Figure 3.1, there are sharp peaks and deep valleys in the three lines that plot the values of the overall complexity measures in the three participants' data. Although most of the values fluctuated between 10 and 20, there were a few points beyond this range – for example, in Jaeri's essays no. 6 and 19, as well as in Yingying's essays no. 5, 11, and 14.

In order to understand what motivates the changes in the overall/sentential complexity measures, it is essential to look beyond the sentential level to the other two levels that are nested within it, i.e. the clausal and the phrasal levels, as the changes in either or both of these levels would most certainly affect the structural manifestation of a sentence, and hence changes in the overall complexity.

Table 3.3 Measures of syntactic complexity used in the case studies

Type of measure	Syntactic level	Code	Operationalisation
Frequency-count	Sentential	Si	The number of simple sentences
		Co	The number of compound sentences
		Cx	The number of complex sentences
		CoCx	The number of compound complex sentences
	Clausal	IC	The number of independent clauses
		DepC	The number of dependent clauses
		AdvC	The number of adverbial clauses
		RelC	The number of relative clauses
		NomC	The number of nominal clauses
		NFC	The number of non-finite clauses
	Phrasal	PP	The number of prepositional phrases
		AdjP	The number of adjective phrases
		AdvP	The number of adverb phrases
		FVP	The number of finite verb phrases
		CNS*	The number of complex nominal structures
	Connector	C	The number of conjunctions
Mean-length	Clausal	MLS	Mean Length Sentence (the total number of words divided by the total number of sentences)
	Phrasal	MLC	Mean Length Clauses (the total number of words divided by the total number of clauses)
Ratio	Sentential (Overall)	FVTR**	Finite Verb Token Ratio (the total number of words divided by the total number of finite verbs)

*CN-pre: premodified CNS; CN-post: postmodified CNS; CN-pre&post: pre- and post- modified CNS; CN-NomC, CN-RelC, and CN-NFC are all post-modified CNS that are modified by a nominal clause, relative clause, and non-finite clause respectively.
**For more discussion on the measure of FVTR, please refer to Verspoor, Lowie & van Dijk (2008).

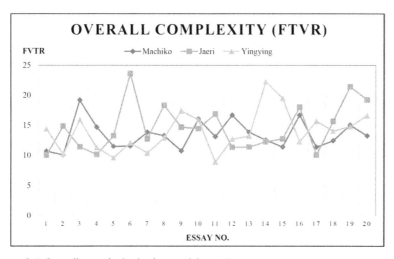

Figure 3.1 Overall complexity in the participants' essays

Case 1: Machiko's writing

The overall complexity measure (FTVR) in Machiko's writing fluctuated between 10 and 20 and reached a peak in essay no. 3, which remained as the highest peak for Machiko throughout the data from the two semesters. This peak was then followed by a large degree of fluctuation, although relatively lower in magnitude when compared to the fluctuation within the first three essays in this data set.

As can be seen from Figure 3.2, the high spike of sentential complexity in Machiko's essay no. 3 seemed to be mainly motivated by high clausal complexity, which also reached a conspicuous peak in the same essay: in essay 3, both sentential complexity and clausal complexity were high. A sample sentence from this essay is presented in Figure 3.3 to illustrate the manifestation of syntactic complexity construction in this piece of writing. The multilevel synchrony method was applied to analyse this sentence. As this method depicts complexification at all levels simultaneously, it not only offers visual access to the causes of complexity manifestation, but also makes it easier to explore the syntactic makeup of the learners' sentence.

The sample sentence in Figure 3.3 is a compound-complex sentence, made up of two independent clauses with seven dependent clauses. Having seven independent clauses within a sentence that has only two T-units has inflated the subordination measure (DepC/T) causing it to shoot up to a high index of 3.5 for the clausal complexity of this sentence. Applying the multilevel synchrony method to this sentence, makes it possible to see that phrasal complexity does not play much of a role in producing high sentential complexity in this sentence.

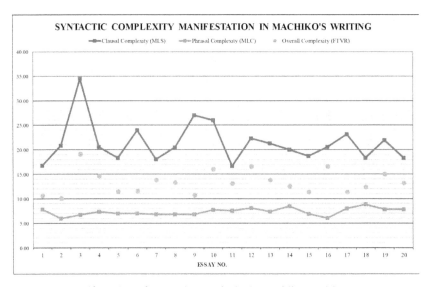

Figure 3.2 Manifestation of syntactic complexity in Machiko's writing

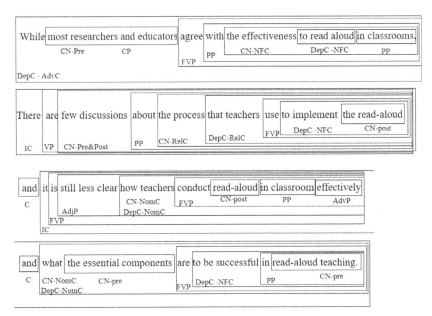

Figure 3.3 A sample sentence from Machiko's essay no. 3 (Word count = 56; FV = 6; T-unit = 2; compound-complex sentence = 2 IC + 7 DepC). Reprinted from 'Profiling the dynamic changes of syntactic complexity in L2 academic writing: A multilevel synchrony method. In G. Fogal and M. Verspoor, *Complex Dynamic Systems Theory and L2 Writing Development*, 2020, p. 121. Reprinted with kind permission from John John Benjamins Publishing Company, Amsterdam/Philadelphia. [www.benjamins.com]

Further exploration of the latter half set of the data reveals that complexity in Machiko's writing during this period might be driven by phrasal complexity, as can be seen by the increase in MLC values. For example, in essay no. 12, 14, 17, 18, the MLC index was above the value of 8. In order to understand what caused such a high value, it is essential to look into the subconstructs of phrasal complexity.

Figure 3.4 shows the token count of some of the phrasal complexity measures in Machiko's essays. It indicates that phrasal complexity in Machiko's essay no. 14, for example, was mainly driven by the high use of complex nominal structures, adjectival phrases and prepositional phrases. Figure 3.5 is a sentence from this essay and demonstrates how the multilevel synchrony method presents a clearer visual inspection of the manifestation of phrasal complexity.

The multilevel synchrony method gives a clear visual mapping of a phrase that is nested within a larger phrase, iteration being possible, creating a long complex nominal structure. In the sample sentence in Figure 3.5, the two (shorter) prepositional phrases are nested within the complex nominal structure which is a post-modified noun phrase with the two prepositional phrases being the post-modifiers. A further

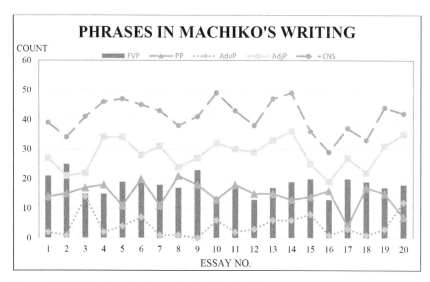

Figure 3.4 Distribution of phrases in Machiko's writing

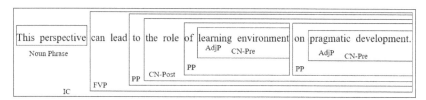

Figure 3.5 A sample sentence from Machiko's essay no. 3 (1 FVP + 3 PP + 2 CN-pre containing AdjP + 1 CN-post). Reprinted from 'Profiling the dynamic changes of syntactic complexity in L2 academic writing: A multilevel synchrony method.' In G. Fogal and M. Verspoor, *Complex Dynamic Systems Theory and L2 Writing Development*, 2020, p. 124. Reprinted with kind permission from John John Benjamins Publishing Company, Amsterdam/Philadelphia. [www.benjamins.com]

exploration of these two prepositional phrases reveals that a complex nominal structure is nested within each of these prepositional phrases and that both these complex nominal structures are pre-modified noun phrases with the pre-modifiers being adjectival phrases. Through the multilevel synchrony mapping method, it is possible to explore visually the manifestation of syntactic complexity in this sentence and to see that the learner (Machiko) applied a pre-modification strategy in making nominal phrases and integrated it into a post-modified nominal phrase making a long and complex nominal structure. These pre-modification and post-modification strategies, which are characteristics of academic writing in English, are prevalent in the learner's writing.

Figure 3.6 shows that Machiko produced many complex nominal structures (CNS) in her essays. This type of structure aligns well with the characteristics of academic writing in English and, since Machiko's

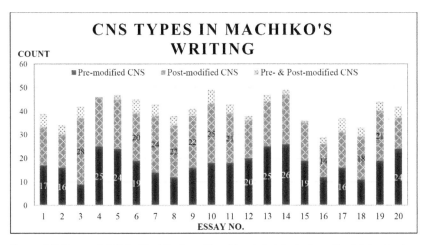

Figure 3.6 Types of CNS in Machiko's writing (the data labels show the highest value among the three strategies within each data point)

essays were academic in nature, a high occurrence of CNSs was not beyond expectation. The multilevel synchrony mapping shows the types of modification Machiko used in forming complex noun structures and reveals that she used a pre-modification strategy in most of the occurrences. As can be seen in Figure 3.6, in 11 of the 20 essays that she wrote, she produced more pre-modified CNSs than post-modified ones. It is worth mentioning that she also employed clausal modification to form complex noun structures and this type of modification featured in all her essays. This strategy was also a relatively large proportion of the modifications used in essay no. 3, where the highest sentential complexity was evident.

When both clausal complexity and phrasal complexity are explored simultaneously through the multilevel synchrony method, it becomes evident that Machiko employed both clausal and phrasal complexification strategies. Figure 3.2 suggests that she used more clausal complexification (through means of subordination) in the first half set of the data and this strategy seemed to decrease as she progressed into the second semester and became more familiar with the features of academic writing. Such familiarity was also evident from the increased phrasal complexity in the second half set of the data. This developmental path seems to suggest that Machiko's writing was progressing towards more alignment with the characteristics of academic writing in English.

Case 2: Jaeri's writing

Jaeri's developmental profile is different from Machiko's. As can be seen in Figure 3.1, Jaeri's sentential complexity measure reflects a relatively higher value than Machiko's. There were two occasions where this value exceeded 20, i.e. in essays no. 6 and no. 19, and even at its lowest point, this value never fell below 10. This means that Jaeri used at least a ratio of 10 words per one finite verb in her writing, and, in the most complex cases, more than 20 words per one finite verb. A further exploration of the distribution of sentence types in her writing reveals that compound-complex sentences accounted for a relatively large proportion (nearly 40% on average) of her writing. They were present in nearly all the essay samples examined in this study, except in essay no. 9. There were two essays which contained more compound-complex sentences than any other type of sentence, i.e. essays no. 17 and no. 18. In these two essays, compound-complex sentences made up more than half the essays, up to as high as 80%.

Given the high ratio of compound-complex sentences, one would expect a correspondingly high value of either clausal subordination or clausal coordination in these essays. The multilevel synchrony mapping of Jaeri's essays revealed that, in Jaeri's case, it seemed to be the latter. However, an analysis of the measures of clausal complexity and phrasal complexity in Jaeri's writing shows that the clausal coordination index for Jaeri's essays was always greater than 1. This means that on average there was more than one T-unit being joined through coordination in a sentence. Indeed, the high proportion of complex sentences and compound-complex sentences in both essays no. 17 and no. 18 corresponded to clausal coordination. However, this does not imply low production of subordinate clauses. In fact, it is the opposite.

It is evident, from the multilevel synchrony mapping, that Jaeri produced many subordinate clauses as well in her writing. In essay no. 13, the subordination index showed a sharp upsurge to a value as high as 9.33, which equates to an average of approximately 9 dependent clauses embedded in each T-unit. Figure 3.7 is a sentence from Jaeri's essay no. 13 and illustrates the heavy use of subordinate clauses in this essay.

Besides subordination and coordination strategies, Jaeri also employed complex nominalisation strategies in her writing, which was to be expected as all these essays were of an academic nature. As can be seen from Figure 3.8, the CNS count started relatively high at the beginning of the first semester but quickly dropped throughout the semester. It rose steadily towards the end of the first semester but dropped again at the beginning of the second semester. It was towards the middle of the second semester that it gradually rose and eventually reached a peak value at essay no. 17 (see Figure 3.8). Interestingly, essay no. 6 essay, where the highest value for the overall complexity measure was obtained, did not reflect the highest usage of complex nominal structures, subordination, or coordination (see the section on Limitation for further explanation). Multilevel synchrony mapping of the data from Jaeri showed that the type of complex nominalisation strategy that Jaeri

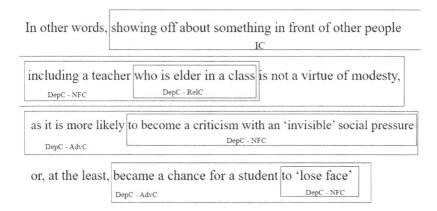

Figure 3.7 A sample sentence from Jaeri's essay no. 13 (grammatical error(s) not corrected) (T-unit count = 1; dependent clause count = 7; DepC/T = 7)

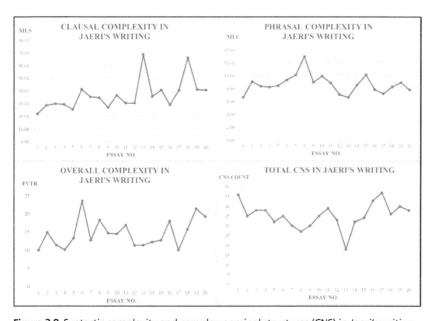

Figure 3.8 Syntactic complexity and complex nominal structures (CNS) in Jaeri's writing

deployed most frequently was the pre-modification strategy as well as clausal modification in forming complex nominals.

When compared to Machiko's writing, Jaeri's writing showed a different makeup of syntactic complexity. The data suggest that her major strategy for making the syntax more complex was elaboration at the clausal level, while Machiko preferred to use clausal elaboration at the beginning but shifted more towards phrasal elaboration as she progressed.

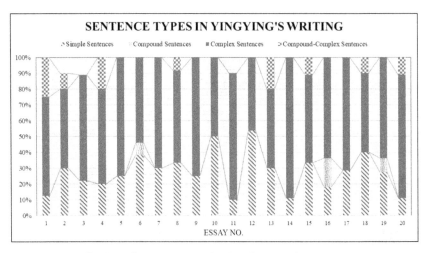

Figure 3.9 Distribution of sentence types in Yingying's writing

Case 3: Yingying's writing

Yingying's writing displayed yet a different pattern. The measure of sentential complexity in Yingying's writing fluctuated over a small range during the first semester, but the magnitude of this fluctuation expanded in the second semester, signalling more variability towards the second half of the data set. As can be seen in Figure 3.1, both the lowest and the highest values were reached in the second half set of the data, i.e. in essays no. 11 and no. 14 respectively. Looking at the types of sentences that Yingying produced in her writing, as shown in Figure 3.9, it is evident that her essays were mainly made up of complex sentences. This was to be expected as Yingying was an advanced learner, as were all the other participants, and the nature of the essays was academic. However, unlike the other two participants in this study, Yingying produced a large number of simple sentences (see Figure 3.9). Also, she sometimes produced incomplete sentences/fragments – for example, in essays no. 2, 3 and 11.

A further examination through the multilevel synchrony method of the subordination strategy Yingying employed in her writing shows that this index was relatively low, especially when compared to the other two participants in this study. While other participants' writing had a higher subordination index, the highest value obtained for this index in Yingying's writing was 2.6, and that was the only occasion on which the value exceeded 2. This means that most of the time she produced fewer than two dependent clauses in every sentence. This converges with the distribution of sentence types evident in her sentences, which shows a rather large proportion of simple sentences. Indeed, a closer look at the

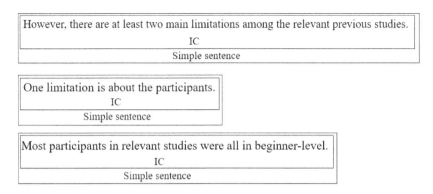

Figure 3.10 A sample sentence from Yingying's essay no. 18 (errors not corrected) (Independent clauses = 3; dependent clauses = 0; all simple sentences)

excerpts from Yingying's essays revealed that many of them contained chunks of consecutive simple sentences, as illustrated in Figure 3.10.

The three sentences cited in Figure 3.10 could have been compacted into two sentences (or even one) by means of subordination, coordination and/or complex nominalisation. However, Yingying did not employ these strategies very frequently and she seemed to be content with producing simple sentences, therefore resulting in the relatively high proportion of simple sentences in her writing (see Figure 3.9).

In fact, not only was the subordination index low in Yingying's writing, her clausal coordination index was also relatively low compared to the other two participants. This index fluctuated between 0.9 and 1.2 in her writing, suggesting that, at its maximum, she produced only one pair of coordinated clauses in every four sentences. However, despite the low evidence of subordination and coordination in Yingying's writing compared with the other participants', her overall complexity index was not very far below that of the other two participants'. One possible explanation is that she produced a large number of complex nominals in her writing. Indeed, she did produce many such constructions and the number became even larger towards the end of the second semester.

Further exploration, using the multilevel synchrony method, into the type of complex nominalisation strategy Yingying deployed reveals that, like the other two participants in this study, she used pre-modification most frequently. It was the most dominant strategy employed in her writing. The mapping further reveals that, although Yingying also used clausal modification to form complex nominals, the frequency with which she used it was very low. This is in line with the results discussed above and suggests that subordination was not Yingying's preferred strategy. This finding shows that, unlike the other two participants' writing, Yingying's essays showed a different makeup of syntactic complexity and were highly idiosyncratic.

Discussion

The findings of this study confirm a number of major propositions in the L2 writing research field. Firstly, they support the proposition that academic writing at the advanced level displays characteristics of concise/compact language with high complexity at the phrasal level, particularly in terms of complex nominal structures (Biber & Gray, 2016; Biber *et al.*, 2011; Biber *et al.*, 2016). The essays written by the participants in this study all displayed a variety of complex nominalisation strategies which they employed in making their writing more complex and more academic. These strategies included the use of pre-modifiers (e.g. adjectives), post-modifiers (e.g. prepositional phrases, relative clauses), and the simultaneous use of pre- and post-modifiers, which are also cited as typical characteristics of academic prose in Biber *et al.* (1999). In particular, the use of prepositional phrases as post-modifiers in complex nominal structures, as detected in many other studies such as Casal and Lee (2019), Jiang *et al.* (2019), and Taguchi *et al.* (2013), is also evident in the academic writing produced by the three participants in this study.

Secondly, the manifestation of syntactic complexity in each participant's writing was different. Machiko tended to modify complexity at the clausal level and use strategies like subordination to lengthen her sentences in the first semester although she gradually progressed towards phrasal complexification in the second semester. Applying the multi-level synchrony mapping method to her texts allowed for visual representation of the complexification strategies that she used in her writing and showed that Machiko used many dependent clauses in the texts she produced during the first semester but gradually shifted to using more complex nominals, adjectival phrases and prepositional phrases in the second semester. This is in line with Norris and Ortega's (2009) suggestion on the progression of elaboration strategies from coordination to subordination and eventually towards phrasal complexification as learners progress toward the higher end of the proficiency spectrum. Jaeri, on the other hand, showed a different pattern of syntactic complexity in her writing. Using multilingual synchrony mapping, it can be seen that Jaeri employed clausal coordination in combination with subordination to make her sentences more complex whilst also using complex nominalisation strategy quite frequently. Towards the end of the data collection period, her writing showed high indices of elaboration at both the clausal and the phrasal levels (see Figure 3.8). Such increases in both clausal and phrasal complexities closely align with the findings in Lahuerta Martínez (2018), who demonstrated significant increases in subordination as well as in the length of noun phrases, detected using different measures of clausal and phrasal complexity from those employed in the current study.

A different pattern again was shown in the essays produced by Yingying, the third participant in this study. When her texts were mapped using the multilingual synchrony mapping method, it became visually obvious that Yingying's writing not only showed low subordination and coordination but also was characterised by a high proportion of simple sentences, which was rather unexpected given that the nature of the essays was academic prose. However, she produced many complex nominal structures in her essays and mainly used the pre-modification strategy in making the nominal structures longer and more complex. This finding is in line with Yoon (2017), who noticed a possibly general pattern of complexification at the phrasal level in Chinese students' academic writing. However, Yingying's MLS measure is slightly higher than that reported in Yoon (2017), although the MLC measure is comparable in both studies.

Use of the multilevel synchrony mapping method affords the synchronous mapping of a construct and its subconstructs simultaneously. It enables a visual inspection of the complexification strategies used in the texts and hence captures a more nuanced picture of the profiles of syntactic complexity in the texts produced by each learner. In this study, it is evident that each learner's writing shows different and rather idiosyncratic profiles of syntactic complexity. Such differences in usage pattern are in line with the proposition of CDST that each learner is an idiosyncratic entity (de Bot & Larsen-Freeman, 2011; Lowie *et al.*, 2009; van Dijk *et al.*, 2011). Idiosyncrasy has been highlighted not only in the field of language learning in particular (Lowie, 2012) but also in the field of human development in general (Kunnen, 2012; Smith & Thelen, 2003; Spencer *et al.*, 2006). Language use and development, which is an aspect of human development, is to be understood as an individual matter and explained within the boundary of its context (Lowie & Verspoor, 2014; Lowie *et al.*, 2009).

Lastly, the data in this study demonstrate the feature of 'nestedness' and hence lend support to the CDST proposition that language is a fractal in which lower-level subsystems are nested in higher level systems, which are in turn nested in yet another, even higher level, system. In other words, the data in this study confirm that such a feature is indeed an inherent property of language and hence confirm this aphorism, among the 30 that Larsen-Freeman (2017) mentioned.

Implications

This study contributes to enriching the description of L2 learners' academic writing through a detailed exploration of the diverse syntactic structures that advanced L2 learners used in their academic writing and the changes in their use of these structures over time. It also highlights several important findings which have direct pedagogical implications.

Firstly, the overuse of simple sentences in the writing of one of the participants may hint at a possible challenge that the student faced in her writing. The student may not have felt comfortable with joining ideas with coordination or subordination, or both, in a logical way and presenting them in a more complex sentence. This might have been due to the student's lack of confidence in selecting the most appropriate/ logical connectors, or to a lack of awareness of syntactic variations in academic writing. While it is not possible to pinpoint the cause by looking at the texts they produced, text exploration, as conducted in this chapter, provides a window through which potential challenges in a student's writing can be identified. Once identified, the issue can be raised with the student to initiate an exploration into the potential cause(s) and to devise ways to address it (them).

Similarly, the overuse of clausal elaboration in the other participant's writing may also hint at low awareness of the concise phrasal discourse style of academic prose. The student might not be aware of these styles, and awareness-raising feedback/training might prove fruitful in helping improve academic literacy even at the very advanced end of proficiency spectrum as such explicit instruction not only raises the salience of the target forms but also helps learners notice the gap in their knowledge (Ellis, 2006), which frequently has a facilitative role in learning (e.g. Bu, 2012). Thus, explicit teaching of the differences between two languages in terms of their syntactic constructions should perhaps be given more consideration as a pedagogical strategy when teaching academic writing in English, thereby helping to make students aware of, and gradually develop familiarity with, the norms of writing academically in English.

Secondly, the idiosyncratic profiles of each of the learners studied in this chapter warrant the need for more caution, in teaching as well as in research, and the need to see beyond the standardised frame of proficiency levels into which the students are categorised and appreciate the individual in them. Each learner is an individual, whose learning experience and language development are unique to themselves and who may, therefore, display a different pattern of language use from their peers in the same proficiency group. They may also be facing and dealing with different challenges despite being in the same proficiency group and will therefore need different assistance/instruction. Similarly, it is important to note that findings from group studies need to be carefully considered and flexibly adapted to teaching, taking care not to dismiss the individuality of the students in their L2 learning journey and in their preferred way of using the L2.

Finally, the multilevel synchrony method employed in this chapter offers an effective pedagogical tool for explaining the concept of syntax and syntactic complexity to L2 learners. The method provides a visual map of sentence components and their syntactic functions and can therefore be utilised in the pedagogy both as a teaching tool when explaining to students how to make their writing more complex as well as a means of self-reflection for students to explore the distribution of syntactic constructions in their writing. It can also serve as a tool for checking grammatical accuracy, as the explicit mapping of the sentence components to their syntactic functions enhances the visibility of the grammatical relationship between components.

Limitations and Future Directions

There are a number of limitations to this study which restrict the scope within which interpretations of the findings can be made. Firstly, the occurrence of complex nominal structures in the data were coded with the coding schema indicated in Table 3.3, without noting whether they were a first mention or a subsequent mention of a referent. Biber *et al.* (1999) pointed out that first mentions of a referent in academic texts are usually post-modified noun phrases, while pre-modified noun phrases are used in both first mentions as well as subsequent mentions of a referent. In other words, the distribution patterns of these two types of modification are different depending on whether the referent is newly introduced or has been previously mentioned in the text. Therefore, the counts of different types of CNS in this study that were tallied without noting this information did not contain enough granularity to enable more in-depth interpretation of the data beyond the discussion above.

Similarly, no separate observation was made regarding the sections of the texts analysed in this study. Hutter (2015) noted that patterns of modification for complex noun phrases varied depending on the sections of the text in which the noun phrases occurred. Through a corpus-based analysis of articles published in the field of applied linguistics as well as language teaching, she demonstrated that the types of noun modification that occur in different sections of a text are not uniform. In other words, the sections from which the sample texts in this study were extracted would have had an impact upon the pattern of CNS usage captured and discussed here. However, as information on which sections the texts were extracted from was not available, this study did not capture such fine-grained details to allow construction of a more nuanced picture of the CNS usage pattern in the participants' academic writing.

Lastly, the interpretations that were made of the data in this study were subject to the inherent limitation of the currently available measures of syntactic complexity, which sets restrictions on the information that can be extracted from the numerical values these measures produce. For example, in Jaeri's essay no. 16, the overall complexity measure showed the highest value. However, the measures of clausal complexity, phrasal complexity, and complex nominal structures did not show any correspondingly high value. This is an interesting yet puzzling phenomenon because it leads to the question: what is it that caused the high index in the overall complexity measure? One might argue that it was perhaps a combination of all these strategies (complexification at the clausal and the phrasal levels) that inflated the overall complexity measures. However, this does not address the inherent limitation of the measures regarding the amount of information they capture. Further contemplation on this limitation point will likely lead to a series of questions on the validity of the measures. For example, 'What is it that the numerical value of the measure(s) actually tells us in terms of the syntactic make-up of the sentences in a learner's writing?', 'Are the measures formulated in a way that accurately gauge the constructs they are designed to measure?', etc. Most importantly, given that syntactic complexity is multifaceted and that components of language are nested within one another, it is perhaps necessary to design a measure that incorporates these characteristics and can hence better capture the information on 'how' students' writing is complex.

Notes

(1) For more discussion on CDST in language studies see de Bot (2017), Han and Liu (2019) and Larsen-Freeman (1997).
(2) To name a few, these include low proficiency in English, low (or lack of) awareness of different interdisciplinary conventions, intercultural rhetoric, etc.

References

Biber, D. and Gray, B. (2016) *Grammatical Complexity in Academic English: Linguistic Change in Writing*. Cambridge: Cambridge University Press.
Biber, D., Gray, B. and Poonpon, K. (2011) Should we use characteristics of conversation to measure grammatical complexity in L2 writing development? *TESOL Quarterly* 45 (1), 5–35. doi:10.5054/tq.2011.244483.
Biber, D., Gray, B. and Staples, S. (2016) Predicting patterns of grammatical complexity across language exam task types and proficiency levels. *Applied Linguistics* 37 (5), 639–668. doi:10.1093/applin/amu059.
Biber, D., Reppen, R., Staples, S. and Egbert, J. (2020) Exploring the longitudinal development of grammatical complexity in the disciplinary writing of L2-English university students. *International Journal of Learner Corpus Research* 6 (1), 38–71. doi: 10.1075/ijlcr.18007.bib.
Biber, D., Johansson, S., Leech, G., Conrad, S. and Finegan, E. (1999) *Longman Grammar of Spoken and Written English*. Harlow: Pearson Education.
Bu, J. (2012) A study of the effects of explicit and implicit teachings on developing Chinese EFL learners' pragmatic competence. *International Journal of Language Studies* 6 (3), 57–80.
Bulté, B. and Housen, A. (2012) Defining and operationalising L2 complexity. In A. Housen, F. Kuiken and I. Vedder (eds) *Dimensions of L2 Performance and Proficiency: Complexity, Accuracy and Fluency in SLA* (pp. 21–46). Amsterdam/Philadelphia: John Benjamins.
Bulté, B. and Housen, A. (2014) Conceptualizing and measuring short-term changes in L2 writing complexity. *Journal of Second Language Writing* 26, 42–65. doi: 10.1016/j.jslw. 2014.09.005.
Bulté, B. and Housen, A. (2019) Beginning L2 complexity development in CLIL and non-CLIL secondary education. *Instructed Second Language Acquisition* 3 (2), 153–180. doi: 10.1558/isla.38247.

Casal, J.E. and Lee, J.J. (2019) Syntactic complexity and writing quality in assessed first-year L2 writing. *Journal of Second Language Writing* 44, 51–62. doi:10.1016/j.jslw.2019.03.005.

de Bot, K. (2017) Complexity theory and dynamic systems theory: Same or different? In L. Ortega and Z. Han (eds) *Complexity Theory and Language Development: In Celebration of Diane Larsen-Freeman* (pp. 51–58). Amsterdam/Philadelphia: John Benjamins.

de Bot, K. and Larsen-Freeman, D. (2011) Researching second language development from a dynamic systems theory perspective. In M.H. Verspoor, K. de Bot and W. Lowie (eds) *A Dynamic Systems Approach to Second Language Development* (pp. 5–23). Amsterdam/Philadelphia: John Benjamins.

Ellis, N. (2006) The weak interface, consciousness, and form-focused instruction: Mind the doors. In S. Fotos and H. Nassaji (eds) *Form-focused Instruction and Teacher Education:Studies in Honor of Rod Ellis* (pp. 17–34). Oxford: Oxford University Press.

Ellis, R. (2003) *Task–based Language Learning and Teaching*. Oxford: Oxford University Press.

Fogal, G. (2020) Unpacking 'simplex systems': Curricular thinking for L2 writing development. In G. Fogal and M.H. Verspoor (eds) *Complex Dynamic Systems Theory and L2 Writing Development* (pp. 271–294). Amsterdam/Philadelphia: John Benjamins.

Godfrey, L., Treacy, C. and Tarone, E. (2014) Changes in French second language writing in study abroad and domestic contexts. *Foreign Language Annals* 47 (1), 48–65. doi: 10.1111/flan.12072.

Han, Z. and Liu, J. (2019) Profiling learner language from a complex dynamic system perspective: An introduction. In Z. Han (ed.) *Profiling Learner Language as a Dynamic System* (pp. 1–16). Bristol: Multilingual Matters.

Hickey, R. (2020) The colonial and postcolonial expansion of English. In D. Schreier, M. Hundt and E. Schneider (eds) *The Cambridge Handbook of World Englishes* (pp. 25–50). Cambridge: Cambridge University Press.

Housen, A. and Kuiken, F. (2009) Complexity, accuracy, and fluency in second language acquisition. *Applied Linguistics* 30 (4), 461–473. doi:10.1093/applin/amp048

Hutter, J.-A. (2015) A corpus-based analysis of noun modification in empirical research articles in applied linguistics. Master's thesis, Portland State University, PDXScholar database. Paper 2211.

Hyland, K. (2011) Learning to write: Issues in theory, research, and pedagogy. In R. Manchón (ed.) *Learning to Write and Writing to Learn in an Additional Language* (pp. 17–35). Amsterdam/Philadelphia: John Benjamins.

Jiang, J., Bi, P. and Liu, H. (2019) Syntactic complexity development in the writings of EFL learners: Insights from a dependency syntactically-annotated corpus. *Journal of Second Language Writing* 46, 1–13. doi:10.1016/j.jslw.2019.100666.

Kim, M. and Crossley, S.A. (2018) Modeling second language writing quality: A structural equation investigation of lexical, syntactic, and cohesive features in source-based and independent writing. *Assessing Writing* 37, 39–56. doi:10.1016/j.asw.2018.03.002.

Kunnen, S. (ed.) (2012) *A Dynamic Systems Approach to Adolescent Development*. New York: Routledge.

Lahuerta Martínez, A. (2018) L2 writing: A comparison of upper intermediate and advanced EFL learners. *European Journal of Language and Literature Studies* 4 (4), 17–21. doi:10.26417/ejls.v4i4.p17–21.

Larsen-Freeman, D. (1997) Chaos/complexity science and second language acquisition. *Applied Linguistics* 18 (2), 141–165. doi:10.1093/applin/18.2.141.

Larsen-Freeman, D. (2017) Complexity theory: The lessons continue. In L. Ortega and Z. Han (eds) *Complexity Theory and Language Development: In Celebration of Diane Larsen-Freeman* (pp. 11–50). Amsterdam/Philadelphia: John Benjamins.

Larsson, T. and Kaatari, H. (2020) Syntactic complexity across registers: Investigating (in)formality in second-language writing. *Journal of English for Academic Purposes* 45, 100850. doi: 10.1016/j.jeap.2020.100850.

Leki, I. (2011) Learning to write in a second language: Multilingual graduates and undergraduates expanding genre repertoires. In R. Manchón (ed.) *Learning to Write and Writing to Learn in an Additional Language* (pp. 85–109). Amsterdam/Philadelphia: John Benjamins.

Lowie, W. (2012) The CEFR and the dynamics of second language learning: Trends and challenges. *CercleS: Language Learning in Higer Education* 2 (1), 17–34. doi:10.1515/cercles–2012–0002.

Lowie, W. and Verspoor, M.H. (2014) Variability and learning mechanisms. Paper presented at the American Association for Applied Linguistics 2014, Portland, Oregon.

Lowie, W. and Verspoor, M.H. (2015) Variability and variation in second language acquisition orders: A dynamic reevaluation. *Language Learning* 65 (1), 63–88. doi:10.1111/lang.12093.

Lowie, W., Verspoor, M.H. and de Bot, K. (2009) A dynamic view of second language development across the lifespan. In K. de Bot and R.W. Schrauf (eds) *Language Development Over the Lifespan* (pp. 125–145). New York: Routledge.

Lu, X. (2011) A corpus-based evaluation of syntactic complexity measures as indices of college-level ESL writers' language development. *TESOL Quarterly* 45 (1), 36–62. doi:10.5054/tq.2011.240859.

Lu, X. and Ai, H. (2015) Syntactic complexity in college-level English writing: Differences among writers with diverse L1 backgrounds. *Journal of Second Language Writing* 29, 16–27. doi:10.1016/j.jslw.2015.06.003.

Manchón, R. (2015) The linguistic component of L2 written literacy in academic settings: Advancing research agendas on the interaction between writing and language. Paper presented at the 2015 Symposium on second language writing, Auckland, New Zealand.

Neary-Sundquist, C.A. (2016) Syntactic complexity at multiple proficiency levels of L2 German speech. *International Journal of Applied Linguistics* 27 (1), 242–262. doi:10.1111/ijal.12128.

Norris, J.M. and Ortega, L. (2009) Towards an organic approach to investigating CAF in instructed SLA: The case of complexity. *Applied Linguistics* 30 (4), 555–578. doi:10.1093/applin/amp044.

Ortega, L. (2015) Syntactic complexity in L2 writing: Progress and expansion. *Journal of Second Language Writing* 29 (1), 82–94. doi:10.1016/j.jslw.2015.06.008.

Paltridge, B. (2017) Context and the teaching of academic writing: Bringing together theory and practice. In J. Bitchener, N. Storch and R. Wette (eds) *Teaching Writing for Academic Purposes to Multilingual Students* (pp. 9–23). New York: Routledge.

Penris, W. and Verspoor, M. (2017) Academic writing development: A complex, dynamic process. In S. Pfenninger and J. Navracsics (eds) *Future Research Directions for Applied Linguistics* (pp. 215–242). Bristol: Multilingual Matters.

Phan, L. (2017) Global English, postcolonialism, and education. In M. Peters (ed.) *Encyclopedia of Educational Philosophy and Theory* (pp. 932–937). Singapore: Springer.

Rosmawati (2014) Second language developmental dynamics: How dynamic systems theory accounts for issues in second language learning. *The Educational and Developmental Psychologist* 31 (1), 66–80. doi: 10.1017/edp.2013.22.

Rosmawati, R. (2020) Profiling the dynamic changes of syntactic complexity in L2 academic writing: A multilevel synchrony method. In G. Fogal and M.H. Verspoor (eds) *Complex Dynamic Systems Theory and L2 Writing Development* (pp. 109–131). Amsterdam/Philadelphia: John Benjamins.

Smith, L.B. and Thelen, E. (2003) Development as a dynamic system. *TRENDS in Cognitive Sciences* 7 (8), 343–348. doi:10.1016/S1364–6613(03)00156–6.

Spencer, J.P., Clearfield, M., Corbetta, D., Ulrich, B., Buchanan, P. and Schöner, G. (2006) Moving toward a grand theory of development: In memory of Esther Thelen. *Child Development* 77 (6), 1521–1538. doi:0009–3920/2006/7706–0001.

Sum, Y. and Cong, Y. (2005) The study of nominalization acquisition in Chinese EFL learners. *CELEA Journal* 28 (6), 89–94.

Taguchi, N., Crawford, W. and Wetzel, D. (2013) What linguistic features are indicative of writing quality? A case of argumentative essays in a college composition program. *TESOL Quarterly* 47 (2), 420–430. doi:10.1002/tesq.91.

van Dijk, M., Verspoor, M.H. and Lowie, W. (2011) Variability and DST. In M.H. Verspoor, K. de Bot and W. Lowie (eds) *A Dynamic Approach to Second Language Development: Methods and Techniques* (pp. 55–84). Amsterdam/Philadelphia: John Benjamins.

Verspoor, M.H. (2017) Complex dynamic systems theory and L2 pedagogy. In L. Ortega and Z. Han (eds) *Complexity Theory and Language Development: In Celebration of Diane Larsen-Freeman* (pp. 143–162). Amsterdam/Philadelphia: John Benjamins.

Verspoor, M.H. and Behrens, H. (2011) Dynamic systems theory and a usage-based approach to second language development. In M.H. Verspoor, K. de Bot and W. Lowie (eds) *A Dynamic Approach to Second Language Development: Methods and Techniques* (pp. 25–38). Amsterdam/Philadelphia: John Benjamins.

Verspoor, M., Lowie, W. and van Dijk, M. (2008) Variability in second language development from a dynamic systems perspective. *The Modern Language Journal* 92 (2), 214–231. DOI: https://doi.org/10.1111/j.1540–4781.2008.00715.x.

Verspoor, M.H., Schmid, M.S. and Xu, X. (2012) A dynamic usage based perspective on L2 writing. *Journal of Second Language Writing* 21 (3), 239–263. doi:10.1016/j.jslw.2012.03.007.

Verspoor, M.H., Lowie, W., Chan, H. and Vahtrick, L. (2017) Linguistic complexity in second language development: Variability and variation at advanced stages. *Recherches en Didactique des Langues et des Cultures* 14 (1), 1–27. Retrieved from doi:10.4000/rdlc.1450.

Wang, Y. and Chen, J. (2013) Differences of English and Chinese as written languages and strategies in English writing teaching. *Teaching and Practice in Langauge Studies* 3 (4), 647–652. doi:10.4304/tpls.3.4.647–652.

Wolfe-Quintero, K., Inagaki, S. and Kim, H.Y. (1998) *Second Language Development in Writing: Measures of Fluency, Accuracy, and Complexity*. Manoa, Hawai'i: Second Language Teaching and Curriculum Center, University of Hawai'i.

Wu, X., Mauranen, A. and Lei, L. (2020) Syntactic complexity in English as a lingua franca academic writing. *Journal of English for Academic Purposes* 45, 100789. doi: 10.1016/j.jeap.2019.100798.

Yang, W., Lu, X. and Weigle, S.C. (2015) Different topics, different discourse: Relationships among writing topic, measures of syntactic complexity, and judgments of writing quality. *Journal of Second Language Writing* 28 (1), 53–67. doi:10.1016/j.jslw.2015.02.002.

Yin, S., Gao, Y. and Lu, X. (2021) Syntactic complexity of research article part–genres: Differences between emerging and expert international publication writers. *System* 97, 102427. doi: 10.1016/j.system.2020.102427.

Yoon, H.J. (2017) Linguistic complexity in L2 writing revisited: Issues of topics, proficiency, and construct multidimensionality. *System* 66, 130–141. doi:10.1016/j.system.2017.03.007.

4 Writing in School Science for EAL Students: Linguistic Challenges and Pedagogical Response

Zhihui Fang
University of Florida, USA

Guofang Li
University of British Columbia, Canada

Introduction

The recent emphasis on disciplinary literacy in American K-12 schooling, endorsed by the *Common Core State Standards* (www. corestandards.com), the *Next Generation of Science Standards* (www. nextgenscience.org) and the *Career, College, and Civic Life Framework for Social Studies* (www.socialstudies.org/c3), has placed greater cognitive and linguistic demands on students, who are now urged to read, write and think like scientists, mathematicians, historians and other disciplinary experts. In particular, writing in the core curriculum content areas of science, social studies/history, and mathematics is the most challenging for students, especially those learning English as an additional language (EAL), who are expected to learn the subject content while also developing language and literacy proficiency (Fang & Schleppegrell, 2008; Wilcox & Jeffrey, 2015). To help EAL students develop the academic language/literacy proficiency needed to engage effectively with content learning, it is crucial to be precise and specific about the linguistic challenges they face and to be linguistically responsive in the pedagogy proposed (Fang, 2020). Our chapter answers this need by identifying some of the linguistic challenges demonstrated by adolescent EAL learners in their school science writing and by describing a genre-based approach to teaching writing that promotes content learning and language/literacy development at the same time.

Writing and Science

Writing is central to both the conception of science and the work of practicing scientists (Fang, 2010; Hand, 2017). On one hand, science is a form of discourse involving the use of language, particularly written language (Norris & Phillips, 2003; Wellington & Osborne, 2001). On the other hand, scientists write in order to keep records of observations/experiments and to communicate their own views and findings to peers and the general public (Yore *et al*., 2004).

Because of its importance, writing has been seen by the science education community as a key component of science literacy that every student is expected to master (Yore *et al*., 2003). The *Next Generation of Science Standards*, for example, requires students to engage in language-intensive activities such as writing and reading as they develop models, present ideas, offer explanations, and engage in evidence-based reasoning (Lee *et al*., 2013). The *Common Core State Standards* (CCSS), likewise, emphasizes the essential role of writing in disciplinary learning, noting that students should demonstrate increasing sophistication in writing as 'a key means of asserting and defending claims, showing what they know about a subject, and conveying what they have experienced, imagined, thought, and felt' (see CCSS Appendix A, www.corestandards.org). Students are expected to write argumentative texts to support knowledge claims and informational texts to examine and convey complex ideas clearly, accurately, and logically. To meet these goals, the CCSS recommends that students 'devote significant time and effort to writing, producing numerous pieces over short and long time frames throughout the year' (see CCSS Appendix A, www.corestandards.org).

The Challenges of Writing in School Science

Despite the importance of writing to science and science learning, many students struggle with writing in science (e.g. Avalos *et al*., 2017; Seah *et al*., 2015). The problem is especially acute for EAL learners, as they face the double challenge of developing academic language and literacy at the same time they are learning subject content (August & Shanahan, 2006). While it can be argued that the vast majority of students are not likely to become practicing scientists and will, thus, not be expected to write the range of genres scientists use to construct and communicate their understanding or in a style typical of the discipline-legitimated discourse, there is still a critical need for them to develop the scientific habits of mind (e.g. curiosity, skepticism, creativity, openness to new ideas, intellectual honesty, ethical responsibility) and academic language/literacy skills that are essential for school success, career readiness, and democratic citizenship.

For this reason, school science is not equivalent to professional science; it is, instead, professional science recontextualized for educational purposes (Halliday & Martin, 1993). As such, school science has its own goals and genres. In addition to learning science content (e.g. big ideas, unifying themes, and key relationships), K-12 students are also expected to develop an understanding of science as inquiry, science in personal and social perspectives, and the history and nature of science (National Research Council, 2012). Some of the common school-based genres for fostering scientific knowledge and understanding are procedure, procedural recount, report, biography, explanation and argument, each of which has a specific purpose and draws on a distinct set of linguistic resources (Christie & Derewianka, 2008). Developing control over the lexicogrammatical resources for writing these genres is, therefore, an important task in K-12 science teaching and learning (Fang, 2006, 2010). This task becomes even more crucial for EAL students, who generally require more linguistic support in disciplinary literacy learning (de Oliverira & Schleppegrell, 2015; Fang, 2021a; Gebhard, 2019).

Theoretical Grounding of Linguistic Analysis

In the next section, we identify some of the linguistic issues EAL students face. We do so through an analysis of the writing they produced in the context of science learning. Our analysis is informed by systemic functional linguistics, or SFL (Halliday & Matthiessen, 2014). SFL is a meaning-based theory of language use. It sees language not as a set of prescriptive rules to be followed, but as a creative resource for making meaning. According to the theory, language use is functional: people use language to get things done, such as explaining a phenomenon, making a request, describing an object, arguing for/against a particular point of view, and performing a ritual. In this sense, language use is a semiotic process in which people make meaning by choosing from the various options that the lexis and the grammar in a language make available. Moreover, language use varies across cultural and situational contexts. People use language in different ways depending on the topic they are dealing with, the task they are engaging in, the audience they are addressing, and the broader and immediate contexts of their social interaction.

Two concepts that are central to SFL and particularly relevant to language and literacy education are genre and register. They are the focus of our analysis in this chapter. From an SFL perspective, genres are textual realizations of recurring, recognizable communicative events that enact the social practices of a given culture (Martin & Rose, 2008). Each discipline as a culture has its own genres that inventorize its social practices and codify its content. Each of these genres marshalls a distinct, relatively stable constellation of structural and linguistic features that enables it to achieve its purpose. Learning a discipline is, thus, synonymous with learning to write (and read) these discipline-legitimated genres (Hasan, 1996).

Register, on the other hand, refers to functional variation in language use across situational contexts (Halliday & Hasan, 1985). People make different language choices in different contexts depending on what they are talking about (field), whom they are interacting with (tenor), and the channel of communication (mode). Learning discipline-legitimated genres in school requires students to make linguistic choices that not only realize the purposes of these genres but also meet the demands of specific tasks in academic contexts (e.g. displaying knowledge, establishing authoritative voice, creating well-organized text that flows, adhering to grammatical conventions). This means that in addition to genre mastery, students also need to have a firm control over register in order to develop academic writing proficiency (Fang, 2021b).

Linguistic Issues in Two EAL Writing Samples

In this section, we draw on the SFL concepts of genre and register to analyze two writing samples produced by two EAL students in their science class. The writing samples were selected from a larger corpus collected as part of a larger research project aimed at improving secondary (middle/high) school students' science literacy through reading/literacy infusion (Fang, 2006; Fang & Wei, 2010; Fang *et al.*, 2008; Fang *et al.*, 2017; Patrick & Fang, in press). While the issues identified are based on only two writing samples by only two students, they are by no means unique to the samples or the students. Both pieces of writing were completed as a take-home assignment in a sixth-grade science unit on scientists and their careers. A popular and important part of the middle school science curriculum in the US, this nine-week unit was designed to increase students' understanding of Nature of Science (NOS) and their interest in pursuing science-related careers. In the unit, students read and discussed biographies of famous scientists, learning about the life stories of scientists, their science careers, the trials and tribulations in their scientific inquiries, the impact of their discoveries, and the personal and professional attributes that contributed to their success. They were expected to develop an understanding of NOS, which includes, among others, (a) scientific knowledge is simultaneously reliable and tentative, (b) science is not just for the genius, (c) science is not always clean and unequivocal, (d) science knowledge is a combination of observations and inferences, and (e) contributions to science can be, and have been, made by people all over the world. As a culminating project for the unit, each student was required to write a biography of a scientist who interested them or a report about a science career that they were interested in pursuing in the future. Apart from reviewing the two handouts, reproduced in Figure 4.1, that presented guidelines and grading rubrics for the task, the teacher provided no further explicit writing instruction related to the assignment or the unit of study. In other words, there was no

9 Weeks Project

Student Name: _____   Block: ___   Date: _____

Parts of the Project completed	Points available	Points earned
Schedule/Career choice with parent's signature	10 points	
Outline with parent's signature	20 points	
Written Report with parent's signature	30 points	
Presentation to class	40 points	Finish March 10

Written Report Grading Sheet

Category	Description	points
Parent Signature (1 point)	3. Parent signature on report (1 point)	
Format (4 points)	1. 12- point font if typed or blue or black ink if hand- written (1 point) 2. 2 pages double spaced if typed or 3 pages handwritten up to half a page = ½ point ½ - 1 page = 1½ points 1½ - 1¾ = 2 points 2-3 pages = 3 points	
Introduction (3 points)	1. Has a statement that tells what the paper is about (1 point) 2. Has an attention grabber to peak the reader's interest (1 point) 3. Tells what information will be covered in the paper (1 point)	
Body of paper (13 points)	1. Paragraphs have a topic sentence (3 points) 2. Paragraphs contains supporting sentences (3 points) 3. Information is organized in a logical sequence (2 points) 4. 20 facts from outline are in paper (5 points) ¼ of a point for every fact	
Conclusion (3 points)	1. Summarizes information covered in the paper. up to 10- 15 points 1½ × 2 points at = 3 points	
Works cited (3 points)	1. Has three different resources listed (½ point for each) 2. Has resources in the correct format (½ point for each)	
Mechanics/ Grammar (3 points)	1. Correct spelling of words (1 point) 2. Complete sentences (2 points)	
Turned in on time	1. 10% off for each day late day(s) late ___ × 10% = ___	

Total points earned _____

Subtract _____

Total points earned _____

How do I write a report?!

1. **Compose a thesis statement**
   a. Tells the reader what the essay will be about
   b. Part 1 states the topic
   c. Part 2 states the point of the essay

2. **Introduction**
   a. Begin with an attention grabber!
      1. Startling information or an anecdote (a short, to the point, and relevant to your topic)
   b. Summary Information: a few sentences explaining your topic in general terms.
   c. Finish the paragraph with your thesis statement

3. **Body Paragraphs**
   a. Start with a main idea in sentence form.
   b. Write down each of your supporting points for that main idea
   c. Elaborate or expand on supporting points
   d. Optional: include a summary sentence for each paragraph

4. **Conclusion**
   a. Sum up your points or main ideas
   b. Three or four strong sentences which do not need to follow any set format.
   c. Review the main points (being careful no to restate them exactly) or briefly describe your feelings about the topic.

Figure 4.1 Guidelines and grading rubrics for the writing assignment

explicit discussion of the specific linguistic expectations in terms of genre, register, or grammatical conventions for completing the assignment.

The first piece of writing, reproduced in Figure 4.2, is a biography of a famous scientist completed by Jaehyun. Jaehyun came from South Korea and spoke Korean as his first language. He had been in the US for less than two years and was still in the process of developing oral English fluency at the time the text was produced. The second piece of writing, reproduced in Figure 4.3, is a report about a science career completed by Rosa. Rosa came from Brazil and spoke fluent Portugese as her first language. She had been in the US for a little over five years and was fluent in spoken English at the time the text was produced. While both students showed considerable knowledge of the topic they were writing about, their writing was problematic from the perspectives of genre, register and grammatical conventions, as discussed below.

Genre

According to Rose and Martin, a genre is a type of text that represents 'a staged, goal oriented social process' (2012: 1). Each genre serves a specific social purpose, usually takes more than one phase to unfold, and marshals a particular set of linguistic resources. For example, a biography tells the life story of a significant individual, such as a famous scientist or an influential historical figure. The purpose of the genre is achieved by moving through three stages: an orientation that locates the person in time/space and provides a synopsis of his/her significant accomplishments, a sequence of events that highlights important moments or turning points in the person's life and/or career, and an evaluation that assesses the person's legacy (Coffin, 2006). It uses concrete nouns to refer to a specific individual (e.g. *Albert Einstein, Marie Curie*), action and relational verbs (e.g. *attended, was*) to describe what the individual did and to attribute qualities to the individual, past tense to indicate past actions or states, evaluative word choices (e.g. *wildly unrealistic, an incredible honor*) to appraise the individual and his/her accomplishments, and temporal sequence markers (e.g. *beginning in the late 1950s … after he proved that … before the Cambridge PhD program*) to chronicle the individual's life events.

A report, on the other hand, presents and organizes factual information on a topic. The purpose of the genre is accomplished through three stages: a general statement that classifies or defines the topic being discussed, a collection of facts about various aspects of the topic that are thematically organized, and a summary statement about the topic at the end (Fang, 2010). It uses generic participants (e.g. *engineers, a scientist*) to make non-specific statements about a class of things/people, relational verbs (e.g. *be, belong to, consist of*) to define, classify, and characterize the class of things/people, simple present tense (e.g. *is, have, treat*) to indicate

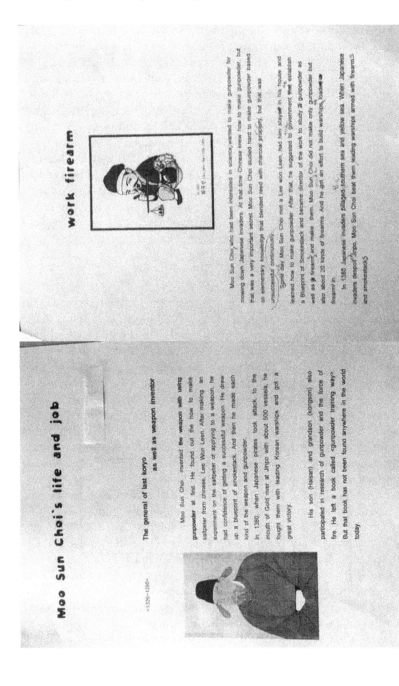

Figure 4.2 Jaehyun's writing (with teacher markings): Biography of a Scientist

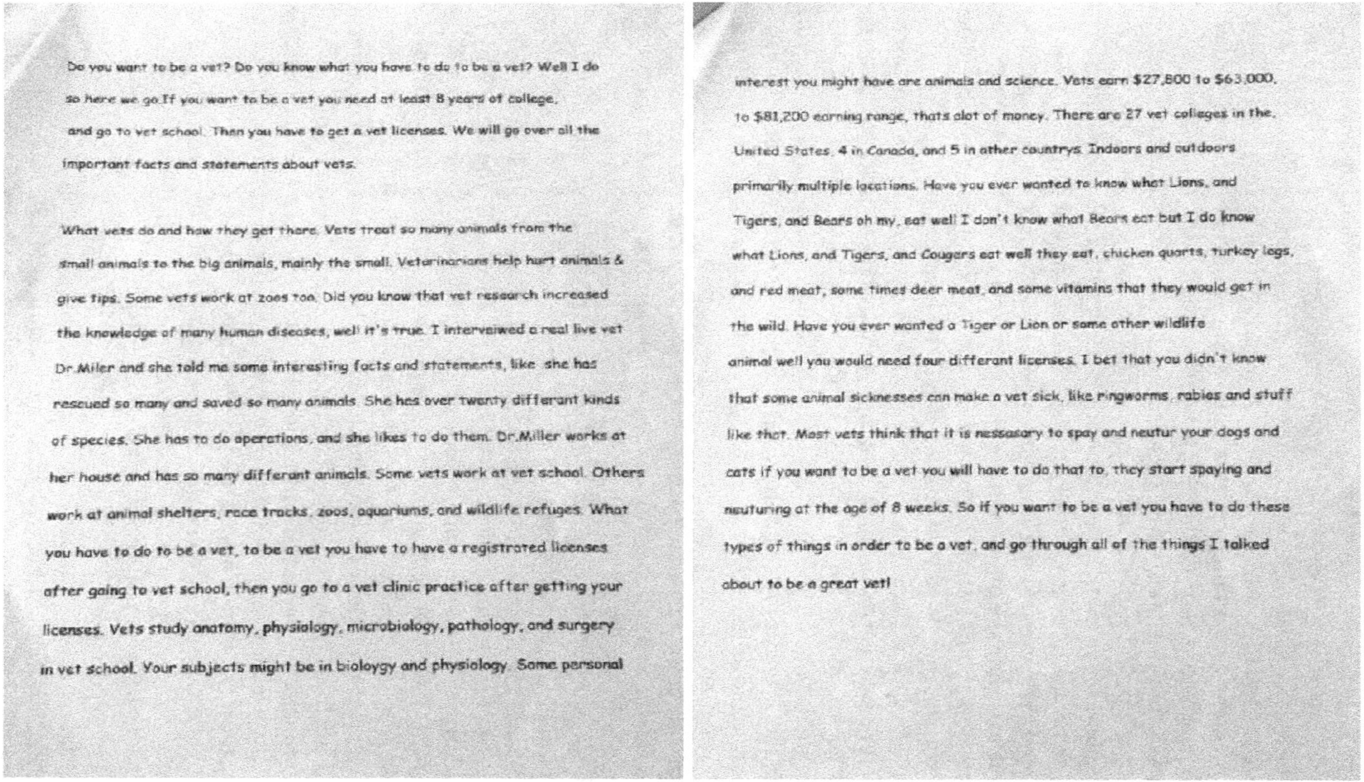

Do you want to be a vet? Do you know what you have to do to be a vet? Well I do. So here we go. If you want to be a vet you need at least 8 years of college. and go to vet school. Then you have to get a vet licenses. We will go over all the important facts and statements about vets.

What vets do and how they get there. Vets treat so many animals from the small animals to the big animals, mainly the small. Veterinarians help hurt animals & give tips. Some vets work at zoos too. Did you know that vet research increased the knowledge of many human diseases, well it's true. I interviewed a real live vet Dr. Miller and she told me some interesting facts and statements, like she has rescued so many and saved so many animals. She has over twenty different kinds of species. She has to do operations and she likes to do them. Dr. Miller works at her house and has so many different animals. Some vets work at vet school. Others work at animal shelters, race tracks, zoos, aquariums, and wildlife refuges. What you have to do to be a vet, to be a vet you have to have a registrated licenses after going to vet school, then you go to a vet clinic practice after getting your licenses. Vets study anatomy, physiology, microbiology, pathology, and surgery in vet school. Your subjects might be in biology and physiology. Some personal

interest you might have are animals and science. Vets earn $27,800 to $63,000. to $81,200 earning range, that's alot of money. There are 27 vet colleges in the United States. 4 in Canada, and 5 in other countrys. Indoors and outdoors primarily multiple locations. Have you ever wanted to know what Lions, and Tigers, and Bears oh my, eat well I don't know what Bears eat but I do know what Lions, and Tigers, and Cougars eat well they eat, chicken quarts, turkey legs, and red meat, some times deer meat, and some vitamins that they would get in the wild. Have you ever wanted a Tiger or Lion or some other wildlife animal well you would need four different licenses. I bet that you didn't know that some animal sicknesses can make a vet sick, like ringworms, rabies and stuff like that. Most vets think that it is necessary to spay and neutur your dogs and cats if you want to be a vet you will have to do that to, they start spaying and neutering at the age of 8 weeks. So if you want to be a vet you have to do these types of things in order to be a vet. and go through all of the things I talked about to be a great vet!

Figure 4.3 Rosa's writing: Report on a Science Career

universal qualities and habitual activities, and specialized vocabulary (e.g. *acidity*, *genetics*) to construe technical knowledge.

Jaehyun's biography of an ancient Korean scientist, Moo Sun Choi, does not seem to follow the schematic conventions of a biography. The biography begins with a statement that summarizes Moo Sun Choi's key accomplishment (*Moo Sun Choi invented the weapon with using gunpowder at first.*), but does not locate the scientist in historical time and context. Instead, it provides a brief summary of how the scientist made the weapon with gunpowder that helped the Koreans drive the Japanese pirates away. The third paragraph mentions the fact that the scientist wrote a book on gunpowder that could not be found nowadays. The next three paragraphs repeat what has already been stated in the first two paragraphs of the essay by providing more details about how Moo Sun Choi made the gunpowder and firearms that helped the Koreans defeat the Japanese invaders.

Despite the lack of a complete, clearly discernible schematic structure that is typical of a biography, the text uses linguistic features specific to the genre, including proper nouns to refer to specific individuals (e.g. *Moo Sun Choi, Lee Won Leen*), action verbs to describe what the scientist did (e.g. *invented, drew up, met*), and relational verbs to characterize the scientist (e.g. *had* confidence, had *been* interested). The story about the scientist is told in the past tense to indicate the historical nature of the scientist's invention. Evaluative phrases – such as *a successful weapon, a great victory, a very important secret* – are used to appraise the worth and impact of the invention. Temporal markers, such as *in 1380, and then, at that time, some [one] day*, and *after that*, are used to sequence the events related to the invention.

Rosa's essay has the shape and look of a report. It begins with a short paragraph that identifies the topic (veterinarian) and questions to be addressed (*Do you want to be a vet? Do you know what you have to do to be a vet? We will go over all the important facts and statements about vets.*). The rest of the report presents various facts about veterinarians in one long paragraph. These facts are sorted into topical areas such as what vets do, what training is needed to become a vet, how much a vet earns annually, and what vets can do to prevent getting sick from exposure to animals; however, the boundaries among these topical areas are not always clearly indicated. The last sentence of the long paragraph (*So if you want to be a vet you have to do these types of things … to be a great vet.*) appears to serve as a conclusion that wraps up the presentation of information about vets.

The report uses generic participants (*a vet, vets*) for the most part to talk about veterinarians as a group, but also mentions a specific veterinarian (Dr Miller) to give an example of what veterinarians typically do. Present tense is used primarily to indicate the habitualness of veterinarians' activities. Action verbs (e.g. *treat, study, earn*) are used heavily to describe what veterinarians do in their professional preparation and practice, but relational verbs (e.g. *are*) are rarely used to define, characterize or classify veterinarians.

To summarize, both texts appropriate some schematic elements and lexicogrammatical features characteristic of their respective genres, but they do not incorporate other structural and linguistic features associated with these genres. They reflect different degrees of familiarity with the two school-based genres on the part of their authors, with Rosa appearing to be reasonably knowledgeable about the report genre and Jaehyun demonstrating a more nascent sense of the biography genre. It is also possible that they reflect different cultural traditions in the students' first language literacy practices, a conjecture not explored in this chapter. While the assignment guidelines (see Figure 4.1) might have given the students some sense of the expected shape of their text, the fact that these guidelines are not genre-specific (i.e. not differentiating biography from report) renders them less helpful than they could have been. Clearly, both EAL students need more specific support to develop control over the two valued genres in school science.

Register

Register refers to the manner of speaking or writing characteristic of a certain situational context (Bussman, 1998). Formal contexts such as schooling often require that students make meaning in ways that are different from what they would normally do in informal contexts such as playgrounds, dinner tables, birthday parties, and sporting events, where everyday registers are typically used. In the schooling context, students are expected to make meanings in ways that feature greater density, formality, precision, generalization, compactness, authoritativeness, and flow (Biber & Gray, 2010; Christie & Derewianka, 2008; Fang, 2021b; Schleppegrell, 2004). This means they must develop new language resources (i.e. academic registers), beyond those they have already been using in everyday social interactions (i.e. everyday registers), in order to take on more technical and abstract meanings that are necessary for construing uncommon-sense knowledge in disciplinary learning.

For example, to display disciplinary knowledge in school, students must learn to use complex nominal groups with specialized terminology and to reason within, rather than between, clauses with nouns, verbs, and prepositions. To be authoritative in knowledge presentation and reasoned in argument development, students must learn to use declarative sentences, modal verbs, and other attitudinal resources. To create tightly-knit texts, students must learn to use internal conjunctions and other cohesive devices, as well as the clause-combining strategies of embedding and condensing. Meeting these expectations is a tall order for many students, especially EALs.

An examination of the sample biography and report shows that the two texts juxtapose academic registers and everyday registers in

Table 4.1 Academic and everyday registers in Jaehyun's writing

Feature Register	Features with examples
Academic Register	• academic vocabulary (e.g. *firearms, saltpeter, smokestack, warships, vessels, weapon, suggest, property, research, invent, blueprint, participate, establish, pillage, despoil*) • nominalizations (e.g. *confidence, victory, effort, force*) • expanded nominal groups (e.g. *an experiment on the saltpeter, confidence of getting a successful weapon, a very important secret, about 20 kinds of firearms, warships armed with firearm and smokestack*) • appositive (*He found out the how to make saltpeter from chinese, <u>Lee Won Leen</u>.*), • non-restrictive relative clause (i.e. *[,]who had been interested in science[,]*), • nonfinite clause (i.e. *[...], leading warships armed with firearm and smokestack*), • interruption construction (i.e. *Moo Sun Choi studied hard to make gunpowder[,] <u>based on elementary knowledge</u>[,] that blended reed with charcoal property,..*)
Everyday Register	• multi-word verb (e.g. *found out, drew up*) • colloquial expression (e.g. <u>*got*</u> *a victory,* <u>*got*</u> *an effort*) • sentence beginning with a conjunction or a conjunctive adverb (e.g. <u>*And then*</u> *he made each kind of the weapon and gunpowder.* <u>*But*</u> *that book has not been found anywhere in the world today.* <u>*And*</u> *he got an effort to build warships.*) • sentence ending with a preposition (e.g. *And he got an effort to build warships loaded a firearm* <u>*in*</u>.) • run-on sentence (e.g. *After that, he suggested to government that establish a Blueprint of Smokesrack and became director of the work to study a gunpowder as well as a firearm and make them.*)

ways that prevent authoritative, compact and precise presentation of information. Table 4.1 shows some of the language resources used in Jaehyun's biography.

Unlike Jaehyun's biography, Rosa's report relies much more heavily on the linguistic resources of everyday registers and much less frequently on the linguistic resources of academic registers, as can be seen in Table 4.2.

To summarize, the two sample texts draw on the lexical and grammatical resources of both academic and everyday registers, resulting in a writing style that is rhetorically problematic and does not meet typical school expectations for language use. The sample biography shows impressive efforts to use academic registers, although traces of everyday registers are also evident. By contrast, the sample report makes extensive use of the interpersonal and interactive resources of everyday registers, sounding remarkably similar to spontaneous speech written down, despite the presence of several features of academic registers. These findings suggest that both students are in need of developing more mature control over academic registers.

Grammatical Conventions

Adherence to grammatical conventions is another writing ability that students are expected to develop in school. The biography text has many grammatical issues that suggest its author is still in the process of developing firm control over grammatical conventions. One such issue has to do with the distinction between restrictive and non-restrictive relative

Table 4.2 Academic and everyday registers in Rosa's writing

Feature Register	Features with examples
Academic Register	• academic vocabulary (e.g. *licenses, veterinarians, diseases, species, wildlife refuges, anatomy, physiology, microbiology, pathology, surgery*) • nominalization (e.g. *statements, operations, sicknesses*) • expanded nominal group (e.g. *all the important facts and statements about vets, knowledge of many human diseases, over twenty different kinds of species, some vitamins that they would get in the wild, all of the things I talked about*) • hedge (e.g. *...you need <u>at least</u> 8 years of college. Your subjects <u>might</u> be in biology and physiology. Some personal interest you <u>might</u> have...*)
Everyday Register	• interrogative sentence (e.g. *Do you want to be a vet? Do you know what you have to do to be a vet?*) • first or second personal pronoun (e.g. *If <u>you</u> want to be a vet <u>you</u> need at least 8 years of college. <u>We</u> will go over all the important facts and statements about vets.*) • discourse filler (e.g. *<u>Well</u> I do. <u>Well</u> it's true.*) • exclamation (e.g. *Have you ever wanted to know what Lions, and Tigers, and Bears <u>oh my</u>, eat[?]*) • colloquial expression (e.g. *so here we go. thats a lot of money. ... and she told me some interesting facts and statements, <u>like</u> she has rescued <u>so many</u> and saves <u>so many</u> animals.*) • reference to writer's mental process (e.g. *<u>I don't know</u> what Bears eat <u>but I do know</u> what Lions, and Tigers, and Cougers eat. <u>I bet</u> you didn't know that some animal sickness can make a vet sick...*) • contraction (e.g. *don't, didn't, it's*) • run-on sentence (e.g. *I interviewed a real live vet Dr Miller and she told me some interesting facts and statements, like she has rescued so many and save so many animals. Have you ever wanted to know what Lions, and Tigers, and Bears oh my, eat well I don't know what Bears eat but I do know what Lions, and Tigers, and Cougers eat well they eat, chicken quarts, turkey legs, and red meat, some times dear meat, and some vitamins that they would get in the wild.*) • pronoun with ambiguous referent (e.g. *Most vets think that it is necessary to spay and neutur your dogs and cats if you want to be a vet you will have to do that to, <u>they</u> start spaying and neutering at the age of 8 weeks.*) • sentence starting with a conjunction or conjunctive adverb (e.g. *<u>So</u> if you want to be a vet you have to do these types of things in order to be a vet, ...*) • amplificatory phrase tag (e.g. *Vets treat so many different animals from the small animals to the big animals, <u>mainly the small</u>. I bet you didn't know that some animal sicknesses can make a vet sick, <u>like ringworms, rabies and stuff like that</u>.*) • hortatory sentence (e.g. *... to be a vet you <u>have to have</u> a registrated licenses ... So if you want to be a vet you <u>have to do</u> these types of things...*)

clauses. In the beginning sentence of the fourth paragraph – *Moon Sun Choi who had been interested in science wanted to make gunpowder for mowing down Japanese invader.* – a comma should have been inserted immediately preceding '*who*' and right after '*science*' (as the correction marks by Jaehyun's teacher indicate in Figure 4.2). The clause, *who had been interested in science*, does not define the meaning of the noun preceding it; rather, it provides non-essential information about Moon Sun Choi and should, thus, be used as a non-restrictive relative clause. A similar problem exists in the use of the nonfinite clause. In the sentence '*Moon Sun Choi beat them leading warships armed with firearm and smokestack.*' (last paragraph), a comma should have been used before the nonfinite clause '*leading warships armed with firearm and smokestack*'.

Another issue with grammar relates to articles (*a/an, the*), determiners (e.g. *the, some*), capitalization, and the singular vs. the plural form

Table 4.3 Sample grammatical issues in Jaehyun's Biography of a Scientist

What Jaehyun wrote	What Jaehyun should have written
make saltpeter from <u>chinese</u>, Lee Won Leen (first paragraph)	make saltpeter from <u>a Chinese</u>, Lee Won Leen
<u>Some</u> day Moo Sun Choi met a Lee won Leen… (fifth paragraph)	<u>One</u> day, Moon Sun Choi met Lee Won Leen…
After that, he suggested to <u>government</u> that… (fifth paragraph)	After that, he suggested to <u>the government</u> that…
… became director of the work to study <u>a gunpowder as well as a firearm</u> and make them (fifth paragraph)	… became <u>the</u> director of the work to study and make <u>gunpowder and firearms</u>
In 1380 Japanese invaders pillaged <u>southern sea</u> and <u>yellow sea</u>. (last paragraph)	In 1380, Japanese invaders pillaged <u>the South Sea</u> and <u>the Yellow Sea</u>.
…warships armed with <u>firearm</u> and <u>smokestack</u> (last paragraph)	…warships armed with <u>firearms</u> and <u>smokestacks</u>

of the noun, whose uses present headaches for even proficient native English speakers. Table 4.3 presents what Jaehyun wrote, along with the corrections of his writing.

Constructing syntactically well-formed sentences with idiomatic expressions is an additional area of challenge evidenced in the sample biography. The sentence that starts the first paragraph (*Moon Sun Choi invented the weapon with using gunpowder at first.*) could have been reworded as '*Moon Sun Choi invented the first weapon that used gunpowder*'. The second sentence in the fifth paragraph – *After that, he suggested to government that establish a Blueprint of Smokestack and became director of the work to study a gunpowder as well as a firearm and make them…* – could have been reworked into '*After that, he suggested to the government that a blueprint of smokestack be established, and subsequently, he directed the work to study and make gunpowder and firearms*'. Further, phrases such as '*took attack to*' (second paragraph), '*was unsuccessful continuously*' (fourth paragraph), and '*got an effort*' (fifth paragraph) could have been more idiomatically expressed as '*attacked*', '*was continuously unsuccessful*', and '*made an effort*', respectively.

Rosa's report demonstrates comparatively greater control over grammatical conventions. It does not have the same issues that confront Jaehyun. Instead, its main problem appears to reside in the use of punctuation, capitalization (e.g. words such as *Lions, Tigers* and *Bears* do not need to start with an upper-case letter.) and word choice (e.g. '*registrated*' should have been '*registered*'), as well as paragraph structure. Although most sentences in the text are syntactically well formed, portions of the text are not appropriately punctuated, resulting in run-on sentences. For example, '*Well I do so here we go*'. (first paragraph) should have been '*Well, I do. So here we go*'. More such examples can be found in Table 4.2. In addition, the second paragraph could have been broken into several smaller paragraphs, with each paragraph focusing on one idea or subtopic, such as what vets do, how much vets earn, and what it takes to become a vet.

To summarize, the two samples of writing exhibit different degrees of conformity to grammatical conventions. The biography has a plethora of grammatical issues at the word, phrase, and sentence levels. On the other hand, the main problem with the report is the use of run-on sentences without proper punctuation. These difficulties, indicative of the students' language proficiency levels, impact the clarity and flow of writing in the two texts. It is obvious that both authors, especially Jaehyun, still have much to learn about grammatical conventions in the process of developing academic literacy.

Promoting Language/Literacy in Disciplinary Learning

The foregoing analysis of two writing samples indicates that the two EAL students face considerable challenges in producing texts that realize the purpose of discipline-legitimated genres and meet the linguistic expectations of formal schooling. These challenges are linguistic in nature, suggesting that both students need to expand their linguistic repertoires for making meaning in academic and disciplinary contexts.

To promote the sort of language learning that supports the development of academic and disciplinary literacy, teachers need to go beyond a mere focus on grammatical conventions to an emphasis on how language choices realize genre and register in ways that meet the demands of schooling and conform to disciplinary conventions. This shift requires a reconceptualization of what language is. Traditionally, language has been conceived of as a set of grammatical rules, and language learning believed to primarily involve mastery of these rules. This approach, which has been documented to be largely ineffective in promoting language learning or literacy development (see Locke, 2010), may help Jaehyun and Rosa address some of the grammatical issues identified above, but it will not empower them to produce high-quality texts that meet academic expectations and disciplinary norms. On this note, it is worth pointing out that Jaehyun was receiving stand-alone ESOL (English for Speakers of Other Languages) instruction (focused mainly on traditional English grammar and culture) provided by the school district at the time of the study; and Rosa had received the same service during her elementary school years, but her English was judged to be proficient enough to no longer require the service in middle school.

An alternative perspective, advocated by functional linguists (Christie & Derewianka, 2008; Fang, 2021a; Schleppegrell, 2004), posits that language consists of interlocking systems of grammatical choices, and these choices are creative resources for making meaning. From this perspective, learning to use language, or learning to make meaning with language (e.g. writing), is a matter of learning to make lexicogrammatical choices that realize the purpose of a particular social interaction and are appropriate to the context in which language is used. Because grammar is the powerhouse for making meaning (Halliday, 2007), a focus on grammar is warranted in language and literacy development work. Attention to purpose (genre) and context (register) in language use necessitates a move away from teaching grammar as a set of prescriptive rules through isolated, drill-like exercises to teaching grammar in context and from a functional point of view. It foregrounds the role of grammatical choices in shaping meaning to meet the demands of specific tasks and contexts.

In this connection, Myhill and colleagues have described a pedagogy for writing that promotes 'playful explicitness with grammar' (Myhill *et al.*, 2013: 103). This pedagogy uses a grammatical metalanguage purposefully in relevant contexts, with grammatical terminology explained through examples rather than definitions. It establishes a link between the grammatical feature introduced and the writing context, showing students how the use of the grammatical feature enhances the quality or effectiveness of writing. The pedagogy engages students in explicit discussion about the structure, meaning and effects of the grammatical feature being introduced, and encourages creative imitation and experimentation by offering model grammatical patterns for students to emulate in their own writing. It also makes meaningful connections between reading and writing by using examples from authentic texts that students read, and uses activities that nurture students' ability to both make informed grammatical choices in their writing and to see writing as a process of designing meaning. In short, the goal of grammar instruction here is to help students recognize how grammatical choices shape the text and fashion the meaning in a way that satisfies the author's rhetorical intentions and addresses the needs of context.

The sort of grammar instruction envisioned by Myhill and her colleagues can be embedded in the broader context of academic experiences, or what Fisher (2018) called the 'activity systems' of disciplinary learning, where students are learning to write and read different school-based genres at the same time they are building content knowledge, forming disciplinary habits of mind, and developing advanced language/literacy skills. A pedagogical heuristic for accomplishing these goals simultaneously is the genre teaching-learning cycle, illustrated in Figure 4.4 (Fang, 2021a).

Informed by Sydney School genre-based literacy pedagogy (Rose & Martin, 2012) and the American register-based literacy pedagogy (de Oliveira & Schleppegrell, 2015; Fang & Schleppegrell, 2008), the cycle consists of four stages: building knowledge and context, analyzing model text(s), playing with language, and constructing text(s). In

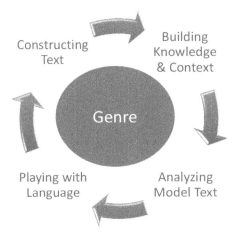

Figure 4.4 Genre teaching-learning cycle (Fang, 2021a: 168)

Stage 1, students explore a question or an issue that is of interest to them or of significance to their discipline (e.g. What contributions to science have women and people of color made? What does a veterinarian do?). The exploration may involve reading, writing and viewing, as well as observation, experiment, field trips and interviews. Through these activities, some of which involve interaction with academic and disciplinary texts, students develop the content knowledge and language resources needed to write about the topic in the target genre (e.g. biography or report).

In Stage 2, well-written texts in the target genre (e.g. model biographies of famous scientists) are selected for detailed analysis. Specifically, the teacher engages students in analyzing and discussing the meaning and craft in these exemplar texts, drawing attention to their purpose, schematic structure and grammatical features. For example, the class can discuss how the author structures their text to achieve its purpose (e.g. orientation – sequence of events – evaluation, general statement – detailed descriptions – summary). The class can also examine, from an SFL perspective, how the author uses:

- technical vocabulary to build technical taxonomy and construct specialized knowledge;
- general academic vocabulary to construe formality and generalization;
- embedded clauses and expanded nominal groups to pack dense information and infuse evaluation;
- the passive voice to bury agency or facilitate discursive flow;
- the present tense to denote habitual activities or universal characteristics;
- the past tense to chronicle past events;

- thematic prominence to foreground certain concepts or ideas;
- nonfinite clauses and non-restrictive relative clauses to introduce, compact and background ancillary information;
- appositives to rename, define, explain, or clarify another noun within a sentence;
- hedging devices to show caution about knowledge claims and generalizations; and
- nominalizations to distill information, build abstraction, bury agency, embed ideology, coin technical terms, and create discursive flow.

The analyses and discussions will develop students' awareness and understanding of how English grammar is used as a productive resource for making discipline-relevant, genre-specific, and register-appropriate meanings in academic contexts.

In Stage 3, the teacher designs tasks that highlight or reinforce key grammatical patterns identified in the mentor text(s) that the class has examined. These tasks can focus on key, unfamiliar, or challenging ways that language is deployed to make meaning in the target genre. They give students the opportunity to 'play' with the specific language features used in the texts they have been reading closely, further cementing their understanding of the structure, logic, meaning and function of these features and developing their facility to use them for authentic purposes and meaningful contexts. For example, given Jaehyun's (and likely other students') confusion between restrictive and non-restrictive relative clauses, examples of both types of clause from the texts that students have read or written can be identified and discussed to show how they are different in structure, function and effect. For students like Rosa, exercises on select linguistic markers of formality and informality can be designed to increase awareness and understanding of academic registers.

In the final phase, the teacher encourages students to use some of the key or unfamiliar language features discussed earlier as they attempt to compose a new text in the target genre. Students are guided through the composing process of generating ideas, creating drafts, making revisions and submitting/publishing their work. An emphasis can be placed on revision during this process, with special attention given to the power of grammar in shaping, clarifying and manipulating meaning. When providing feedback for revision, it is important not to overcorrect students' writing, as this can shatter their confidence and overwhelm their learning capacity. The academic preparedness of students in a class can vary considerably, so the amount and nature of the feedback provided should vary accordingly. For example, the linguistic issues identified in Jaehyun's and Rosa's writing do not all have to be addressed at one time and in one assignment. Instead, the most salient, significant, relevant or persistent issues (e.g. organization of biography for Jaehyun, use of informality markers for Rosa) can be tackled first. At the same time, it is worth keeping in mind that 'a few concepts taught well and a few pieces done well can be much more important for a student writer's growth than many concepts and lessons taught superficially and many pieces of writing assigned without much guidance' (Weaver, 2010: 195). To reduce writing anxiety, the teacher can first work with students (or have students work collaboratively) to compose the new text before letting them work individually on the new text.

Through these four stages, students learn to write the genre in the register expected of them and at the same time use writing to consolidate, demonstrate and communicate what they have learned about curriculum content and academic language. This means the genre teaching-learning cycle can be particularly helpful to EAL learners, who generally require greater support in developing the language and literacy proficiency needed to engage in disciplinary learning. The benefits of such support can be maximized when the cycle is delivered through collaboration between content area (e.g. science) teachers and EAL specialists. In fact, collaboration should be encouraged because content area teachers rarely possess the language expertise needed to scaffold writing and EAL specialists seldom have the requisite content knowledge to make the language/literacy work meaningful and engaging. A recent study by Gibb *et al.* (2020), for example, suggests that such collaboration is not only beneficial but also feasible. Specifically, the researchers describe how an EAL teacher and a science teacher collaborated in designing and delivering a content-based writing lesson for a ninth-grade unit on mitosis that explicitly taught students the grammatical skills needed to write a well-crafted lab report. This success example suggests that school-based interdepartmental teacher collaboration can facilitate the implementation of the genre teaching-learning cycle to more effectively address EAL students' writing/literacy needs in disciplinary learning.

Conclusion

Writing in science and other academic disciplines is a demanding task, as it calls for the use of new language resources that many EAL students have yet to develop but which are essential for construing markers of advanced literacy such as technicality, density, abstraction, generalization, compactness, elaboration, argumentation, objectivity, formality, rigor and flow (Fang, 2021b). Students need support in developing these language resources in disciplinary learning. This development work requires experience, practice and motivation, as well as opportunities to negotiate meaning in authentic contexts for which writing is functional (Schleppegrell, 2004). A genre-based pedagogical cycle that embeds contextualized grammar instruction by explicitly linking form with meaning/function promotes deeper understanding of the linguistic resources that are significant and effective for realizing and instantiating valued school-based genres, offering teachers a powerful heuristic for supporting students' academic writing development in the context of disciplinary learning.

References

August, D. and Shanahan, T. (2006) *Developing Literacy in Second–language Learners: Report of the National Literacy Panel on Language Minority Children and Youth.* Mahwah, NJ: Lawrence Erlbaum.

Avalos, M., Zisselsberger, M., Gort, M. and Secada, W. (2017) 'Hey! Today I will tell you about the water cycle!': Variations of language and organizational features in third-grade science explanation writing. *Elementary School Journal* 118 (1), 149–176.

Biber, D. and Gray, B. (2010) Challenging stereotypes about academic writing: Complexity, elaboration, explicitness. *Journal of English for Academic Purposes* 9 (1), 2–20.

Bussmann, H. (1998) *Routledge Dictionary of Language and Linguistics.* London: Routledge.

Christie, F. and Derewianka, B. (2008) *School Discourse: Learning to Write Across the Years of Schooling.* London: Continuum.

Coffin, C. (2006) *Historical Discourse: The Language of Time, Cause and Evaluation.* London: Continuum.

de Oliveira, L. and Schleppegrell, M. (2015) *Focus on Grammar and Meaning.* Oxford: Oxford University Press.

Fang, Z. (2006) The language demands of science reading in middle school. *International Journal of Science Education* 28 (5), 491–520.

Fang, Z. (2010) *Language and Literacy in Inquiry–based Science Classrooms, Grades 3–8.* Thousand Oaks, CA: Corwin & Arlington, VA: National Science Teachers Association Press.

Fang, Z. (2020) Toward a linguistically informed, responsive, and embedded pedadgogy in secondary literacy instruction. *Journal of World Languages* 6 (1–2), 70–91.

Fang, Z. (2021a) *Using Functional Grammar in English Literacy Teaching and Learning.* Beijing: Foreign Language Teaching and Research Press.

Fang, Z. (2021b) *Demystifying Academic Writing: Genres, Moves, Skills and Strategies.* New York: Routledge.

Fang, Z. and Schleppegrell, M. (2008) *Reading in Secondary Schools: A Language–based Pedagogy.* Ann Arbor, MI: University of Michigan Press.

Fang, Z. and Wei, Y. (2010) Improving middle school students' science literacy through reading infusion. *Journal of Educational Research* 103 (3), 262–273

Fang, Z., Adams, B., Li, C., Gallingane, C., Jo, S., Fennessy, M. and Chapman, S. (2017) Supporting Els in learning to write scientifically: A genre-based approach. In M. Daniel (ed.) *English Learners at the Top of the Class: Reading and Writing for Authentic Purposes* (pp. 67–82). New York: Rowman & Littlefield.

Fang, Z., Lamme, L., Pringle, R., Patrick, J., Sanders, J., Zmach, C., Charbonnet, S. and Henkel, M. (2008) Integrating reading into middle school science: What we did, found, and learned. *International Journal of Science Education* 30 (15), 2067–2089.

Fisher, R. (2018) Reconciling disciplinary literacy perspectives with genre-oriented activity theory: Toward a fuller synthesis of traditions. *Reading Research Quarterly* 54 (2), 237–251.

Gebhard, M. (2019) *Teaching and Researching ELLs' Disciplinary Literacies.* New York: Routledge.

Gibb, B., Li, G. and Schwartz, T. (2020) Improving ELLs' scientific writing through co-teaching: Collaboration between ESL and science teachers in a secondary school in Canada. In M. Dover and A. Honigfeld (eds) *Co-teaching for English Learners: Evidence-based Practices and Research-informed Outcomes* (pp. 235-244). Greenwich, CT: Information Age Publishing.

Halliday, M. (2007) *Language and Education*. Collected Works of M.A.K. Halliday Volume 9 edited by J. Webster. London: Continuum.

Halliday, M. and Hasan, R. (1985) *Language, Context, and Text: Aspects of Language in a Social–semiotic Perspective*. Geelong: Deakin University Press.

Halliday, M. and Martin, J.R. (1993) *Writing Science: Literacy and Discursive Power*. Pittsburgh, PA: University of Pittsburgh Press.

Halliday, M. and Matthiessen, C. (2014) *An Introduction to Functional Grammar* (4th edn). New York: Routledge.

Hand, B. (2017) Exploring the role of writing in science: A 25-year journey. *Literacy Learning: The Middle Years* 25 (3), 16–23.

Hasan, R. (1996) Literacy, everyday talk and society. In R. Hasan and G. Williams (eds) *Literacy in Society* (pp. 377–424). London: Longman.

Lee, O., Quinn, H. and Valdes, G. (2013) Science and language for English language learners in relation to next generation science standards and with implications for common core state standards for English language arts and mathematics. *Educational Researcher* 42 (4), 223–233.

Locke, T. (ed.) (2010) *Beyond the Grammar Wars*. London: Routledge.

Martin, J. and Rose, D. (2008) *Genre Relations: Mapping Culture*. London: Equinox.

Myhill, D., Jones, S., Watson, A. and Lines, H. (2013) Playful explicitness with grammar: A pedagogy for writing. *Literacy* 47 (2), 103–111.

National Research Council (2012) *A Framework for K–12 Science Education: Practices, Crosscutting Concepts, and Core Ideas*. Washington, DC: National Academies Press.

Norris, S. and Phillips, L. (2003) How literacy in its fundamental sense is central to scientific Literacy. *Science Education* 87 (2), 224–240.

Patrick, J. and Fang, Z. (in press) High school science teachers learning to teach science reading through a functional focus on language: Toward a grounded theory of teacher learning. In L. Seah, R. Silver and M. Baildon (eds) Teachers' Knowledge of the Role of Language in Content Pedagogy. Singapore: Springer.

Rose, D. and Martin, J.R. (2012) *Learning to Write, Reading to Learn: Genre, Knowledge and Pedagogy in the Sydney School*. Bristol, CT: Equinox.

Schleppegrell, M. (2004) *The Language of Schooling: A Functional Linguistics Perspective*. Mahwah, NJ: Lawrence Erlbaum.

Seah, L., Clarke, D. and Hart, C. (2015) Understanding middle school students' difficulties in explaining density differences from a language perspective. *International Journal of Science Education* 37 (14), 2386–2409.

Weaver, C. (2010) Scaffolding grammar instruction for writers and writing. In T. Locke (ed.) *Beyond the Grammar Wars* (pp. 185–205). London: Routledge.

Wellington, J. and Osborne, J. (2001) *Language and Literacy in Science Education*. Philadelphia, PA: Open University Press.

Wilcox, K. and Jeffery, J. (2015) Adolescent English language learners' stances toward disciplinary writing. *English for Specific Purposes* 38, 44–56.

Yore, L., Bisanz, G. and Hand, B. (2003) Examining the literacy component of science literacy: 25 years of language arts and science research. *International Journal of Science Education* 25 (6), 689–725.

Yore, L., Hand, B. and Florence, M. (2004) Scientists' views of science, models of writing, and science writing practices. *Journal of Research in Science Teaching* 41 (4), 338–369.

5 Supporting EAL Writing Development in the Early Stages of the Doctorate: Candidates from the East Writing in the West

Morena Botelho de Magalhães
University of Auckland, New Zealand

Introduction

Higher education students have been crossing borders in increasing numbers since the mid-1990s. The internationalisation of higher education has impacted on doctoral programmes around the globe, which have had to change and adapt to the needs of students, who are increasingly diverse culturally and linguistically. International students are a considerable source of income to universities in neoliberal times (Shore, 2010), particularly in English- speaking countries. With English as the lingua franca of academia (so much so that 'international research' is usually seen as research published in English), the varieties of English acquired in students' home countries may differ from the varieties of English used in their new academic environment. Consequently, a wide range of English language proficiency and standards among international applicants is noted, as are the perceived challenges related to language constraints. Doctoral candidates enrolling in English-medium institutions will probably have developed academic literacy in their discipline through earlier studies. However, those with English as an Additional Language (EAL) might face additional language demands, especially if studying through English-medium programmes for the first time (Read, 2016).

EAL doctoral candidates from the Global South and the Global East, new to unfamiliar contexts, may be unacquainted with the norms in place in the Global North and the West. When doctoral candidates relocate to study, new sociocultural spaces and discourse norms are likely to be in place. Adapting to unfamiliar discourse conventions may require training, which is not always available, and additional work. In the contemporary Anglophone academic world, English language constraints can impact on students' experiences of academia, their progress and academic success. However, conducting research through the medium of English, especially in 'desirable locations' (Findlay *et al.*, 2012: 122), may be exactly what motivates EAL candidates' relocation. In the doctoral educational scenario, a common narrative of doctorates abroad 'in the Global North' being 'rewarded with status upon their return to work in the Global South' (Burford, 2018: 493) reflects the current values regulating global science. Even if the North–South geographical sense does not apply to students from the East studying in New Zealand, for example, the dichotomy between the East and West is still prevalent and can influence some EAL candidates' experiences of learning to adapt to their new contexts.

At the doctoral level, 'inappropriate' academic literacy affects candidates' writing development and their experiences of the doctoral degree as a whole. Having an adequate understanding of the levels of academic literacy required to produce a doctoral thesis or articles for publication in English, which will eventually award candidates a doctoral degree, is essential (Paré, 2010). But how can we support doctoral candidates in developing the expected academic literacy in a given local context when there are so many varieties of English being acquired in diverse environments and at various proficiency levels? One possibility is to assess doctoral candidates' academic English language needs upon admittance to the degree programme and to offer access to various forms of support from the early stages of the doctorate.

This chapter focuses on four EAL doctoral candidates and their experiences of accessing support for writing development during the first year of their PhD. The four candidates began their PhD studies with inadequately developed academic writing skills in English, according to the institution where they enrolled. An examination of their experiences of accessing language and writing support, after a compulsory assessment of their English language skills, can offer insights into the circumstances that affected the candidates' writing development. By analysing the experiences shared by the participants, the similarities and idiosyncrasies of their stories, this chapter aims ultimately to identify affordances for EAL writing development in the early stages of the study for the doctoral degree.

Previous Research

The first doctoral year is critical for candidates. Not only is it generally considered the most challenging by doctoral students (Golde, 1998), but it also usually indicates whether candidates are likely to complete their degree studies successfully (Lovitts, 2001). The initial phase of doctoral studies can be particularly challenging: time pressure, uncertainty about processes, not feeling part of an academic community, and financial pressures, have all been identified as key stressors for beginning doctoral candidates (Cornwall *et al.*, 2019). While these initial challenges may affect students regardless of their cultural or language background, inadequate language proficiency may impact negatively on candidates' enculturation process (Laufer & Gorup, 2018; Sawir *et al.*, 2012) and bring more stress to the doctoral experience (Kuwahara, 2008; Li & Casanave, 2008). Cultural differences may account for candidates' difficulties in adapting to their new academic environment, but language barriers may intensify their struggles (Hennebry *et al.*, 2012; Li & Casanave, 2008). Moreover, EAL writers may feel that they are 'at a certain deficit' (Langum & Sullivan, 2017: 24) in comparison with native English speakers.

Little research has been published on the writing development experiences of commencing EAL doctoral candidates. Even though some recent studies have focused on EAL doctoral writing (e.g. Ma, 2019; Mochizuki, 2019; Thurlow *et al.*, 2019; Xu & Zhang, 2019), not many researchers have investigated EAL writing development in the first doctoral year. Read and von Randow's (2016) study is an exception, as the researchers interviewed 20 international PhD candidates to gain insights into their perceptions of being required to participate in an English language enrichment and academic writing programme. Read and von Randow's research examined their participants' reactions to a compulsory language goal (described in the Background section of this chapter) and to the resources provided by the institution for the completion of the goal.

The suite of institutional resources to support doctoral candidates across disciplines is usually referred to as generic support. In the case of EAL doctoral candidates, this support is often associated with grammar-focused and language-related workshops or courses organised around the literacy demands of doctoral research (Carter & Laurs, 2014). Generic support usually covers language needs as well as other aspects of doctoral writing (Lee & Murray, 2015). Whereas language support may help candidates improve their confidence in their language ability (Hennebry *et al.*, 2012; Read & von Randow, 2016), writing support accessed by participation in multi-disciplinary writing groups, for example, can expand candidates' understanding of general research writing principles (Aitchison, 2010, 2014). Generic support can be particularly important in the early stages of the doctorate as it assists EAL candidates develop general academic English language proficiency as well as strengthen their writing skills.

However, while doctoral candidates may begin their PhD by meeting expectations common to all areas, they will conclude their degree by making an original research contribution to their disciplinary field. In this process, candidates usually go through 'formal acquisition of core disciplinary knowledge' but they must also familiarise themselves with disciplinary writing conventions, which are often not spoken about and are acquired informally (Maher *et al.*, 2014: 701). Differences in style, positioning, academic attribution (Hyland, 2004), and rhetoric (Tardy, 2005) within wider discourse communities, such as Sciences or Arts, as well as in particular fields (Hyland, 2012) makes learning the discourse norms of their discipline a long and demanding process for doctoral candidates (Aitchison *et al.*, 2012). Support to develop academic literacy within disciplines is therefore essential.

As key players in the overall doctoral journey, supervisors also play a significant role in their students' disciplinary enculturation process. Supervisors can facilitate doctoral candidates' adaptation to the new academic environment as well as introduce them to the literacy conventions of their disciplinary community (Ali & Kohun, 2007; Lee, 2008; Maher *et al.*, 2014; Ohashi *et al.*, 2008; Owens, 2007). Doctoral candidates may need 'an insider's knowledge' to learn about their 'discipline's genres, its arguments, its distinct styles, its key thinkers and theories' (Paré, 2010: 31) so that they can start to grasp the nuances of disciplinary discourse and begin participating in conversations within their disciplines. Supervisors can provide access to such conversations; their feedback and support are vital in their students' writing development.

Writing plays a central part in the construction of an academic identity (Kamler & Thomson, 2014), which is key in doctoral learning (Cotterall, 2015). Understanding how academic identity develops can help elucidate the kinds of support that can be offered to EAL doctoral candidates to assist them develop as writers (and as academics). I see academic identity as 'associated with the feeling of belonging to a community of researchers and scholars', with its development observed in the doctoral candidate's ability to contribute to discussions within the academic community (Botelho de Magalhães *et al.*, 2019: 5). For doctoral candidates, their academic identity construction process, and the creation of a desired researcher self (Xu & Zhang, 2019), are developed mainly through the writing of a PhD thesis, which will represent their original contribution to disciplinary knowledge. Writing affirms the identity that doctoral candidates construct for themselves but, for some EAL doctoral candidates, their language proficiency is likely to impact on their identity development process.

As noted by Flowerdew and Wang:

> EAL novice scholars have to face two problems at the same time – lack of experience in academic writing and limited proficiency in English – a situation that originates from their dual identities as new members of the academic community and as EAL writers. (2015: 84, 85)

English language proficiency in modern academia and its Anglophone dominance are thus paramount. If language prevents EAL candidates from participating in disciplinary conversations, they will need to improve their English language ability in order to engage in more advanced literacy activities, which will in turn enable their participation in international academic communities. This participation, i.e. the realisation of an academic identity, is enabled through writing (Aitchison, 2018).

However, while 'writing is identity work' (Paré, 2019: 81), doctoral candidates also develop their identity as they perform other academic activities. Writing may be 'the thread which links everything [doctoral candidates] do in their PhD' (Botelho de Magalhães *et al.*, 2019: 6), but scholarly activities other than writing, e.g. doing lab work, reading papers, collecting data, working with participants and discussing research (Mantai, 2017), contribute to their growth as researchers. Teaching during the doctorate also helps candidates 'feel like an academic' and is usually a positive experience (Emmioğlu *et al.*, 2017: 86). Moreover, learning that can positively influence doctoral writing development and, ultimately, academic identity, also occurs through participation in conferences (Kuzhabekova & Temerbayeva, 2018), research group meetings and peer discussions (Archer, 2008; McAlpine *et al.*, 2009). Access to as many academic practices as possible from the early stages of the doctorate can enrich the doctoral experience and facilitate disciplinary enculturation. For EAL doctoral writers with limited English proficiency, such practices can afford further opportunities for engagement with academic discourse.

Contextual Background

Assessing candidates' English language ability at the beginning of the doctorate can facilitate access to language development resources and writing support opportunities. Post-entry language assessment (PELA) programmes aim to identify English language deficiencies early for subsequent language and writing training to be offered (Read, 2016). However, international candidates who go through the process of presenting evidence of English language proficiency prior to commencing their PhD programme may feel disheartened when they learn that their English language skills are deemed as lower level and needing improvement (Chatterjee-Padmanabhan, 2014; Read & von Randow, 2016). Furthermore, the perceived language insufficiency may affect how candidates see themselves in relation to their English language ability and have an impact on their confidence to participate in academic practices; it may also affect their developing academic identity.

At a large research university in New Zealand, all doctoral candidates take a PELA as they begin their studies. Participation in the PELA programme is required of all commencing doctoral candidates regardless of their language background or previous academic and professional experience. The assessment is one of the compulsory goals that doctoral candidates must complete within their first year of study; the goals were established with a view to assist candidates in their enculturation process and to gauge their readiness to conduct research independently (University of Auckland, 2016). The PELA goal was a measure taken in response to concerns about language difficulties impacting 'effective relationships between supervisors and their doctoral candidates, and progress in general' (Read & von Randow, 2016: 137). The goal serves as an introduction to language demands and academic literacy expectations at the doctoral level. The PELA takes a generic approach to assessing language needs, thus mirroring the generic resources delivered centrally by the university: language-related online resources and workshops, as well as workshops on doctoral writing (e.g. thesis proposals and literature reviews) and on communicating research. Upon taking the PELA, candidates receive feedback on their performance and are advised on the resources they must engage with for the betterment of their English language skills, especially academic writing.

The study

In this chapter, I discuss the writing development experiences of four EAL doctoral candidates at the beginning of their doctoral degree. In doing so, I draw on my PhD research (Botelho de Magalhães, 2019), for which I collected the data presented here. The research was a longitudinal narrative inquiry study in which I investigated the language learning and literacy activities the doctoral candidates engaged in as they began their doctoral studies, and the impact these activities had upon the candidates' identity construction process.

The research question guiding this chapter is:

- What experiences contribute positively to the writing development of early-stage EAL doctoral candidates?

The participants volunteered to take part in the study after responding to an advertisement placed in various locations on campus. Thus a convenience sampling method was adopted (Mackey & Gass, 2005). To be selected for the research, the doctoral candidates had to be:

- new to the university (i.e. have joined the university upon commencing the PhD)
- required to work on their English language skills, as per their PELA results
- in the initial stages of the PhD.

Table 5.1 Summary of participants' profiles (all names are pseudonyms)

Name	PhD area	Country of origin	L1	Gender	Future intention/Career ambition
Heather	Physics	India	Tegululu	F	Undertake postdoctoral studies and work as an academic/ researcher internationally
Lottie	Linguistics	China	Mandarin	F	Undertake postdoctoral studies and work as an academic/ researcher (in China or internationally)
Ruth	Bioengineering	Iran	Farsi	F	Work as an academic/researcher internationally and preferably not return to Iran
Victor	Geography	China	Mandarin	M	Work as an academic internationally and preferably not return to China

The four participants in this chapter come from diverse disciplinary areas and cultural backgrounds. Table 5.1 summarises their profiles.

Interviews were my sole method of data collection. This is because my focus was on the participants' experiences during their first doctoral year, narrated in stories constructed in interactions with me via research interviews (Kasper & Prior, 2015). I, too, was a doctoral candidate pursuing a degree in a second language and trusted that having this in common would help me bond with my participants and develop a close relationship with them. In narrative inquiry, this proximity between researcher and participant is crucial for exploring situations and events (Clandinin & Connelly, 2000). Therefore, rather than removing myself from the research context, I acknowledged the subjectivity of my research process and my position as a researcher investigating her peers. When collecting data, I prompted my participants with questions but remained open to converse about matters they wished to discuss (Richards, 2009). In other words, I invited my participants to share their stories (Chase, 2003) while making sure we also focused on issues pertinent to my research project. I counted on the 'magic' of interviewing (Brinkmann, 2018: 578) and on me successfully establishing communicability (Briggs, 2007) with my participants, especially given our proximity as fellow doctoral candidates.

Almost all interviews took place during the participants' first doctoral year. I interviewed Heather and Lottie three times and Ruth and Victor four times. There was an interval of about nine months between the first and the last interview with Heather, Ruth and Victor, and 13 months between Lottie's first and last interview. The interviews were carried out in informal settings and were flexible in terms of the topics discussed so that the participants could feel comfortable in sharing their stories with me (Chase, 2003; Riessman, 2008). Our dialogues were a site of co-constructed knowledge (Talmy, 2010), which I later explored.

The interviews were analysed thematically (Murray, 2009) and their content also summarised in story form (Chik & Benson, 2008; Polkinghorne, 1995). Incorporating narrative writing as an analytic tool enabled me to identify critical events in my participants' stories (Webster & Mertova, 2007) thus allowing me to gain more in-depth understanding of their experiences (Benson, 2013). I also sent the narrative summaries to participants so that they could confirm I had recreated their stories accurately (Polkinghorne, 2007).

The participants

Heather, Lottie, Ruth and Victor were international students who had recently arrived in New Zealand when they started their doctoral degree. The four candidates relocated from the Global East to gain research and work experience in the West through English-medium instruction. None had lived in an English-speaking country before or had much experience with academic English writing. They took the PELA upon commencing their doctoral degree and were then required to work on their English language skills. The four candidates were working towards meeting their compulsory first-year doctoral goals when we first met and had successfully completed their first doctoral year when the last interview took place. I present the participants in cameos that provide a brief introduction to who they are and their reasons for doing a PhD in New Zealand. Further insights into the participants' writing development experiences are discussed in the Findings section.

Heather

Heather is a physicist from the southern part of India and comes from a multilingual background. While English was the medium of instruction throughout her education, teachers and pupils also used their mother tongue in the classroom. After graduating from her master's degree, Heather decided to pursue a doctorate overseas and started searching for the top universities in her field. The New Zealand institution that Heather enrolled in featured in her list and, after contacting potential supervisors, she applied for a PhD, was granted a scholarship, and joined a research team working on a large project. Heather was disappointed with her PELA results. She seemed to notice a disconnect between the English she knew and the variety of English expected of her in her new academic environment. Nevertheless, she acknowledged that language expectations at the doctoral level were probably different from her previous academic experiences and recognised aspects in her academic writing that needed improvement. Working in a research group meant that Heather had regular meetings with the team, which she really enjoyed.

Lottie

Lottie is originally from a very small Chinese town but went to university in a larger city. She was only 25 years old when she started her PhD in linguistics. She chose to study in New Zealand to work with her main supervisor, but the availably of funding was also a factor in her decision. Coming to New Zealand (as opposed to England or the USA) meant that she was able to secure a Chinese scholarship, which made it possible for her to study overseas. As a result of the PELA, Lottie was required to participate in various English language enrichment workshops and to complete an academic English writing course. Her attitude towards the language requirements was positive and she seemed thankful for the opportunity to improve her English language skills. Lottie took the writing course willingly. As well as participating in the required workshops, she also attended PhD departmental seminars as often as she could and met with Chinese colleagues on weekends to discuss their research. She felt well supported overall and thought the services and resources she accessed were very good.

Ruth

Ruth left Iran to accompany her husband, who had been accepted into a PhD programme in New Zealand. She had a Master of Physics and wanted to pursue further studies in the area but could not secure funding to do so. It was through making contacts that she was made aware of a large-scale bioengineering research project taking place in an institute associated with the university. She was able to join the project because of her physics background. Ruth would conduct specific research for part of the larger project as a doctoral student. Her research was funded by one of the institute's research partners. Ruth performed well in the PELA but realised that her academic writing needed improving. She appreciated taking the assessment and receiving feedback after it. Ruth's supervisor took an interest in helping her with her English after being notified of her results, which really impressed Ruth. The recommendations for Ruth's language goal were for her to attend writing workshops and to work on her English language skills independently.

Victor

Victor had been living in Shanghai before he started his PhD in geography. Upon finishing his master's degree, he applied for several PhD programmes in different English-speaking countries and chose New Zealand because of its casual lifestyle, the natural environment and its clean air. The university he chose had a very good reputation and Victor found a potential supervisor in the field he wanted to work in, so he proceeded with a formal application. Victor took the PELA within the first two months of starting his PhD and attended several language workshops as well as study skills workshops following the PELA. He also joined in other activities to socialise and to have the opportunity to practise English (e.g. English lessons at church), and he sought opportunities to network within the university. Victor was funding his own studies but his finances did not seem to worry him. His priority was advancing his career and he wanted to gain as much academic experience as he could during his PhD.

Findings

In this section, I identify the circumstances and experiences that contributed positively to the writing development of Heather, Lottie, Ruth and Victor in the initial year of their PhD. I first discuss the participants' engagement with generic support that afforded opportunities for English language enrichment and writing improvement. I then discuss the role the participants' supervisors played in supporting their students' writing development in the early stages of the PhD. I also consider the participation of Heather, Lottie, Ruth and Victor in academic activities that provided further opportunities for engagement with academic discourse during their first PhD year.

Generic support for English language enrichment and writing development

Heather, Lottie, Ruth and Victor completed the PELA at the beginning of their doctoral degree, as required, and followed specific English language enrichment recommendations as a result of their performance in the assessment. Most recommendations were for the participants to access generic resources (Carter & Laurs, 2014) made available centrally by the institution. Lottie was the only participant whose programme included completing a for-credit English writing course. Participating in the PELA process was seen as an overall positive experience by the four doctoral candidates. Even Heather, who was initially puzzled by her results, eventually acknowledged that the process had been beneficial. In Read and von Randow's (2016) study, their participants also found the PELA to be 'a fair assessment of their language ability' (2016: 145) and were happy to have participated in the programme.

Receiving feedback after the assessment and meeting with a language adviser was one of the highlights of the PELA process for the four doctoral candidates. They appreciated the individual consultation with the adviser as, in the one-on-one meeting, they could express concerns and ask questions, which is crucial for increasing learning opportunities (Chanock, 2007). The participants found having resources pointed out to them very useful and they remembered parts of their conversation with the adviser and some of the feedback received. Heather, for instance, began to pay more attention to sentence structure after the meeting. Ruth recalled being told about the importance of clear topic sentences, and Victor learned from his language adviser about a podcast created by another New Zealand university, which he found very helpful and often accessed.

As for the language support on offer at the university, English grammar and writing workshops were the resources accessed the most. Lottie began attending the workshops before she took the PELA and repeated some a few times. Victor also attended several workshops from the beginning of his PhD studies. He felt he was making progress with his writing and credited the language enrichment resources provided by the university for giving him 'more confidence in [his] English' language skills. Victor did not think he would have difficulties with his research or his 'professional knowledge': for him, mastering English was 'the problem'. In his words: 'if I can deal with it, I can deal with my PhD study' (Interview 2, in Botelho de Magalhães, 2019).

As well as English language and writing workshops, the generic resources provided by the university also include conversation groups for EAL students, which are highly popular with doctoral candidates. Lottie and Victor attended the conversation groups as regularly as they could, especially at the beginning of their first year. Victor appreciated the opportunity to 'communicate with real people' (Interview 1, in Botelho de Magalhães, 2019) while Lottie wanted to learn more about New Zealand culture and meet other students. Heather and Ruth were not particularly interested in these meetings. These two candidates belonged to research teams and thus had regular contact with an array of colleagues. Lottie and Victor worked individually on their own research projects; although they also interacted with PhD colleagues and other academics, they felt the need to find further opportunities to converse in English.

As already stated, Lottie also had to take an English writing course in her first year. She gladly accepted the recommendation and was very happy to have such an opportunity. The course focused on writing research reports and Lottie found it very practical as it pushed her 'to learn more about academic writing … the introduction, the literature review … how to describe [the] methodology and results' (Interview 2, in Botelho de Magalhães, 2019). More importantly, the course boosted Lottie's confidence. Before completing the course, Lottie would only write about her doctoral work in Mandarin. After taking it, she began submitting written work in English to her supervisor and was less afraid of making mistakes. She was proud of the full research proposal and the literature review she wrote in her first year and said that she was enjoying the challenges of writing about her research in English (Interview 3, in Botelho de Magalhães, 2019).

My participants' English language and development was discussed in our conversations quite often. This is not surprising given that they were aware of my research interests. The participants were open about their language-related difficulties and eager to talk about them. Their living, studying and working in New Zealand was a new experience and, while operating in English was exciting, it was also challenging at times. The generic support my participants accessed helped them to cope more easily with the challenges they faced in the initial stages of their doctoral journey. Research shows that when candidates engage with the resources on offer, their doctoral experience is likely to be enhanced and their chances of succeeding academically increase (Fotovatian, 2012; Read & von Randow, 2016; Sawir *et al.*, 2012). Moreover, accessing support for the general development of English language proficiency can strengthen candidates' academic writing skills, therefore facilitating their development as writers.

The supervisors' role in their students' writing development

Supervisory guidance enabling writing development was apparent in the stories of the four participants. Heather, Ruth, Lottie and Victor were relatively new to the discourse norms of their disciplines and the conventions of academic English since none had had much experience with academic writing prior to beginning their doctorate. While they experienced different degrees of difficulty with English, they were all aware of language issues that interfered, to some extent, with their ability to write clearly. All supervisors focused on the development of their student's research, but some also incorporated comments about language use when giving feedback.

Heather's supervisor commented on language and style features of her texts from the early stages of her PhD. Heather did not always understand her supervisor's comments but still appreciated his dedication to helping her and his other students. Heather was highly proficient in English, given her cultural and educational background, but she often made remarks about her desire to sound less Indian and more native-like, both in her speaking and writing. Comments from her supervisor that she did not have 'a strong accent' (Interview 2, in Botelho de Magalhães, 2019) and that he did not see 'a strong influence of [her] mother tongue on [her written] English' (Interview 1, in Botelho de Magalhães, 2019) made her happy. Heather was concerned about fitting in with her research team and about producing texts to the standard she believed was expected of her – direct and objective writing characteristic of the natural sciences (Casanave, 2010). She relied on her supervisor's feedback to guide her in that regard.

Heather made a conscious effort to make her writing more 'scientific'. When writing a research report for one of her experiments, for example, she worked on several drafts, trying to refine her writing, until the final version was ready. Her supervisor remarked that there were 'still some blemishes in English', but his feedback was unclear as Heather thought that 'what he meant was not English' but rather a lack of experience with 'scientific writing' (Interview 2, in Botelho de Magalhães, 2019). Heather realised that there was 'no change in the meaning' of the passages her supervisor corrected, but also acknowledged that his style was not hers: 'if I read the sentence, I wouldn't have written in this way'. Still, she accepted all his suggestions as, after all, he was 'a native speaker, of course, so he would know better' (Interview 2, in Botelho de Magalhães, 2019). Certain standard language ideologies pervade the current monolingual 'international' research community and Heather seemed aware of 'the power of the written medium to transmit information to the global community' (Canagarajah, 2002: 5). Heather imagined her future self (Markus & Nurius, 1986) working in academia, but not in her country of origin: she aspired to an international academic career, for which understanding the norms of academic English writing and the place it holds 'in the process of constructing, disseminating, and legitimizing knowledge' (Canagarajah, 2002: 6) is vital.

Ruth's supervisors also contributed to Ruth's writing development. Her main supervisor seemed very committed to assisting with the improvement of her writing and language skills: 'My supervisor said, I'll do everything that I can do to help you to improve your English' (Interview 2, in Botelho de Magalhães, 2019). Furthermore, Ruth was doing her PhD with publications and was expected to co-write with her main and co-supervisor throughout her doctorate, with at least one article being ready for submission by the end of her first PhD year. In co-writing, Ruth showed her first drafts to her main supervisor, who would correct grammar mistakes, suggest alternative ways of expressing ideas, and also offer comments on content. Ruth then revised the draft until she felt confident enough to present it to both supervisors. After subsequent revisions, the trio considered possible avenues for publishing the work.

In working together with her supervisors, Ruth was exposed to a pedagogy that facilitated growth in her confidence and ability as a writer. Her supervisors edited her writing and provided models of the expected academic discourse, since the three worked together in crafting academic texts. Ruth could observe how their drafts evolved; she experimented with her own writing and learned in the process. In engaging in joint writing (Kamler & Thomson, 2014), Ruth's supervisors were socialising her into the discourse of their discipline. Although academic writing can be learned by accessing other forms of support, the traditional doctoral candidate–supervisor pedagogy may still remain the principal site for learning disciplinary writing conventions (Aitchison *et al.*, 2012). Ruth certainly benefited from her supervisors' pedagogical approach.

Lottie and Victor were also supported by their supervisors but their experiences were quite distinct. Lottie's supervisor focused on content and not so much on her language when giving feedback. Victor's supervisor, on the other hand, provided advice on text structure and the organisation of ideas as well as feedback at paragraph and sentence levels. Both Chinese participants were supervised by Chinese researchers but their supervisors had different attitudes towards language. Lottie's supervisor would only discuss her doctoral work in Mandarin while Victor's supervisor would never resort to their shared mother tongue. Whereas Lottie gained from her supervisor's content-oriented approach, his limited focus on language made her feel as if he did not have high expectations for her written work. Lottie did not have confidence in her writing skills and thought that academic writing was her 'biggest problem' (Interview 2, in Botelho de Magalhães, 2019). Although her supervisor's approach was intellectually rewarding, Lottie may have missed out on early opportunities to experience the heuristic power of writing and speaking about her research (Paré, 2010) in English. It is understandable that Lottie may have experienced a certain frustration with her supervisor's attitude given that her doctoral thesis was going to be written and defended in English.

The approach to language taken by Victor's supervisor contrasted to that of Lottie's. Victor had difficulties in refining his research topic at the beginning of his PhD and thought that he and his supervisor had 'wasted a lot of time communicating': 'maybe it's because of the language … he is also from China, but he never spoke in Chinese to me' (Interview 1, in Botelho de Magalhães, 2019). Despite sounding somewhat disappointed with his supervisor's approach, Victor appreciated the fact that his supervisory meetings were all conducted in English. He agreed with his supervisor's position, as they were 'working in [a] business environment and, business is business' (Interview 1, in Botelho de Magalhães, 2019). One of Victor's main difficulties was using 'western logic' to express himself; for him, writing in English was like 'someone tie your hands, asking you to just use your feet' (Interview 2, in Botelho de Magalhães, 2019). The language prerogative of Victor's supervisor may have worked as an affordance for Victor's writing development as it pushed him to find ways of expressing himself in 'western logic'.

While the language attitude of Victor's supervisor may seem unnatural, Victor considered it commendable. Like Heather, Victor imagined his future self as a member of an international academic community. Discussing his work in English from the early stages of his research could potentially contribute to the crafting of a successful doctoral thesis. Victor seemed aware that thesis writing, a form of social practice, needs to be learned (Basturkmen *et al.*, 2014; Bitchener, 2016; Kamler & Thomson, 2014; Paltridge & Starfield, 2007), and that his supervisor could play a key role in introducing him to the discourse of their discipline (Paré, 2010). Victor held his supervisor as a role-model for expertise performance in the 'Anglophone university system' (Casanave, 2019: 58), a system representing today's hegemonic scientific world and one in which Victor hoped to participate.

Academic practices as opportunities for engagement with academic discourse

The participation of Heather, Lottie, Ruth and Victor in academic activities during their first PhD year varied considerably. All participants took part in departmental seminars and had supervisory meetings regularly. Their supervisors, as seen in the previous section, provided important support. However, the opportunity to interact with researchers other than their supervisors, for example, was not uniform. Heather and Ruth, the two participants whose research was part of a larger project, belonged to research teams and thus had regular team meetings, which senior academics often joined. Ruth was also the only participant who had the opportunity to participate in a regular writing group, whereas Heather and Victor were the only ones to experience teaching undergraduate students from early on in their doctorates.

Although Heather and Ruth mainly relied on their supervisors for writing support, the two also benefited from interacting with senior researchers. Regular team meetings meant that they were informed about other researchers' work and frequently participated in discussions. Victor also often interacted with academics in his department. Despite working on an individual research project and being supported mainly by his supervisor, Victor felt comfortable with approaching senior academics and discussing his research with them. Lottie, on the other hand, did not usually discuss her research with other academics in her department even though she interacted socially with them quite often. Department functions were common in Lottie's faculty and students and lecturers shared communal areas, such as the kitchen, on a daily basis. Lottie had a good relationship with her PhD colleagues and preferred to approach them for support and assistance with PhD matters.

Of the four candidates, Ruth's experiences of engaging with scholarly activities were the most remarkable. This is because in Ruth's work environment, novice and more expert researchers constantly interacted and collaborated. Regular activities included a writing club, sessions for researchers to bring in a piece of writing for others to read and critique, and weekly journal club meetings for the discussion of relevant journal articles previously selected by one of the club members. Opportunities for researchers to present their work in research forums on campus and externally were also offered regularly. Doctoral candidates and researchers at various levels took part in all activities. Participating in groups and activities with senior academics made Ruth feel an equally valued member of her research community.

Ruth's work environment seemed to emulate values characteristic of a community of practice (Lave & Wenger, 1991). Experts welcomed novice researchers and supported their situated learning process so that they could gradually move from the periphery to more independent and more confident participation in the community (e.g. taking the lead in the writing and journal clubs). Ruth felt supported and empowered by her new academic community – positive emotions also noted in other doctoral candidates participating in communities of practice (Shacham & Od Cohen, 2009) and experiencing a strong sense of scholarly community (Stubb *et al.*, 2011).

Learning from senior academics was an invaluable experience for Ruth. The regular writing group meetings, for example, gave Ruth the opportunity to critique other researchers' writing and to have her texts equally evaluated. The journal club provided Ruth with a platform for her to discuss research articles relevant to her doctoral project. Participants took turns in selecting the materials to be read and discussed and the longer Ruth participated, the more confident she felt in selecting articles that were relevant to her own work. Ruth's significant growth in confidence and ability to work independently translated into development as a writer. The more literacy practices she participated in, the more she learned about academic writing and the disciplinary discourse of her academic community.

Victor and Heather were the only participants who had the opportunity to teach early in their doctoral degrees. Victor applied to become a tutor in his first year and taught two undergraduate courses within the first 18 months of his PhD. He saw teaching as crucial for his academic career development, especially since the experience could help him improve his communication skills. Having to instruct others in English helped with his confidence. Heather also taught undergraduate students during her first doctoral year. She started teaching within her first six months at the university and was involved in the supervision of undergraduate students' compulsory lab work. Teaching can contribute to a doctoral student's sense of being an academic (Emmioğlu *et al.*, 2017; Mantai, 2018) and the experience provided Victor and Heather with the opportunity to explain familiar concepts to students in English, therefore affording another avenue for engagement with scientific academic discourse.

Discussion

My participants' experiences of accessing support for the development of their writing skills in the first doctoral year, albeit similar in some aspects, were different. One common experience was that they all accessed generic support to work on their English and writing skills following the PELA recommendations. The four participants seemed aware that developing their English proficiency and writing would in turn assist them to cope with the other tasks they would need to fulfil in the initial stages of the doctorate (e.g. writing a research proposal). Having to comply with compulsory goals may limit doctoral candidates' autonomy (Burford, 2016) but it can also facilitate the transition process for candidates who may find the early stages of the PhD quite stressful (Cornwall *et al.*, 2019). Even though Heather, Lottie, Ruth and Victor completed their goals successfully and within the expected timeframe, that is not to say they did not find the first doctoral year demanding. The PELA goal probably helped them to better manage their writing tasks in the initial phase of the doctorate.

The four participants also counted on supervisory support and feedback for successful academic writing. Supervisors, usually key in socialising doctoral candidates into disciplinary academic discourse (Paré, 2010, 2011), were the principal source of writing support for Heather, Ruth and Victor from the beginning of their degree studies. Dialogue can increase opportunities for academic literacy skills development (Lillis, 2001) and mentoring has an important part in academic discourse socialisation (Duff, 2010). In Ruth's case, she worked together with her supervisors in producing research articles. Ruth's supervisors corrected her writing and provided models of the expected discourse conventions; she could see her drafts evolving with their input. Ruth's experiences of 'situated learning' (Lave & Wenger, 1991) and the pedagogy she was exposed to enabled her confidence to grow and her writing ability to improve.

The writing support that Heather, Lottie and Victor received from their supervisors varied in style and approach. Effective supervision must facilitate conversations about the language that candidates are expected to attain during their doctoral trajectories (Cotterall, 2011b). Victor's supervisor purposefully commented on language use and sentence structure when giving feedback. Heather's supervisor also attempted to provide some language feedback but his comments were not always clear. Furthermore, he seemed to imprint his own voice in her work (even if not on purpose). Lottie's supervisor focused on content and did not comment much on her language or writing skills. Supervisors may not have the expertise to teach their students writing (Casanave, 2019) or they may consider they are 'not good writers themselves' or simply refuse to 'help students with basic English skills' (Aitchison *et al.*, 2012: 441). Whatever the case, there was inconsistency in the writing support my participants' supervisors provided. This variation signals the fact, also pointed out by Cotterall (2011a), that how much supervisory support doctoral candidates receive is not something they can control but is usually the outcome of chance.

The participants' opportunities to take part in diverse scholarly activities also seemed to be a matter of chance. For example, the institute where Ruth was researching offered writing groups as well as meetings to discuss relevant research articles on a regular basis. The other participants' departments had no such offerings. On the other hand, Heather and Victor were given the opportunity to teach. Writing groups support doctoral candidates' writing development and growth as researchers (Aitchison & Guerin, 2014). Activities such as teaching and participation in discussion groups also help doctoral candidates feel like academics (Emmioğlu et al., 2017; Mantai, 2017, 2018) and can afford another level of engagement with academic discourse. Access to a variety of academic practices not only enhances the doctoral experience but also supports doctoral candidates' disciplinary enculturation, which in turn affords writing development.

The unpredictability of the affordances the participants experienced in the first year of their PhD illustrates the idiosyncrasy of the doctorate. The doctoral experience is idiosyncratic in nature as each individual navigates the doctorate motivated by personal intentions and future aspirations. But the differences in the support offered by the candidates' new academic environment reinforce how distinctive the experience can be. While Ruth's experiences of collaborative work and inclusion in various activities may seem ideal, the fact that she was the only participant to co-write with supervisors and to take part in a regular writing group demonstrates the lack of equal opportunities for early-stage doctoral candidates across the university.

One final consideration is the participants' desire to join international academia. Their decision to pursue a doctorate in New Zealand, a Western English-speaking country, was probably influenced by the possibility of researching and writing in English, thus helping them enter the Anglophone scientific world, synonymous with international research. Heather's and Victor's stories reveal (even if only subtly touched on here) their wish to comply with particular discourse norms. Heather wanted her writing to be 'more scientific' whereas Victor wanted his to be expressed in 'western logic'. Both were clear about their intention to pursue an international career and so was Ruth. While English language proficiency is not essential for intellectual progress, the opportunity to improve one's English language ability is a common reason to relocate for study (Findlay et al., 2012). Academic English writing pervades the construction and dissemination of knowledge in today's monolingual global science arena (Canagarajah, 2002). My participants' relocation choice seems to corroborate this current scenario.

Conclusion

This chapter has discussed the experiences of four EAL doctoral candidates 'from the Global East' learning to write 'in the West' and has revealed affordances for writing development in the initial phases of the doctorate. While the participants' overall experiences differed, they all had access to support for improving their English and writing skills. Generic resources, such as a PELA and follow-up workshops, as well as writing support from supervisors (even if differing in approach) were available to all. However, other scholarly activities that could also have contributed to the participants' writing development were not. Doctoral candidates are in charge of their progress when they choose the activities they wish to participate in; however, their participation is dependent on the opportunities they encounter. Every doctoral trajectory is unique, and it is virtually impossible to provide an equivalent level of support or experience to all. But for EAL candidates, especially those who are told that their language skills warrant attention, some consistency in terms of department offerings – such as opportunities to teach, for example – or the level of detail in supervisory feedback, would seem more appropriate.

Ultimately, this chapter aimed to provide insights into the writing development of early stage EAL doctoral candidates. In analysing the experiences of Heather, Lottie, Ruth and Victor, my intention has been to link their stories to key elements in successful academic writing pedagogy at the doctoral level, especially in the initial phases of the PhD. What became apparent from their narratives is that while individual experiences differ, EAL doctoral candidates may have common motives for relocating to another country for research and may share some difficulties related to language constraints and adapting to new discourse norms. Participating in a PELA may help candidates become more aware of linguistic issues; however, improving their linguistic performance is only the starting point in candidates' writing journeys. The PELA provides linguistic feedback at the beginning of the PhD, but doctoral candidates also clearly benefit from collaborating with others and from engaging with academic discourse through different activities.

The message for institutions and supervisors is clear: expanding EAL doctoral candidates' opportunities to participate in various academic practices can afford more occasions for their writing development. The more opportunities on offer, the more chances EAL doctoral candidates have to participate in practices that will contribute to their growth as writers. In turn, such growth will enable (more) participation in disciplinary conversations amongst members of the international academic community and therefore the realisation of a desired academic identity.

References

Aitchison, C. (2010) Learning together to publish: Writing group pedagogies for doctoral publishing. In C. Aitchison, B. Kamler and A. Lee (eds) *Publishing Pedagogies for the Doctorate and Beyond* (pp. 83–100). New York: Routledge.

Aitchison, C. (2014) Same but different: A 20-year evolution of generic provision. In S. Carter and D. Laurs (eds) *Developing Generic Support for Doctoral Students: Practice and Pedagogy*. Abingdon: Routledge.

Aitchison, C. (2018) Writing an identity into being. In S. Carter and D. Laurs (eds) *Developing Research Writing: A Handbook for Supervisors and Advisors* (pp. 193–197). Abingdon: Routledge.

Aitchison, C. and Guerin, C. (eds) (2014) *Writing Groups for Doctoral Education and Beyond: Innovations in Practice and Theory.* New York: Routledge.

Aitchison, C., Catterall, J., Ross, P. and Burgin, S. (2012) 'Tough love and tears': Learning doctoral writing in the sciences. *Higher Education Research and Development* 31 (4), 435–447. https://doi.org/10.1080/07294360.2011.559195.

Ali, A. and Kohun, F.G. (2007) Dealing with social isolation to minimize doctoral attrition: A four-stage framework. *International Journal of Doctoral Studies* 2, 33–49. https://doi.org/10.28945/56.

Archer, L. (2008) Younger academics' constructions of 'authenticity', 'success' and professional identity. *Studies in Higher Education* 33 (4), 385–403.

Basturkmen, H., East, M. and Bitchener, J. (2014) Supervisors' on-script feedback comments on drafts of dissertations: Socialising students into the academic discourse community. *Teaching in Higher Education* 19 (4), 432–445. https://doi.org/10.1080/13562517.2012.752728.

Benson, P. (2013) Narrative writing as method: Second language identity development in study abroad. In G. Barkhuizen (ed.) *Narrative Research in Applied Linguistics* (pp. 244–263). Cambridge: Cambridge University Press.

Bitchener, J. (2016) The content feedback practices of applied linguistics supervisors in New Zealand and Australian universities. *Australian Review of Applied Linguistics (ARAL)* 39 (2), 105–121.

Botelho de Magalhães, M. (2019) Narratives of language learning and identity in first-year EAL doctoral candidates' trajectories. PhD thesis, University of Auckland. http://hdl.handle.net/2292/47405.

Botelho de Magalhães, M., Cotterall, S. and Mideros, D. (2019) Identity, voice and agency in two EAL doctoral writing contexts. *Journal of Second Language Writing* 43, 4–14. https://doi.org/10.1016/j.jslw.2018.05.001.

Briggs, C.L. (2007) Anthropology, interviewing, and communicability in contemporary society. *Current Anthropology* 48 (4), 551–580. https://doi.org/10.1086/518300.

Brinkmann, S. (2018) The interview. In N.K. Denzin and Y.S. Lincoln (eds) *The SAGE Handbook of Qualitative Research* (5th edn, pp. 576–599). Thousand Oaks, CA: Sage.

Burford, J. (2016) Doctoral induction day. In J. Smith, J. Rattray, T. Peseta and D. Loads (eds) *Identity Work in the Contemporary University* (pp. 117–127). Rotterdam: Sense Publishers. https://doi.org/10.1007/978-94-6300-310-0_9.

Burford, J. (2018) The trouble with doctoral aspiration now. *International Journal of Qualitative Studies in Education* 31 (6), 487–503. https://doi.org/10.1080/09518398.2017.1422287.

Canagarajah, A.S. (2002) *A Geopolitics of Academic Writing.* Pittsburgh: University of Pittsburgh Press. https://doi.org/10.2307/j.ctt5hjn6c.

Carter, S. and Laurs, D. (eds) (2014) *Developing Generic Support for Doctoral Students: Practice and Pedagogy.* Abingdon: Routledge.

Casanave, C.P. (2010) Taking risks? A case study of three doctoral students writing qualitative dissertations at an American university in Japan. *Journal of Second Language Writing* 19 (1), 1–16. https://doi.org/10.1016/j.jslw.2009.12.002.

Casanave, C.P. (2019) Performing expertise in doctoral dissertations: Thoughts on a fundamental dilemma facing doctoral students and their supervisors. *Journal of Second Language Writing* 43, 57–62. https://doi.org/10.1016/j.jslw.2018.02.005.

Chanock, K. (2007) Valuing individual consultations as input into other modes of teaching. *Journal of Academic Language and Learning* 1 (1), A1–A9.

Chase, S.E. (2003) Taking narrative seriously: Consequences for method and theory in interview studies. In Y.S. Lincoln and N.K. Denzin (eds) *Turning Points in Qualitative Research: Tying Knots in a Handkerchief* (pp. 273–296). Walnut Creek, CA: AltaMira Press.

Chatterjee-Padmanabhan, M. (2014) Transforming texts: Challenges experienced by international doctoral thesis writers. In S. Carter and D. Laurs (eds) *Developing Generic Support for Doctoral Students: Practice and Pedagogy* (pp. 80–82). Abingdon: Routledge.

Chik, A. and Benson, P. (2008) Frequent flyer: A narrative of overseas study in English. In P. Kalaja, V. Menezes and A.M.F. Barcelos (eds) *Narratives of Learning and Teaching EFL* (pp. 155–168). Basingstoke: Palgrave Macmillan.

Clandinin, D.J. and Connelly, F.M. (2000) *Narrative Inquiry: Experience and Story in Qualitative Research*. San Francisco, CA: Jossey-Bass.

Cornwall, J., Mayland, E.C., van der Meer, J., Spronken-Smith, R.A., Tustin, C. and Blyth, P. (2019) Stressors in early-stage doctoral students. *Studies in Continuing Education* 41 (3), 363–380. https://doi.org/10.1080/0158037X.2018.1534821.

Cotterall, S. (2011a) Stories within stories: A narrative study of six international PhD researchers' experiences of doctoral learning in Australia. PhD thesis, Macquarie University.

Cotterall, S. (2011b) Doctoral students writing: Where's the pedagogy? *Teaching in Higher Education* 16 (4), 413–425. https://doi.org/10.1080/13562517.2011.560381.

Cotterall, S. (2015) The rich get richer: International doctoral candidates and scholarly identity. *Innovations in Education and Teaching International* 52 (4), 360–370. https://doi.org/10.1080/14703297.2013.839124.

Duff, P.A. (2010) Language socialization into academic discourse communities. *Annual Review of Applied Linguistics* 30, 169–192. https://doi.org/10.1017/S0267190510000048.

Emmioğlu, E., McAlpine, L. and Amundsen, C. (2017) Doctoral students' experiences of feeling (or not) like an academic. *International Journal of Doctoral Studies* 12, 73–90.

Findlay, A.M., King, R., Smith, F.M., Geddes, A. and Skeldon, R. (2012) World class? An investigation of globalisation, difference and international student mobility. *Transactions of the Institute of British Geographers* 37 (1), 118–131. https://doi.org/10.1111/j.1475-5661.2011.00454.x.

Flowerdew, J. and Wang, S.H. (2015) Identity in academic discourse. *Annual Review of Applied Linguistics* 35, 81–99. https://doi.org/10.1017/S026719051400021X.

Fotovatian, S. (2012) Three constructs of institutional identity among international doctoral students in Australia. *Teaching in Higher Education* 17 (5), 577–588. https://doi.org/10.1080/13562517.2012.658557.

Golde, C.M. (1998) Beginning graduate school: Explaining first-year doctoral attrition. *New Directions for Higher Education* 101, 55–64.

Hennebry, M., Lo, Y.Y. and Macaro, E. (2012) Differing perspectives of non-native speaker students' linguistic experiences on higher degree courses. *Oxford Review of Education* 38 (2), 209–230. https://doi.org/10.1080/03054985.2011.651312.

Hyland, K. (2004) *Disciplinary Discourses: Social Interactions in Academic Writing*. Ann Arbor, MI: University of Michigan Press.

Hyland, K. (2012) *Disciplinary Identities: Individuality and Community in Academic Discourse*. Cambridge: Cambridge University Press.

Kamler, B. and Thomson, P. (2014) *Helping Doctoral Students Write: Pedagogies for Supervision* (2nd edn). London: Routledge.

Kasper, G. and Prior, M.T. (2015) Analyzing storytelling in TESOL interview research. *TESOL Quarterly* 49 (2), 226–255. https://doi.org/10.1002/tesq.169.

Kuwahara, N. (2008) It's not in the orientation manual: How a first-year doctoral student learned to survive in graduate school. In C.P. Casanave and X. Li (eds) *Learning the Literacy Practices of Graduate School: Insiders' Reflections on Academic Enculturation* (pp. 186–200). Ann Arbor, MI: University of Michigan Press.

Kuzhabekova, A. and Temerbayeva, A. (2018) The role of conferences in doctoral student socialization. *Studies in Graduate and Postdoctoral Education* 9 (2), 181–196. https://doi.org/10.1108/SGPE-D-18-00012.

Langum, V. and Sullivan, K.P.H. (2017) Writing academic English as a doctoral student in Sweden: Narrative perspectives. *Journal of Second Language Writing* 35, 20–25. https://doi.org/10.1016/j.jslw.2016.12.004.

Laufer, M. and Gorup, M. (2018) The invisible others: Stories of international doctoral student dropout. *International Journal of Higher Education Research* 78 (1), 165-181 https://doi.org/10.1007/s10734-018-0337-z.

Lave, J. and Wenger, E. (1991) *Situated Learning: Legitimate Peripheral Participation.* Cambridge: Cambridge University Press.

Lee, A. (2008) How are doctoral students supervised? Concepts of doctoral research supervision. *Studies in Higher Education* 33 (3), 267–281. https://doi.org/10.1080/03075070802049202.

Lee, A. and Murray, R. (2015) Supervising writing: Helping postgraduate students develop as researchers. *Innovations in Education and Teaching International* 52 (5), 558–570. https://doi.org/10.1080/14703297.2013.866329.

Li, X. and Casanave, C.P. (2008) Introduction. In C.P. Casanave and X. Li (eds) *Learning the Literacy Practices of Graduate School: Insiders' Reflections on Academic Enculturation* (pp. 1–11). Ann Arbor, MI: University of Michigan Press.

Lillis, T.M. (2001) *Student Writing: Access, Regulation, Desire.* London: Routledge.

Lovitts, B.E. (2001) *Leaving the Ivory Tower: The Causes and Consequences of Departure from Doctoral Study.* London: Rowman & Littlefield.

Ma, L.P.F. (2019) Academic writing support through individual consultations: EAL doctoral student experiences and evaluation. *Journal of Second Language Writing* 43, 72–79. https://doi.org/10.1016/j.jslw.2017.11.006.

Mackey, A. and Gass, S.M. (2005) *Second Language Research: Methodology and Design.* Mahwah, NJ: Lawrence Erlbaum.

Maher, M.A., Feldon, D.F., Timmerman, B.E. and Chao, J. (2014) Faculty perceptions of common challenges encountered by novice doctoral writers. *Higher Education Research and Development* 33 (4), 699–711. https://doi.org/10.1080/07294360.2013.863850.

Mantai, L. (2017) Feeling like a researcher: Experiences of early doctoral students in Australia. *Studies in Higher Education* 42 (4), 636–650. https://doi.org/10.1080/03075079.2015.1067603.

Mantai, L. (2018) 'Feeling more academic now': Doctoral stories of becoming an academic. *The Australian Educational Researcher* 46 (1), 137–153. https://doi.org/10.1007/s13384-018-0283-x.

Markus, H. and Nurius, P. (1986) Possible selves. *American Psychologist* 41 (9), 954 and 954–969.

McAlpine, L., Jazvac-Martek, M. and Hopwood, N. (2009) Doctoral student experience in education: Activities and difficulties influencing identity development. *International Journal for Researcher Development* 1 (1), 97–109.

Mochizuki, N. (2019) The lived experience of thesis writers in group writing conferences: The quest for 'perfect' and 'critical'. *Journal of Second Language Writing* 43, 36–45. https://doi.org/10.1016/j.jslw.2018.02.001.

Murray, G. (2009) Narrative inquiry. In J. Heigham and R.A. Croker (eds) *Qualitative Research in Applied Linguistics: A Practical Introduction* (pp. 45–65). New York: Palgrave Macmillan.

Ohashi, J., Ohashi, H. and Paltridge, B. (2008) Finishing the dissertation while on tenure track: Enlisting support from inside and outside the academy. In C.P. Casanave and X. Li (eds) *Learning the Literacy Practices of Graduate School: Insiders' Reflections on Academic Enculturation* (pp. 218–229). Ann Arbor, MI: University of Michigan Press.

Owens, R. (2007) Valuing international research candidates. In C. Denholm and T. Evans (eds) *Supervising Doctorates Downunder: Keys to Effective Supervision in Australia and New Zealand* (pp. 146–154). Camberwell, Victoria, Australia: ACER Press.

Paltridge, B. and Starfield, S. (2007) *Thesis and Dissertation Writing in a Second Language: A Handbook for Supervisors.* London: Routledge.

Paré, A. (2010) Slow the presses: Concerns about premature publication. In C. Aitchison, B. Kamler and A. Lee (eds) *Publishing Pedagogies for the Doctorate and Beyond* (pp. 30–46). New York: Routledge.

Paré, A. (2011) Speaking of writing: Supervisory feedback and the dissertation. In L. McAlpine and C. Amundsen (eds) *Doctoral Education: Research-based Strategies for Doctoral Students, Supervisors and Administrators* (pp. 59–74). Dordrecht: Springer.

Paré, A. (2019) Re-writing the doctorate: New contexts, identities, and genres. *Journal of Second Language Writing* 43, 80–84. https://doi.org/10.1016/j.jslw.2018.08.004.

Polkinghorne, D.E. (1995) Narrative configuration in qualitative analysis. *International Journal of Qualitative Studies in Education* 8 (1), 5–23. https://doi.org/10.1080/0951839950080103.

Polkinghorne, D.E. (2007) Validity issues in narrative research. *Qualitative Inquiry* 13 (4), 471–486. https://doi.org/10.1177/1077800406297670.

Read, J. (2016) Some key issues in post-admission language assessment. In J. Read (ed.) *Post-admission Language Assessment of University Students* (pp. 3–20). Cham: Springer.

Read, J. and von Randow, J. (2016) Extending post-entry assessment to the doctoral level: New challenges and opportunities. In J. Read (ed.) *Post-admission Language Assessment of University Students* (pp. 137–156). Cham: Springer. https://doi.org/10.1007/978-3-319-39192-2_7.

Richards, K. (2009) Interviews. In J. Heigham and R.A. Croker (eds) *Qualitative Research in Applied Linguistics: A Practical Introduction* (pp. 182–199). Basingstoke: Palgrave Macmillan.

Riessman, C.K. (2008) *Narrative Methods for the Human Sciences*. Los Angeles, CA: Sage Publications.

Sawir, E., Marginson, S., Forbes-Mewett, H., Nyland, C. and Ramia, G. (2012) International student security and English language proficiency. *Journal of Studies in International Education* 16 (5), 434–454. https://doi.org/10.1177/1028315311435418.

Shacham, M. and Od Cohen, Y. (2009) Rethinking PhD learning incorporating communities of practice. *Innovations in Education and Teaching International* 46 (3), 279–292. https://doi.org/10.1080/14703290903069019.

Shore, C. (2010) The reform of New Zealand's university system: 'after neoliberalism'. *Learning and Teaching* 3 (1), 1–31. https://doi.org/10.3167/latiss.2010.030102.

Stubb, J., Pyhältö, K. and Lonka, K. (2011) Balancing between inspiration and exhaustion: PhD students' experienced socio-psychological well-being. *Studies in Continuing Education* 33 (1), 33–50. https://doi.org/10.1080/0158037X.2010.515572.

Talmy, S. (2010) Qualitative interviews in applied linguistics: From research instrument to social practice. *Annual Review of Applied Linguistics* 30, 128–148. https://doi.org/10.1017/S0267190510000085.

Tardy, C.M. (2005) 'It's like a story': Rhetorical knowledge development in advanced academic literacy. *Journal of English for Academic Purposes* 4 (4), 325–338. https://doi.org/10.1016/j.jeap.2005.07.005.

Thurlow, S., Morton, J. and Choi, J. (2019) You can't be Shakespearean talking about the institutionalisation of sex offenders: Creativity and creative practices of multilingual doctoral writers. *Journal of Second Language Writing* 43, 46–56. https://doi.org/10.1016/j.jslw.2017.11.002.

University of Auckland (2016) *Statute and Guidelines for the Degree of Doctor of Philosophy (PhD)*. https://cdn.auckland.ac.nz/assets/policyhub/2016%20Statute%20website%20version.pdf.

Webster, L. and Mertova, P. (2007) *Using Narrative Inquiry as a Research Method: An Introduction to Using Critical Event Narrative Analysis in Research on Learning and Teaching*. London: Routledge.

Xu, L. and Zhang, L.J. (2019) L2 doctoral students' experiences in thesis writing in an English-medium university in New Zealand. *Journal of English for Academic Purposes* 41, 100779. https://doi.org/10.1016/j.jeap.2019.100779.

6 Agency in L2 Academic Literacies: Immigrant Students' Lived Experiences in Focus

Kirsi Leskinen
University of Jyväskylä, Finland

Introduction

Reading and writing in academic contexts are often challenging for students using their second or additional language to do so. Furthermore, academic literacy practices vary across cultures and disciplines, which means that even students with a background in higher education have to appropriate new ways of making meaning in new academic environments (Kim & Belcher, 2018; Wette & Furneaux, 2018). These perspectives intersect in this chapter, which approaches the experiences of immigrant students in Finland who had already completed some university studies before emigrating. They wanted to develop their language and literacy skills in Finnish to get access to and succeed in academic life and professional careers in their new home country, and they took part in a tailored training programme that integrated language and content studies in different disciplines. Such a setting is significantly different from previous research on learning academic reading and writing in a second or additional language, which has focused on advanced second language users, mainly English language users, who already have access to academia, such as exchange students (e.g. Kim & Belcher, 2018) or international degree students (e.g. Lee & Maguire, 2011).

Morrice (2013) emphasizes the importance of understanding past experiences when exploring the experiences of highly educated refugee professionals who enter higher education in their new country to find employment and re-establish their professional identity. However, hardly any research on adult immigrant students in the context of academic literacies has paid attention to students' lived experiences. This study therefore aims to explore how students experience, perceive and negotiate new reading and writing practices and academic genres in their L2 Finnish, allowing for their relevant life experience and previous knowledge. To understand how they experience the new literacy practices, the study draws on a dialogical view of agency (Dufva & Aro, 2015; Sullivan & McCarthy, 2004; Vitanova, 2005, 2010), which is based on Mikhail Bakhtin's work (e.g. 1981, 1986). In a broad, sociocultural definition, agency refers to an individual's 'socioculturally mediated capacity to act' (Ahearn, 2001: 112), and, in the dialogical approach, the emphasis is especially on the individual's lived and felt experience (Sullivan & McCarthy, 2004). In this view, agency is seen from a holistic perspective, as dynamic but also continuous and semi-permanent (Dufva & Aro, 2015). This means that, to understand an individual's sense of agency, one has to understand the role of earlier experience and future hopes, as well as the current social context.

In this study, academic literacy practices are considered as a wide range of language-using situations in academic settings, from writing emails to reading scientific articles. In addition to basic reading and writing skills, also digital, numerical and visual literacies are to be employed to accomplish these tasks. Therefore, literacies are understood in a broad sense and conceptualized as multiliteracies, which means that the multimodal and multilingual aspects of meaning making are taken into account (Cope & Kalantzis, 2009). The focus is on three literacy practices that are commonly used in higher education courses in Finland, namely summary writing, participating in a discussion forum in an online learning environment, and writing a learning journal. Participants' agency with these three practices is approached through their spoken narratives. In line with the small-stories perspective (Georgakopoulou, 2015), narratives are seen as tellings of past, ongoing or future events in an interactive environment. The research questions are:

How is agency displayed in immigrant students' spoken narratives on academic literacy practices in L2 Finnish?

How are immigrant students' beliefs and lived experiences reflected in the spoken narratives displaying agency?

The chapter is structured as follows. First, there is a discussion of prior research relevant to the current study. Then, the theoretical framework, the analytical concepts, and the methodology of the current study are introduced. This is followed by an analysis of the narratives of six focal participants, in order to explore their experiences of agency in the three literacy practices. Finally, the findings are discussed in the framework of academic literacies, and their pedagogical, theoretical and policy implications are explored.

Literature Review and Theoretical Framework

Prior research on academic literacies in a second language

In this study, the notion of literacy practice is used to conceptualize the link between the activities of reading and writing and the social structures surrounding them (Barton & Hamilton, 1998). The study draws on the academic literacies perspective (Lea & Street, 1998; Lillis & Scott, 2007) which, in line with New Literacy Studies (e.g. Barton & Hamilton, 1998), sees reading and writing as social practices. The approach is interested in meaning making, power relations, identities and institutional practices in academic settings, and therefore sees literacy practices as situated, dynamic and complex (Lea & Street, 1998). It is also transformative in nature; this means, for example, that new ways have to be found of meaning making in academic contexts, using students' own resources as tools (Lillis & Scott, 2007: 13).

Academic reading and writing in a second language have been studied intensively in various frameworks. Based on a synthesis of previous research, Hyland (2011: 31) identified five kinds of knowledge involved in learning second language writing. These are (1) content knowledge; (2) system knowledge, which refers to language and the surface level of the text; (3) knowledge of the writing process; (4) genre knowledge; and (5) context knowledge, such as readers' expectations and cultural preferences. In a new academic setting, writers actively repurpose and reconstruct their prior knowledge and combine it with new knowledge (Kim & Belcher, 2018). The more socially emphasized research has focused on students' experiences and perceptions. For example, Lee and Maguire (2011) found that their research participants, two South Korean students in a Canadian university, were struggling with the new writing norms because these norms conflicted with their identities.

In Anglo-Western academic contexts, the majority of writing activities are of the 'reading-to-write' type (Nesi & Gardner, 2012), such as the three literacy practices analysed in this study. However, students with prior university-level studies from non-Western countries are not always familiar with this kind of writing and may find it challenging (Wette & Furneaux, 2018: 190–192). Writing from sources is a complex cognitive process which at different stages involves a variety of reading and writing strategies (e.g. McCulloch, 2013). Interestingly, Bhowmik (2016) found that the conscious use of different strategies throughout the writing process was a major component in L2 writers' agency. He suggested that the enactment of agency allows writers to choose among different ways to complete a task. Wette and Furneaux (2018) did not apply the concept of agency in their study, but their research participants, who were international students, reported using a variety of resources, such as their supervisors or websites, to assist them with their writing and in their studies in general. Finally, Jeffery and Wilcox (2016) investigated adolescent L2 English writers' authorial agency, which they conceptualized as 'the socially mediated inclination to write, sense of purpose in writing, and perceived ability to write well', and argued that such agency is related to writing development.

Common to almost all previous research is that it has focused on academic literacy practices in English, which is a global lingua franca and is often taught in schools around the world as a foreign language. Finnish, in contrast, is a less widely taught language and has majority language status only in Finland. Typically, migrants do not start learning the language until they arrive in the country. However, Finnish language skills are considered essential for succeeding in working life in Finland, and even many academics working in English in a Finnish university agree that one needs Finnish skills to be able to participate fully in society generally and in working life (Nikulin, 2019). Previous research on writing in L2 Finnish has often taken a usage-based approach to language. For example, Ivaska (2015) has explored constructions in academic essays that were part of the Corpus of Advanced Learner Finnish, and he highlights the context-based nature of language learning. Mustonen (2015), in turn, used the CEFLING (Linguistic Basis of the Common European Framework for L2 English and L2 Finnish) corpus, and she notes that the idiomatic use of constructions in written texts reflects the active language use in everyday learning environments. In the current research setting, the students were participating in new academic literacy practices in Finnish, a language they had started to learn in adulthood and in which they were not yet advanced. In the following section, I will introduce how the concept of agency is understood in this study.

Dialogical approach: Agency as lived, experienced and embodied

This study draws on a dialogical approach to agency, which is based on the ideas of Bakhtin (e.g. 1981, 1986) and has been further developed by Vitanova (2005, 2010), Dufva and Aro (2015) and Sullivan and McCarthy (2004), among others. Similar to other sociocultural perspectives, the dialogical approach understands agency as situated between the individual and the environment, but the emphasis is on the individual's views and experiences, and understanding small, personal stories (Sullivan & McCarthy, 2004). From a dialogical perspective, agency is examined 'as both subjectively experienced and as collectively emergent' (Dufva & Aro, 2015: 38). In other words, agency is constructed in dialogue with other people and the environment.

From a dialogical perspective, gaining agency means finding one's own voice (Vitanova, 2005, 2010). In Bakhtin's philosophy, life is understood as dialogic in nature (see, for example, Bakhtin, 1986), and in dialogue with others, people encounter various worldviews, beliefs and ways of acting, which Bakhtin (1981, 1986) refers to as 'voices'. Individuals can choose how they perceive and react to these voices that they encounter. According to Bakhtin (1981), the voices of others can be dealt with in three ways: individuals can ignore them as irrelevant, perceive them as internally persuasive and start using them as their own, or regard them as authoritative, which means that the individuals need to totally accept or totally reject them. Bakhtin also uses the concept of 'word' to describe how the language that we use is never neutral. Words are used to convey meaning and they are laden with intentions and worldviews (Bakhtin, 1981: 293–294). They are always 'half someone else's' (Bakhtin, 1981: 293), which means that the speaker recycles others' ideas and intentions and also adds something of his or her own. The process of making words one's own, that is to say using words with one's own intention, is called appropriation. Second language development as a whole can also be seen as appropriation: learners recycle the words of others to express themselves and to make them their own (Dufva *et. al*, 2014; Suni, 2008). Language learning is thus part of finding one's own voice and gaining agency, in the context of migration in particular (Vitanova, 2005).

According to Dufva and Aro (2015) agency is dynamic: it often changes over time and from one situation to another. However, agency is also seen as continuous, as people regard their life 'as an ongoing narrative' rather than a sequence of random events (Dufva & Aro, 2015: 38). New situations constantly bring new possibilities for change and new possibilities for new interpretations of ourselves (Sullivan & McCarthy, 2004). Sullivan and McCarthy (2004: 296) point out that, in the present, an agentive individual looks in two directions: back to the past and 'their responsibility for their actions' and 'forward towards the potential of the future'. So, agency is part of the continuum of an individual's life but at the same time it is experienced in a particular time and place (see Dufva, 2004). Language-related lived experiences are understood here in line with Busch (2017), who draws on Merleau-Ponty's (e.g. 2009) philosophy. She emphasizes the bodily–emotional dimensions of experience and argues: 'it is the emotionally charged experience of outstanding or repeated situations of interaction with others that keeps alive the process of inscribing language experience into body memory' (Busch, 2017: 352).

To better understand the life experiences of learners as constructing their sense of agency, I adapt the concept of the historical body from the nexus analytical framework (Scollon & Scollon, 2004). Nexus analysis sees social action as an intersection of participants' life trajectories and capacities (the historical body), the participants' interaction order, and those wider discourses that are present in the action (Scollon & Scollon, 2004: 19–20). In the nexus analytical framework, the social action in focus in this study can be defined as participation in a literacy practice, namely, writing an academic text in an L2. The historical body refers to people's 'life experiences, their goals and purposes, and their unconscious ways of behaving and thinking' (Scollon & Scollon, 2004: 46), and these historical bodies have been shaped in particular social spaces (Blommaert & Huang, 2009: 7); in the context of language learning, this could mean classrooms, supermarkets, libraries and so on. Finally, both frameworks applied in this study share a similar socio-cognitive understanding of embodiment: from a dialogical perspective, agency is embodied (Sullivan & McCarthy, 2004), and in nexus analysis the individual's lived experience is located in the body (Scollon & Scollon, 2004; see also Busch, 2017; Dufva, 2004).

Data and Methods

The context of the study is a nine-month training programme that was designed for migrants who have completed university-level studies before migration and who aim to work in their own field or continue their studies in Finland. The programme was conducted in a higher education institution in the latter half of the 2010s and language studies were integrated with studies on civic and working life skills as well as content studies. This meant that the students mainly studied Finnish in language classes that were focused on the most common academic literacy practices and academic language and, in addition, they could select and complete some university-level content studies in their own or other relevant disciplines. These content studies were for independent study, such as writing essays or completing online assignments, and they were the same as for students who were not from the programme. However, the students could bring materials and themes from these courses to the Finnish classes and use them for the learning tasks, such as for writing a summary in Finnish. In addition, students had meetings with mainstream degree students, who acted as their tutors; in these meetings they could receive further support with the materials and tasks and where they mainly spoke Finnish. I had a dual role in the training, in that I was one of the five teachers of Finnish as a second language and I gathered data as a researcher.

Conducted in this educational setting, the current study is part of a larger ethnographically oriented multidisciplinary research project which draws on the nexus analytical framework (Scollon & Scollon, 2004). As already explained above, the aim of nexus analysis is to investigate a social action at a nexus point, which is an intersection of the life experiences and historical trajectories of the participants (historical bodies) with discourses and interactional elements (Scollon & Scollon, 2004: 19–20). The social action in the current study is writing as participating in a literacy practice, and the focus is on the historical bodies of the participants. During the training programme, I interviewed some of the students and collected their oral and written course work, as well as course material and interaction data from their student tutor group meetings. The interviews had many of the features of ethnographic interviews, since we had shared many classroom situations. There was mutual trust, but my dual role also affected the nature of the interviews. The participants often seemed to treat me as their teacher – for example, when asking about their word choices in Finnish. I was not in a position to formally grade or assess the students, but it is possible that they still thought it was important that they should make a good impression on me. I tried to be sensitive in handling the interview questions, because they were either closely related to course work or were very open-ended, and I did not want the participants to feel that they were obliged to talk about personal things that they would rather not talk about with their teacher. In the interviews, the participants and I shared two common languages: Finnish, which was my first language and the participants' second language, and English, which was a lingua franca for all of us. All participants chose to use Finnish. The reason might have been that they saw the interviews as an opportunity to practise speaking Finnish, or that they were used to speaking Finnish with me. Being so used to communicating together in Finnish helped us to find mutual understanding in the interview interaction, even though it sometimes took some time. However, the choice of language further contributed to the already existing asymmetrical power relationship between me and the participants.

The analysis started with mapping the academic literacy practices that were part of the training. Three literacy practices were selected for further analysis based on the many different experiences that the students expressed in their narratives throughout the data. These practices were writing a summary of a field-specific text for the Finnish class, participating in a discussion forum in an online learning environment as an assignment for a content course, and writing a learning journal for the Finnish class. The analysis is based on the participants' spoken narratives on the three literacy practices. (See Table 6.1. All names are pseudonyms chosen by the participants or by the author.) These narratives are from four data types: their pair discussions, and individual, pair and group interviews. The summary writing and the forum discussion data were both gathered approximately halfway through the programme, while the learning journal data were gathered at the end of the programme. In addition, the students' pieces of writing as well as interaction data from a student tutor group meeting were used as a secondary data source to contextualize the narratives. Oral data were transcribed, and relevant data excerpts were translated into English for the purpose of this chapter. In the translation process, some elements of the learner language were lost, and the speech in the

Table 6.1 Participants by group (A/B) and data types (pair discussion, individual/pair/ group interview) concerning different literacy practices

	Group	Summary writing	Forum discussion	Learning journal
Olga	B	Pair discussion		Individual interview
Faisal	B	Pair discussion		
Waseem	B	Pair discussion		
Adam	B		Group interview	Pair interview
Mostafa	A		Group interview	
Adnan	A			Individual interview

translated excerpts may seem more fluent and more target-like than in the original narratives.

The key participants (see Table 6.1), all 25–35 years old, were from different fields. They had migrated to Finland for a variety of reasons, but in no case was studying a major reason for migrating. Some of the participants had come to Finland as refugees. At the beginning of the training, students were divided into two Finnish classes, based on their language skills. Students at the estimated A1 and A2 levels in the CEFR were in group A, and students at the B1 and B2 levels were in group B (see Council of Europe, 2001). Olga was from Russia, Mostafa was from an African country, and Faisal, Waseem, Adam and Adnan were from Middle Eastern countries.

After mapping the three literacy practices from the whole data set, I analysed the narratives that were related to those practices, in order to identify the different aspects of agency that were involved. I draw on the ideas of the small-stories approach (Georgakopoulou, 2015) in understanding the nature of narratives as part of the ongoing interaction. From the small-stories perspective, everything that is told is worth analysing, not only traditional, long, chronological stories of past experiences (Georgakopoulou, 2015: 258). In the actual analysis, I analysed the content combined with the form and structure of the narrative (Riessman, 2008). This meant paying attention to word choices, such as repetitions and verb forms, bearing in mind the fact that the participants were speaking their second language (see Vitanova, 2005).

Barkhuizen (2013: 6–7) identifies three interconnected levels of context in narrative study, which I also took account of in the analysis. The first level refers to the interactional context of the narrative, such as the speaker's role in the interaction. The second level is the local context of the narrative, which includes for example the physical setting and language choice. The third level refers to the larger sociohistorical and sociocultural context. Vitanova (2010: 30) also remarks on the context of narrative and suggests that Bakhtin's philosophy enables the researcher to analyse the dialogic interplay between the individual and the context. Following Vitanova (2005, 2010) the data of the current study are analyzed from a dialogical perspective by seeing the narratives as polyphonic interactions. In practice this meant, for example, identifying the different voices that were present in the narratives.

Findings

Beliefs and prior knowledge shaping the experience of writing a summary

It was evident that, with the summary task, the participants' beliefs about language and language learning were related to their sense of agency, and it seemed that their beliefs also had an impact on how they decided to take action (see also Aro, 2009). The students also perceived their prior knowledge as a resource, and their lack of prior knowledge as a hindrance, when writing the summary. The aim of the task was to learn reading strategies, summarizing, paraphrasing and writing from a source text. The students chose texts such as scientific articles that were related to the content courses they were attending or their own academic field more generally. The summary (*referaatti*) they wrote had a word limit of 500 words. Afterwards, they had an oral task in pairs in which they reflected on the reading and writing processes and their reading and writing skills. As a guideline for their discussion, students had a handout with a list of questions, and they recorded the pair-work with their own cell phones.

In the discussions, students expressed various beliefs about second language learning. These beliefs seemed to reflect common views, or authoritative voices in Bakhtin's (1981) terms (see also Aro, 2009). In the first example, Olga and Faisal are identifying what they want to practise next in reading and writing, and they also explain why. These students follow their handout closely, and Olga is taking the leading role in the discussion.

Example 1

Olga: - - ja mitä sä haluat harjoitella (.) se on kaks bee
Faisal: miten haluat erityisesti harjoitella (.) minä haluan (.) harjoitella kielioppi, minä pitän minun pitää ensimmäi- ensimmäiseksi pitää ymmärtää kielioppi, ja lauserakentaa sitten mä voin ymmärtää lause lauseita
Olga: mhy
Faisal: jos minä en tiedä, mikä tämä pääte on, sitten minä en osaa (.) ymmärtää
Olga: no mä haluan, kun mä oon jo sano- kun oon jo sanoin, lukea enemmän tällaisia tekstejä ja tavallisesti sun ammatissa on, samanlaisia termejä ja jos sä luet ehkä kymmenen tekstiä, varmasti sä muistat kaikki terminit nyt
Faisal: ((naurahtaa))

Example 1 (English translation)

Olga: - - and what do you want to practise (.) it's 2B
Faisal: how do you specifically want to practise (.) I want to (.) practise
         grammar, I have to, I fir- first have to understand grammar, and
         sentence structure then I can understand sentence sentences
Olga: mm
Faisal: if I don't know which ending this is, then I can't (.) understand
Olga: well I want to, as I have already sa- as I already said, to read
         more the kinds of texts that you usually have in your profes-
         sion, similar terms and if you read maybe ten texts, surely you
         remember all the terms now
Faisal: ((laughs))

Faisal's belief about reading in a second language seems to be very grammar oriented. He wants to practise grammar next because he believes that in order to 'understand sentences' (*ymmärtää lauseita*) he needs to 'understand grammar' (*ymmärtää kielioppi*). He goes on to say that if he does not know the ending of a word, he cannot understand. Finnish is an agglutinative language with numerous different endings, which might make it challenging for the learner to know all the endings (see Martin, 1995). Faisal's belief is in line with the traditional, formal conceptualization of language as structures, or monological thinking, in Bakhtin's terms (Bakhtin, 1981, 1986; Dufva *et al.*, 2011: 110–114). Therefore, from a dialogical perspective, Faisal's conceptualization may be an authoritative voice, which he ventriloquates in his narrative (Bakhtin, 1981). Olga, in turn, believes that if she reads 'maybe ten texts' (*ehkä kymmenen tekstiä*) from her field she will learn all the discipline-specific terms. Aro (2009), in her interview research on young learners of English, identified an authoritative belief similar to Olga's, which emphasized the role of reading, practising and memorizing vocabulary in language learning. According to Dufva (2003), beliefs about language learning are both shared and individual at the same time; they are a combination of personal experiences and views from societal contexts, such as school and media. Students' views at any given moment are therefore related to their past experiences and their past contacts with authoritative voices.

Students' beliefs about language learning, reading and writing seemed to have an actual impact on the learner's action. In the next example, the same students talk about planning their own summaries.

Example 2

Olga: - - miten sä suunnitelet sun oma tekstin
Faisal: oikeesti minä haluan (.) lukea vielä, pari ehkä parikymmentä
         ((naurahtaa))
Olga: mhy ((naurahtaa))

Faisal: koska se on todella vaikea teksti, kun minä (.) ymmärrän kaikki sitten minä voin kirjoittaa, mitä tekstissä on, ja voin referoida

Olga: joo (.) no minä taval- mä tavallisesti luen pääotsikko, sitten kun [opettajan nimi] neuvoi meille alaotsikot, ja nyt mä, no ehkä ehkä voin arvata mistä, tuo koko teksti (.) sitten mä luen ja alleviivaan tärkeät kohdat (.) ja sitten aloitan kirjoittaa omin sanoin mistä mä oon jo lukenut ja niitä asiat mistä mä ymmärsin (.) joo ja kun mä luen samaan aikaan mä yritän vaikka jotain vaikka pari sanaa tästä lauseesta kirjoittaa koska jos mä vain luen, sitten mä en voi muistaa mitään, mun pitää samaan aikaan lukea eli nähdä kirjaimet ja itse kirjoittaa, omalla kädellä

Example 2 (English translation)

Olga: how do you plan your own text

Faisal: really I want (.) to read a couple more times, perhaps twenty more times ((a laugh))

Olga: umm ((a laugh))

Faisal: because it's a really difficult text, when I (.) understand everything then I can write what the text is about, and I can summarize

Olga: yeah (.) well I usual- I usually read the title, then the sub-headings as [teacher's name] advised us, and now I, well maybe maybe I can guess what the whole text is about (.) then I read and underline the important parts (.) and then I start to write in my own words what I've read and about the things that I've understood (.) yeah and when I read at the same time I try to write a couple of words from that sentence because if I only read, I can't remember anything, at the same time I have to read or see the letters and write for myself, with my own hand

Summary writing involves both reading and writing, and both students in this excerpt first start to talk about reading. Faisal says that before being able to write, he wants to read the text 'a couple more times, perhaps twenty more times' (*pari, ehkä parikymmentä*) to understand it; his laughter shows that he might exaggerate a little. He seems to believe, however, that reading and writing are two quite separate activities, which is in line with the dominant classification of the four elements of language competence (see Hartley, 2007). According to Faisal, his source text is 'really difficult' (*todella vaikea*), and he cannot proceed to writing or even answer Olga's question about writing before understanding 'everything' (*kaikki*) in the text. Olga, on the other hand, sees reading and writing in a different light, as she regards them as intertwined activities. The practices she talked about in the interview are similar to those described in previous studies on writing from sources in a second language (see, for example, McCulloch, 2013). Olga seems to have a variety of strategies that she uses to approach the task, which Bhowmik (2016) has shown to be a major element in an L2 writer's agency.

In the example, Olga says that she reads and underlines the most important parts and writes 'in her own words' (*omin sanoin*) about what she has understood. From the dialogical perspective, this paraphrasing is part of the process of making another's words her own, and it is also a central element in gaining agency (see Dufva & Aro, 2015). In addition to the ideas in her text, Olga seems to be appropriating the reading and writing practices that she describes. She reads the sub-headings 'as the teacher advised' (*kun opettaja neuvoi*), and thus explicitly refers to an authority whom she has listened to. In addition, Olga's word choice – 'in one's own words' (*omin sanoin*) – is most commonly used in educational settings, such as in assignments and instructions, which also refers to classroom discourse. Olga therefore seems to be following reading and writing practices that she has learned in educational settings. Maybe this strong involvement is related to her profession as a teacher or her possible identity as a 'good student' – or maybe she just finds the practices useful. However, Olga's beliefs about the literacy practice allow her to exercise her agency in the writing task, whereas what Faisal says indicates that his belief about the nature of the summary writing task limits his capacity to act.

In addition, Olga's description of her reading and writing practices in this example is very physical, because she mentions her sight and hands as being crucially involved in the activity. Olga says that if she only reads, she cannot remember anything, because 'at the same time I have to read, see the letters and write for myself, with my own hand' (*mun pitää samaan aikaan lukea eli nähdä kirjaimet ja itse kirjoittaa, omalla kädellä*). Olga's belief, as well as her agency, are thus embodied. In addition, her sense of agency is bound in time and space (see Dufva, 2004). This is evident from another narrative in the same discussion in which she talks about what is easy for her in reading and writing. She ends up describing the ideal reading situation for her: 'I can just sit alone quietly and read very slowly, and at the same time underline familiar phrases or words, it gives me confidence' (*mä voin rauhassa vain yksin istua, ja tosi hitaasti lukea, samaan aikaan alleviivata tuttuja fraaseja vai sanoja, se antaa mulle itsevarmuus*). Her material surroundings, namely having the opportunity to sit alone and underline whatever she wants, as well as having plenty of time, are key elements in shaping her experience.

In addition to their beliefs, students' prior knowledge also emerged as a source of agency in the narratives on summary writing. Olga, for example, says on another occasion that some terms that she had 'already studied in Russia' (*jotka mä oon jo opiskellut Venäjällä*) were easy for her in the summary writing task because she 'could guess what they mean' (*mä voin arvata mitä ne tarkoittavat*). In other words, Olga was somewhat familiar with the content of her text because she had already studied the terms in her first language. Olga also actively made use of her prior knowledge in guessing the meanings.

Waseem, on the other hand, perceived the summary writing task as difficult because of his lack of background knowledge. In the pair discussion with a student called Tatjana, he explains that the reason for his difficulty is that his source text is not from his own field. In the following excerpt, his focus is on understanding the concepts.

Example 3

Waseem: joo, ei vain esimerkiksi se on ei vain, ongelma ei vain ole
Tatjana: lukee ja ymmärtää
Waseem: ymmärtää sanat, se on ei ei suomen kieli onkelma, se on esimerkiksi (.) liberaali asioita että politiikka asioita, he kirjoi- he sanovat sisälle artikkelissa, mä en ymmärrä mä en tiedä mitä on, hyvin mä me tiedä hyvin mitä on liberaali esimerkiksi

Example 3 (English translation)

Waseem: yeah it's not for example, the problem is not just
Tatjana: to read and understand
Waseem: to understand words, it's not not a problem with the Finnish language, it's for example (.) liberal and political things, they wri- they say in the article, I don't understand I don't know what is, I don't know well what liberal is, for example

Waseem says that understanding the text is difficult not only because of the Finnish language, but also because he does not understand what the concepts mean. He repeats the word 'problem' (*ongelma*) and only uses the negative verb form when referring to himself, which might imply that his sense of agency in the situation is rather weak. Waseem makes a distinction between knowing a word and understanding a concept – maybe he knows the equivalent for *liberaali* in some other language. Waseem's example of a concept that he does not know draws attention to his reservoir of previous knowledge. In the Finnish higher education context, 'liberal' is presumably a construct that all students know. Academic texts are full of concepts, some of which are explained thoroughly while some are concepts that readers are expected to be familiar with already. Taking a transformative approach to academic literacies means acknowledging these different knowledge repertoires (see Paxton & Frith, 2015).

Using multilingual and external resources to participate in an online discussion forum

Online learning environments offer students a space to use their multilingual resources and digital skills. As part of the training programme, a few students completed an online course in entrepreneurship. The main task of the course was to post a weekly assignment, using source materials, in an online learning environment, and comment on other students' assignments. This was done in an online discussion forum set up by the learning environment. The material was mainly in Finnish, but students could use either Finnish or English in their assignments and comments. However, most students used Finnish in the discussion forum.

In the following example, Mostafa describes his multilingual practices when completing the tasks.

Example 4

Mostafa: ennen minä käytin kääntäjää minä yritän ymmärtää mitä tämä tarkoittaa, ja kun minä ymmärrän ehkä (.) neljäkymmentä tai viisikymmentä prosenttia, ja sitten minä ota kaikki, ja sitten kääntää, ja ymmärrän mitä tarkoittaa, ja sitten, on kaikki on minun päähän (.) ja sitten voin minä kommentoida mitä tämä tarkoittaa ja, miten mutta (.) minä, en voi (.) myös kirjoittaa suomeksi kommentoita - - minä käytän englanniksi kommentoi mutta minä ymmärrän mitä keskustelevat ja mitä, he sanovat he kommentoita

Example 4 (English translation)

Mostafa: before I use an online translator I try to understand what this means, and when I understand maybe (.) forty or fifty percent, then I take everything, and translate it, and understand what it means, and then, everything is in my head (.) and then I can comment on what this means, and how, but (.) I can't (.) also write the comments in Finnish - - I use English when I comment, but I understand what they discuss and what they say they comment

In this excerpt, Mostafa positions himself in the centre of the action and focuses on describing what he can do: there is only one negative verb form in the whole narrative. Mostafa was able to participate in the discussion because he used both Finnish and English as well as an online translation application. In other words, his 'historical body' (Scollon & Scollon, 2004: 46–49), which includes his language repertoires and skills related to using technology, had a central role in his completion of the task. García and Kleifgen (2019) point out the same issue: multilingual readers and writers benefit from using their linguistic and multimodal repertoires in literacy activities. On the other hand, the structure of the course enabled Mostafa to use all these resources, and therefore his agency was constructed in a dialogue between the environment and his own capacities.

In addition to their multilingual resources, students used their information-searching skills and relied on source texts when participating in the discussion forum. The next example comes from Adam, who had not been involved in digital academic literacy practices during his previous studies at university level. In the interview with me, he describes the online course as 'difficult' (*vaikea*) but also as 'a new and wonderful experience' (*uusi ja ihana kokemus*). Adam usually used English in his own posts and replies but on one occasion he responded to a post about a new business idea in Finnish. In the following, he describes this occasion to me.

Example 5

Adam: yksi kerta minä kommentoin, toinen toinen opiskelija hän on suomalainen opiskelija, ja hänen yrittäjyys oli avaa apteekin, apteekin

Kirsi: mm joo

Adam: ja todella minä luulen että mä (-) noin kolme ehkä neljä tuntia, että mä haluan sanoo, mä haluan tiedä suomen sää- säännöt, suomen säännöt (.) joo kuka haluaa avaa apteekin, ja sitten minä otan vähän, kolme tai neljä lausetta ja laita hänelle ja laitan myös että mistä lähde- lähteet

Kirsi: okei joo

Adam: mutta ota, ota ota aika mulle että kolme tuntia vain että

Kirsi: joo tosi kauan

Adam: miten tämä apteekkiasia kääntäjä

Example 5 (English translation)

Adam: once I commented on a student he was a Finnish student and his business idea was to open a pharmacy

Kirsi: mm yeah

Adam: and really I think I (-) about three maybe four hours, I want to say, I want to know the Finnish ru- rules, Finnish rules (.) yeah for someone who wants to open a pharmacy, and then I take some, three or four sentences and respond to him and also add the sources

Kirsi: okay yeah

Adam: but it takes, takes takes time, three hours only -

Kirsi: yeah that's very long

Adam: to translate this pharmacy thing

In this small story, Adam describes the actions that were involved in his writing process. His main message seems to be that he needed a long time, as he repeats this at the beginning and at the end of his story, and he specifies that it took three or four hours to write three or four sentences. However, in the narrative, Adam positions himself as an active and agentive participant in the discussion forum; he first wanted to know the rules for opening a pharmacy in Finland, so he searched for the information, and, when writing the response, he wanted to add the sources. Adam uses a whole repertoire of skills – in nexus analytical terms, his 'historical body' is involved in the action (see Scollon & Scollon, 2004: 46–49).

In the excerpt, Adam says that he 'took' (*otti*) a few sentences and that he needed several hours 'to translate the pharmacy thing' (*tämä apteekkiasia kääntäjä*). This 'taking' and translating process is visible in the actual response that Adam wrote. The written response contains two sentences; the first one is copy-pasted from his source, and the second one is so complex that he probably has not written it all by himself. He mentions the sources but he does not use quotation marks or otherwise follow the instructions for citing. Previous studies have shown that writing from sources is often challenging for students, and it might be even more challenging in one's second language than in one's first language (e.g. Cumming *et al.*, 2016). It is also influenced by individuals' previous reading and writing knowledge and strategies (e.g. Cumming *et al.*, 2016; Hyland, 2011; Wette & Furneaux, 2018). However, Adam knows the idea of citing, and his response is relevant in content. By depending on the source texts and recycling others' linguistic resources he is able to participate in the discussion (see Suni, 2008), which might not have been possible with only his own productive Finnish skills.

Perceiving a learning journal as a platform for exercising agency

In the case of the learning journal, it was clear that each student developed a personal relationship with this literacy practice and that they perceived it as a source for their agency in different ways. A learning diary is defined as a form of academic writing that helps students to understand the ideas of a course and their own learning processes (Creme, 2008). In the programme, the aim of using a learning journal was also to introduce the genre to the students and practise writing in Finnish. The genre was first explicitly introduced to the students in class, and then their task was to write a short diary entry in Finnish once a week for three weeks. The students could write about anything they had learned during the week, and in the detailed instructions they were encouraged to be reflective. The students were also given some brief feedback on each journal entry.

Adnan perceived the learning journal as a platform to practise his Finnish skills however he chose. In addition to the language class in the programme, he had taken another class in which he had also written entries in a learning journal. In the following interview excerpt, Adnan reflects on how he learns through writing, and I seek confirmation for my interpretations.

Example 6

> Adnan: oppimispäiväkirja minä opin paljon oppimispäiväkirja (.) ja raportti, koska, ajattelen että kirjoittaminen on parempi (.) on parempi puhuminen ja ääntäminen tai lukeminen (.) en tiedä

> ehkä koska, mulla on aikaa kirjoittaa ja ajatella miksi tämä
> sanoja ja miksi *like*, loppu- lopuksi ja, joo joo mutta minä
> ajattelen kirjoittaminen on tosi parempi kuin puhuminen joo

Kirsi: eli sä opit, enemmän kirjoittamalla kun sä saat miettiä, saat
aikaa, saat miettiä saat ajatella

Adnan: joo ehkä mulla on aikaa mä ajattelen mutta puhu (.) ei ei oo ei
ole tarpeeksi aikaa, joo mutta kirjoittaa ja joo ja mun *like*,
like more confidence

Kirsi: mm joo

Adnan: kirjoittaminen joo minä ajattelen (.) käy- käytä uusia sanoja tai
fraaseja, joka oppimispäiväkirja (.) oppia op- oppimaan uusia
sanoja

Example 6 (English translation)

Adnan: learning journal I learned a lot learning journal (.) and report
because I think that writing is better (.) is better than speaking
and pronunciation or reading (.) I don't know maybe because
I have time to write and think about why these words and why
like, final- finally, yeah yeah but I think writing is much better
than speaking yeah

Kirsi: so you learn more by writing when you get to think, get time,
get to think

Adnan: yeah I have time I think but speaking (.) I don't I don't have
enough time yeah but writing and yeah and my *like*, *like more
confidence*

Kirsi: umm yeah

Adnan: writing yeah I think (.) I use new words and phrases, each
learning journal (entry) (.) learn new words

From the dialogical perspective, the process of language learning can be seen as the appropriation of linguistic resources: the language learner recycles the linguistic material of the community (Dufva *et al.*, 2014; Suni, 2008). In this example, Adnan implies that he uses a learning journal as a platform for this kind of recycling, as he 'uses new words and phrases' (*käytä uusia sanoja ja fraaseja*) in his entries in order to learn them. This recycling can also be observed in his actual journal entries, in which he uses some words and phrases that were introduced in language classes.

Adnan also says that he has 'learned a lot' (*opin paljon*) from writing a learning journal. He thinks this is because 'writing is much better than speaking' (*kirjoittaminen on tosi parempi kuin puhuminen*), which might mean either that he likes writing better than speaking or that he considers himself to be better at writing than at speaking. In either case, the reason why writing is better for Adnan is that he has more time to think when writing than when speaking, and this gives him *more confidence*. This belief about himself as a person who learns by writing and who learns when he has time to think has its roots in his previous experience; it might be related to his learning experience or to his interest in literature. Overall, Adnan's beliefs about language learning and himself as a learner seem to frame his experience of agency in writing the learning journal and his perception of this as an affordance for his language learning.

Olga also developed ownership of the same literacy practice, but she perceives it as a platform for reflecting on her life and learning.

Example 7

Olga: oppimispäiväkirja on aika mielenkiintoista koska siellä sä kirjoitat omasta no opiskelusta tai mitä sä valitset se voi olla joku ju- sun oma joka päivä elämän, päiväkirja esimerkiksi, aika mielenkiintoista miettiä miks mä teen sen miks mä herään aamulla ja menen johonkin, onks se on hyödyllistä, olenko opiskellut no ahkerasti tai, olenko samaa mieltä tai tutkijat ovat, no tekevät virheitä vaikka ne on tutkijat mutta ne on henkilöt, aika mielenkiintoisesti

Example 7 (English translation)

Olga: the learning journal is quite interesting because you write about your own studies or what you choose it can be a journal of your everyday life for example, it's quite interesting to think why am I doing this why do I wake up in the morning and go somewhere, if it is useful, have I studied hard, or do I agree with researchers, well they make mistakes even though they are researchers, they are human, quite interesting

In the narrative, Olga repeats the word 'interesting' (*mielenkiintoinen*) three times in various inflected forms and lists six different questions to reflect on in a learning journal. This gives the impression that the learning journal is interesting because it offers a space for dialogue. Following Olga's questions, one can reflect on the choices one makes and become aware of the possible consequences of one's choices. This kind of reflexive awareness is the key feature of agency (Sullivan & McCarthy, 2004: 295–297, 307). On the other hand, the last aspect that Olga mentions as interesting is being critical about what researchers claim, and it might refer to Olga's one diary entry in which she writes about the results of an article that she disagrees with. For Olga, the learning diary seems to be a platform for a dialogue, either with herself or with others. In Bakhtinian terms, this dialogue helps Olga to find her own voice. Olga's goal is eventually to work as a teacher in Finland, but she first has to complete some complementary studies in order to be qualified to teach in Finland and writing a learning diary is a typical activity in the field of education in Finland. Olga might therefore find the learning diary interesting also because it is a purposeful literacy practice for her (see Jeffery & Wilcox, 2016), and she can relate it to her future self or her ideal self (see Virtanen, 2013).

Adam, on the other hand, offers a third perspective. He does not find a learning journal useful for his learning. In the programme, he was writing entries in a learning journal for the first time in his life, and he put some effort into understanding what a learning diary is about, as he talked about it with his tutors. His actual texts were quite short in relation to the instructions they were explicitly given, and the teachers commented almost every week that he could write more about his own thoughts or opinions. In the interview with me, Adam concluded that he did not really like writing the learning journal.

Example 8

Adam: todella mä en (.) se on hyvä idea mutta mä idea tutustuu uusi asia mitä suomalaiset, opiskelijat tehdä yliopistossa mutta mä en tykkää tehdä asi- tästä asiasta
Kirsi: joo oppimispäiväkirjasta
Adam: - - nyt mä ymmärrän millainen oppimispäiväkirja on ja miten pitää tehdä sitä

Example 8 (English translation)

Adam: really I don't (.) it's a good idea to get to know a new thing how Finnish students study at university but I don't like doing thi- this thing
Kirsi: yeah learning journal
Adnan: - - now I understand what a learning journal is like and how I should write it

In the example, Adam is first very forthright about what he feels about writing a learning journal, and then he tries to explain why he does not like it. He says that it is a good idea to learn 'what Finnish students do' (*mitä suomalaiset opiskelijat tehdä*), and these word choices indicate that writing a learning journal is their literacy practice, not his. In this narrative, Adam claims that he has understood what a learning diary is like, but he seems to resist taking ownership of it, or, in other words, he seems to resist being socialized into this literacy practice (see Vitanova, 2010: 145–151). Lee and Maguire (2011) analyse this kind of resistance towards dominant ways of writing as a question of identity.

Interestingly, Adam takes a very different stance toward studying online than he does to writing a learning journal. In Example 5, above, Adam talked about his experience of writing a discussion forum post in Finnish. In the next excerpt, Adam continues his narrative as an afterword to the small story that he told earlier (in Example 5).

Example 9

Adam: se on minulle se on ensimmäinen kerta, verkossa mä tein mä opiskelin yliopistossa (.) mutta ehkä tulevaisuudessa toinen,

toinen (-) tai mitä, joo toinen kolmas neljäs sitten sitten (-) ei ole ottaa paljon aikaa

Example 9 (English translation)

Adam: it is the first time for me to study online in the university, but maybe in the future the second, second (-) or what, yeah the second, third, fourth then then (-) it won't take much time

Adam returns to the time-consuming aspect of writing his response when talking about the future, as he says that maybe after two, three or four times it will no longer take so much time to participate in this kind of activity in Finnish. However, Adam positions himself as possibly studying online again often in the future. An agentive individual looks both at earlier events and towards potential events in the future (Dufva & Aro, 2015: 41). Adam's ideal selves might be shaping the present experience and creating the motivation to invest enough time to complete the online learning assignment (see Virtanen, 2013).

If we compare Adam's two experiences, we see that in both cases he used some external resources (source texts or his tutors) and put some effort into completing the tasks. However, he developed a different kind of relationship with each academic literacy practice. There may be various reasons for that. For example, reflective texts like a learning journal may not be very usual in his field, which is economics, or alternatively, the online forum discussion task was part of an interactive discipline course rather than a language course, which might have made it more meaningful to him; perhaps he just liked one literacy practice better than the other. Whatever the reason, Adam's personal preferences, prior experience or future selves shaped the way he showed agency.

Conclusion

The aim of this study was to explore immigrant students' agency in academic literacies in L2 Finnish by analysing their narratives. The particular focus was on the role of students' beliefs and lived experiences in narratives displaying agency. This was particularly relevant in the current study because the research participants had already completed university-level studies, and they had high goals for their future in Finland.

The results indicate that learners' beliefs about learning, reading and writing in a second language, as well as about themselves as learners, can have a major impact on how they decide to take action (see Mercer, 2012 for similar results). When completing tasks online, students described using their multilingual resources as well as their skills in using external resources, and this seemed to be a crucial part of their strong sense of agency. Finally, the students took different stances on the same literacy practice and perceived it as a source for their agency in a variety of ways, which indicates that each student developed a personal relationship to the new practice with which they were engaged.

Overall, students' prior experiences and life histories, or 'historical bodies' in nexus analytical terms (see Scollon & Scollon, 2004: 46–49), were related to the ways they perceived the new literacy practices. This was evident in the ways the students explicitly referred to their own preferences, prior knowledge or future, but also in the different voices that were present in their narratives. Students' agency was also shown to be embodied and closely connected with time and their material surroundings, such as writing and underlining words by hand, taking time for thinking, and using technology as a mediational means (see Wertsch, 1991) in searching for information and writing.

The results have implications for pedagogy and education policy. Immigrant students' background knowledge might differ a lot from 'traditional' students' knowledge reservoirs – for example, one of the students did not know what the concept 'liberal' meant. However, immigrant students also have their own unique life histories and learning trajectories (see Morrice, 2013). The need that this implies for individual support in academic reading and writing has long been recognized in research. In addition to having their individual capacities and needs, students also perceive new literacy practices in their own individual ways. Sometimes this means that learners do not see the new literacy practice as relevant for their learning or for their life, or they see it as clashing with their identities (see Lee & Maguire, 2011), as was the case with one of the students struggling with learning journals. In the classroom, this kind of agency may come into conflict with the teacher's ideas. It is thus essential to explain the purpose of the exercises carefully and use reflective practice to acknowledge individual perceptions.

The results of this study suggest that the development of immigrant students' agency in academic literacy practices is indeed a complex process, which is shaped by many individual factors (see also Mercer, 2012). Morrice (2013) uses the concept of capital to contextualize the individual resources and capacities that shape refugee students' experiences in higher education, but she also emphasizes that these experiences are linked to the wider societal framework. In many higher education institutions, entrance examinations are designed for first language speakers, or the requirements in terms of language proficiency are very high (e.g. Airas *et al.*, 2019). More sensitivity is therefore needed towards highly skilled immigrants' earlier experiences as well as their capacities and potential.

In this study, the academic literacies perspective helped us to understand literacy practices and students as part of social reality, and to recognize that academic writing always takes place inside power hierarchies. For immigrant students, gaining agency with academic literacies is not only about appropriating new ways of meaning making, but also about gaining access to the academic community. This study has given insights into the everyday reality of students who struggle to find their place, and their voice. The theoretical novelty of this chapter lies in its application of dialogical conceptualizations to the analysis of developing agency in L2 academic literacies. A dialogical approach offered a framework to explore students' strengthening voice – in this case their developing agency both as situated in time and place and as part of their continuum of life. Despite its limitations, such as not analysing the students' actual performance or their observable action, this study reveals how complex and multi-layered a phenomenon immigrant students' agency is.

References

Ahearn, L.M. (2001) Language and agency. *Annual Review of Anthropology* 30, 109–137.
Airas, M., Delahunty, D., Laitinen, M., Shemsedini, G., Stenberg, H., Saarilammi, M., Sarparanta, T., Vuori, H. and Väätäinen, H. (2019) *Taustalla on väliä. Ulkomaalaistaustaiset opiskelijat korkeakoulupolulla* [Background matters. Students with an immigrant background in higher education]. Evaluation report. Julkaisut [Proceedings]22:2019. Helsinki: Kansallinen koulutuksen arviointikeskus [Finnish Education Evaluation Centre]. https://karvi.fi/app/uploads/2019/11/KARVI_2219.pdf.
Aro, M. (2009) Speakers and doers: Polyphony and agency in children's beliefs about language learning. Jyväskylä Studies in Humanities 116. PhD thesis, University of Jyväskylä, Finland.
Bakhtin, M.M. (1981) *The Dialogic Imagination. Four Essays by M.M. Bakhtin*. Edited by Michael Holquist and translated by Caryl Emerson and Michael Holquist. Austin, TX: University of Texas Press.
Bakhtin, M.M. (1986) *Speech Genres and Other Late Essays*. Edited by Caryl Emerson and Michael Holquist and translated by Vern W. McGee. Austin, TX: University of Texas Press.
Barkhuizen, G. (2013) Introduction: Narrative research in applied linguistics. In G. Barkhuizen (ed.) *Narrative Research in Applied Linguistics* (pp. 1–16). Cambridge: Cambridge University Press.
Barton, D. and Hamilton, M. (1998) *Local Literacies: Reading and Writing in One Community*. London: Routledge.
Bhowmik, S.K. (2016) Agency, identity and ideology in L2 writing: Insights from the EAP classroom. *Writing & Pedagogy* 8 (2), 275–308.
Blommaert, J. and Huang, A. (2009) Historical bodies and historical space. *Journal of Applied Linguistics* 6 (3), 11–26.
Busch, B. (2017) Expanding the notion of the linguistic repertoire: On the concept of spracherleben – the lived experience of language. *Applied Linguistics* 38 (3), 340–358.
Cope, B. and Kalantzis, M. (2009) 'Multiliteracies': New literacies, new learning. *Pedagogies: An International Journal* 4 (3), 164–195.
Council of Europe (2001) *Common European Framework of Reference for Languages: Learning, Teaching, Assessment*. Cambridge: Cambridge University Press.
Creme, P. (2008) A space for academic play: Student learning journals as transitional writing. *Arts and Humanities in Higher Education* 7 (1), 49–64.
Cumming, A., Lai, C. and Cho, H. (2016) Students' writing from sources for academic purposes: A synthesis of recent research. *Journal of English for Academic Purposes* 23, 47–58.

Dufva H. (2003) Beliefs in dialogue: A Bakhtinian view. In P. Kalaja and A.M.F. Barcelos (eds) *Beliefs About SLA: New Research Approaches* (pp. 131–152). New York: Springer.

Dufva H. (2004) Language, thinking and embodiment: Bakhtin, Whorf and Merleau-Ponty. In F. Bostad, C. Brandist, L.S. Evensen and H.C. Faber (eds) *Bakhtinian Perspectives on Language and Culture: Meaning in Language, Art and New Media* (pp. 133–146). Basingstoke: Palgrave Macmillan.

Dufva, H. and Aro, M. (2015) Dialogical view on language learners' agency: Connecting intrapersonal with interpersonal. In P. Deters, X. Gao, E.R. Miller and G. Vitanova (eds) *Theorizing and Analyzing Agency and Second Language Learning: Interdisciplinary Approaches* (pp. 37–53). Bristol: Multilingual Matters.

Dufva, H., Aro, M. and Suni, M. (2014) Language learning as appropriation: How linguistic resources are recycled and regenerated. *AFinLA-e: Soveltavan kielitieteen tutkimuksia* 6, 20–31.

Dufva, H., Suni, M., Aro, M. and Salo, O-P. (2011) Languages as objects of learning: Language learning as a case of multilingualism. *Apples – Journal of Applied Language Studies* 5 (1), 109–124.

García, O. and Kleifgen, J.A. (2019) Translanguaging and literacies. *Reading Research Quarterly* 55 (4), 553–571.

Georgakopoulou, A. (2015) Small stories research: Methods – analysis – outreach. In A. De Fina and A. Georgakopoulou (eds) *The Handbook of Narrative Analysis* (pp. 255–271). Malden, MA: Wiley.

Hartley, J. (2007) Reading, writing, speaking and listening: Perspectives in applied linguistics. *Applied Linguistics* 28 (2), 316–320.

Hyland, K. (2011) Learning to write: Issues in theory, research, and pedagogy. In R. Manchón (ed.) *Learning-to-Write and Writing-to-Learn in an Additional Language* (pp. 17–35). Amsterdam: John Benjamins.

Ivaska, I. (2015) Edistyneen oppijansuomen konstruktiopiirteitä korpusvetoisesti: Avainrakenneanalyysi [Corpus-driven approach towards constructional features of advanced learner Finnish: Key structure analysis]. Turun yliopiston julkaisuja C–409. PhD thesis, University of Turku, Finland.

Jeffery, J.V. and Wilcox, K.C. (2016) L1 and L2 adolescents' perspectives on writing within and across academic disciplines: Examining the role of agency in writing development. *Writing & Pedagogy* 8 (2), 245–274.

Kim, M. and Belcher, D.D. (2018) Building genre knowledge in second language writers during study abroad in higher education. *Journal of English for Academic Purposes* 35, 56–69.

Lea, M. and Street, B. (1998) Student writing in higher education: An academic literacies approach. *Studies in Higher Education* 23 (2), 157–172.

Lee, H. and Maguire, M.H. (2011) International students and identity: Resisting dominant ways of writing and knowing in academe. In D. Starke-Meyerring, A. Paré, N. Artemeva, M. Horne and L. Yousoubova (eds) *Writing in Knowledge Societies* (pp. 351–370). Fort Collins, CO: WAC Clearinghouse and Parlor Press.

Lillis, T. and Scott, M. (2007) Defining academic literacies research: Issues of epistemology, ideology and strategy. *Journal of Applied Linguistics* 4 (1), 5–32.

Martin, M. (1995) The map and the rope: Finnish nominal inflection as a learning target. Studia Philologica Jyväskyläensia 38. PhD thesis, University of Jyväskylä, Finland.

McCulloch, S. (2013) Investigating the reading-to-write processes and source use of L2 postgraduate students in real-life academic tasks: An exploratory study. *Journal of English for Academic Purposes* 12 (2), 136–147.

Mercer, S. (2012) The complexity of learner agency. *Apples – Journal of Applied Language Studies* 6 (2), 4–59.

Merleau-Ponty M. (2009) *Phénoménologie de la Perception* [Phenomenology of Perception]. Paris: Gallimard.

Morrice, L. (2013) Refugees in higher education: Boundaries of belonging and recognition, stigma and exclusion. *International Journal of Lifelong Education* 32 (5), 652–668.

Mustonen, S. (2015) Käytössä kehittyvä kieli: Paikat ja tilat suomi toisena kielenä – oppijoiden teksteissä [How language develops through use]. Jyväskylä Studies in Humanities 255. PhD thesis, University of Jyväskylä, Finland.

Nesi, H. and Gardner S. (2012) *Genres Across the Disciplines: Student Writing in Higher Education.* Cambridge: Cambridge University Press.

Nikulin, M. (2019) Akateemisen maahanmuuttajan suomen kielen taidon tarve työssä ja arjessa [The need of Finnish language proficiency in the everyday and working life of non-native academic people in Finland]. *Lähivõrdlusi. Lähivertailuja* 29, 171–203.

Paxton, M. and Frith, V. (2015) Transformative and normative? Implications for academic literacies research in quantitative disciplines. In T. Lillis, K. Harrington, M.R. Lea and S. Mitchell (eds) *Working with Academic Literacies: Research, Theory, Design* (pp. 155–162). Fort Collins, CO: WAC Clearinghouse and Parlor Press.

Riessman, C.K (2008) *Narrative Methods for the Human Sciences.* Los Angeles, CA: Sage.

Scollon, R. and Scollon, S.B.K. (2004) *Nexus Analysis: Discourse and the Emerging Internet.* London: Routledge.

Sullivan, P. and McCarthy, J. (2004) Toward a dialogical perspective on agency. *Journal for the Theory of Social Behaviour* 34 (3), 291–309.

Suni, M. (2008) Toista kieltä vuorovaikutuksessa. Kielellisten resurssien jakaminen toisen kielen omaksumisen alkuvaiheessa [Second language in interaction: Sharing linguistic resources in the early stage of second language acquisition]. Jyväskylä Studies in Humanities 94. PhD thesis, University of Jyväskylä, Finland.

Virtanen, A. (2013) Minä sairaanhoitajana: Tulevaisuuden minuudet motivaatiota muokkaamassa [I as a nurse: Future selves making the motivation]. *Lähivertailuja. Lähivõrdlusi* 23, 403–427.

Vitanova, G. (2005) Authoring the self in a non-native language: A dialogic approach to agency and subjectivity. In J.K. Hall, G. Vitanova and L. Marchenkova (eds) *Dialogue with Bakhtin on Second and Foreign Language Learning: New Perspectives.* Mahwah, NJ: Lawrence Erlbaum.

Vitanova, G. (2010) *Authoring the Dialogic Self: Gender, Agency and Language Practices.* Amsterdam: John Benjamins.

Wertsch, J.V. (1991) *Voices of the Mind. A Sociocultural Approach to Mediated Action.* Cambridge, MA: Harvard University Press.

Wette, R. and Furneaux, C. (2018) The academic discourse socialisation challenges and coping strategies of international graduate students entering English-medium universities. *System* 78, 186–200.

7 Constructing Persuasion: A Cross-cultural Comparison of Chinese and English Student Writings

Jihua Dong
Shandong University, China

Introduction

It is generally accepted that persuasion is an important component of academic writing (Hyland, 1998; Parkinson, 2011). According to Perloff (2003), persuasion is concerned with 'a symbolic process in which communicators try to convince other people to change their attitudes or behaviour regarding an issue through the transmission of a message, in an atmosphere of free choice'. The rhetorical strategies of persuasion are seen to entail 'both rational exposition and the manipulation of rhetorical and interactive features' (Hyland, 1998: 439). Through the use of linguistic devices, writers are able to unfold the possible interpretation, deliver their credibility, communicate their main points efficiently, and navigate readers to accept their claims or spur them to take due action. Such endeavours can function to achieve persuasive 'appeals', a term used by Swales (1990: 144), which in this study is used to refer to the persuasive strategies that can achieve convincingness in the course of persuasion construction.

Such uses also enable authors to project a tone of confidence in their argument and promote the relevance of their contribution to the evolving argument. Meanwhile, L2 students have been reported to have encountered various problems in their argumentative writing, particularly when expressing their persuasive involvement and constructing their nuanced persuasive evaluation and credible writer image (Grant & Ginther, 2000).

The way that writers encode their persuasion has aroused increasing interest from researchers, and substantial attention has been focused on examining how academic persuasion has been constructed in the writings of diverse genres, such as published research articles (Dong & Buckingham, 2018; Hyland & Jiang, 2018; Khedri *et al.*, 2013), postgraduate dissertations (and undergraduate academic essays – see Li & Wharton, 2012), as well as students' argumentative writing (Jiang, 2015; Milagros del Saz Rubio, 2011; Liu & Thompson, 2009).

Meanwhile, a considerable number of studies have been conducted from a cross-cultural perspective to examine various linguistic devices related to persuasion construction. For example, Ädel (2006) examined the evaluative expressions in English argumentative writings of L1 and L2 students and found that L2 students used more personal and interpersonal markers than native students. Similarly, Ädel and Erman (2012) investigated the evaluative extraposed pattern (i.e. *it + link-verb+ adj. + to/that*) in non-native and native student writings in the field of linguistics, and found that native and non-native students vary greatly in terms of the patterns that deliver persuasive expressions. In the same vein, Jiang (2015) compared the nominal stance construction (e.g. *the fact that*) in English and Chinese students' writing, and found that Chinese students use fewer nominal stance constructions but use more attitudinal adjectives and more first person possessives to modify nominal nouns.

While these studies have enriched our understanding of the different practices of native and non-native students in their persuasion construction, most of them have only examined the construction of persuasion in terms of linguistic devices, such as stance and engagement (Hyland, 2005), attitude devices (Ho & Li, 2018), and metadiscourse devices (Çandarli *et al.*, 2015; Crismore *et al.*, 1993; Mu *et al.*, 2015). The linguistics devices that authors utilise to construct their persuasion are still underexplored. Therefore, this study attempts to tease out the common linguistic devices denoting persuasion and to map out the cross-cultural variation in persuasion construction in the argumentative writings of native English students and non-native Chinese students.

The notion of genre denotes 'a class of communicative events, the members of which share some set of communicative purposes' (Swales, 1990: 58), and it is generally regarded as 'highly structured and conventionalised with constraints on allowable contributions in terms of their intent, positioning, form and functional value' (Bhatia, 1993: 13). Genre plays a vital role in our use and choice of language as it activates 'networks of semantic options' (Halliday, 1978: 123), determines the 'range of meaning potential' (Halliday, 1978: 123) and the 'linguistic forms' (Halliday, 1978). Therefore, the exploration of the genre-specific linguistic features could reveal the underlying norms and conventions prioritised in a particular genre and could provide insight into the ways that different communities construct knowledge and shape their value systems within their situational rhetorical contexts.

The argumentative essay is one particular genre among many that has been examined in this way. Characterised by being 'argumentative or expository in character' (Altenberg & Tapper, 1998: 83), this genre is mainly used to 'persuade the reader of the text correctness of a central statement' (Hyland, 1990: 68). An alignment with the generic convention of this genre normally requires writers to present a 'demonstration of facts, propositions and standpoints to their advantages in building their argument and gaining claim plausibility' (Jiang, 2015: 95).

The exploration of persuasive strategies can help to reveal the conventionalised norms in argument construction, as well as the 'repertoire of situationally appropriate responses to recurrent situations' (Berkenkotter & Huckin, 1995: ix). Also, augmentative writing is 'one of the most common forms of curriculum genre that undergraduate students write' (Mei, 2006: 330). Thus, it is useful to explore the discursive practices of persuasion construction figuring in this genre, and to identify the persuasion strategies that are characteristic of argumentative writings. This study aims to tease out the linguistic features related to persuasive strategies in argumentative essays. Specifically, this study will address the following two research questions:

(1) What are the general uses of persuasion devices in the writings of native English-speaking students and non-native English-speaking Chinese students?
(2) What are the differences in the persuasive strategies employed by native English-speaking students and non-native English-speaking Chinese students?

The Theoretical Framework of Persuasion

Aristotle's *Rhetoric* has a great impact on the establishment and development of the art of rhetoric. Classical rhetoric is mainly concerned with the perception of how language works when written or spoken, and the ability to see the available means of persuasion. In contrast, contemporary rhetoric theory views persuasion more broadly as human symbol use and it embraces both verbal, visual and other non-verbal expressions. Since rhetoric practice is seen as disciplinary in nature, great emphasis has been given to examining rhetorical uses within specific, localised discourse communities.

Aristotle's framework encompasses three major aspects in constructing persuasion, namely logos, ethos and pathos, which appeal to readers' rationality, credibility, and emotions respectively, as specified in the following excerpt:

Of the modes of persuasion furnished by the spoken word there are three kinds. The first kind depends on the personal character of the speaker [ethos]; the second on putting the audience into a certain frame of mind [pathos]; the third on the proof, or apparent proof, provided by the words of the speech itself [logos]. Persuasion is achieved by the speaker's personal character when the speech is so spoken as to make us think him credible. (Aristotle, 1954: 8)

More specifically, logos concerns a rhetorical appeal to the audience's rationality, thus constituting an essential element in building up the effectiveness of an argument. The use of logos allows writers to draw clear, logical connections between ideas, which contributes to persuading the audience to agree with the point of view conveyed in the writing. Ethos is mainly concerned with a rhetorical appeal that demonstrates a speaker's knowledge, credibility, and solid moral character. This can be achieved by various means, such as showing the author's expertise in the topic being examined, citing credible sources, using acceptable terminology, and introducing precise and sound data. Such strategies can help to demonstrate academic or authorial credentials, can convey the writer's credibility and authority, and establish trust with the expected readers. Pathos is mainly concerned with an appeal to the audience's emotions. Its use can contribute to creating resonance with the audience and thus elicit feelings that already reside in them. The use of this rhetorical device can arouse the audience's feelings and influence their acceptance of the writer/speaker/ the view conveyed in the text/speech.

The three modes of persuasion have been suggested as one of the most influential theories in persuasion analysis, and have been drawn upon as theoretical underpinning for studies on relevant linguistic constructs, such as the appraisal framework (Martin & White, 2005), and the promotional (meta) discourse in research articles (Afros & Schryer, 2009). For instance, Afros and Schryer (2009) investigated the promotional strategies used in research articles in language and literary studies. Their analysis shows that these disciplinary writers used devices, such as evaluative lexis, coordination, comment clauses, personal pronouns, lexical cohesion, and discourse chunks sequencing to express their promotional stance.

This study is based on the framework of persuasion and analyses the linguistic devices in constructing persuasion in the argumentative writings of native English-speaking and non-native English-speaking Chinese students. Examples are taken from the study to illustrate the three modes of persuasion. As previously suggested, the choice of linguistic device can function to 'change or affect the opinions or behaviors of an audience in terms of positively assessing the research contribution' (Martín & Pérez, 2014: 1). Table 7.1 presents the functions and some typical linguistic devices of the three persuasive strategies. Specifically, logos concerns the linguistic devices used to show

Table 7.1 The categorisation of persuasion expression

Category	Functions	Examples
Logos	Linguistic devices used to construe the logical relationship between clauses or show the presence of their reason-oriented projection	*in addition; even if; result in; on the contrary; in contrast*
Ethos	Concerns the linguistic devices indicating writer's credibility	*according to; described by; it has been demonstrated; it has been found; it has been shown*
Pathos	Linguistic devices that denote writer's endeavours to appeal to readers' emotional response.	*fortunately; it is interesting; important role; happy; surprising; crucial; amazing*

reason-oriented projection. The use of these logos-laden expressions enables readers to see the argument delivered in the writing as credible and convincing.

Examples (1) and (2) illustrate two cases of using the marker *as a result* and the inductive reasoning marker *to sum up* to show the logical connection between two sentences or clauses.

Example (1)

Traditionally the emperor was first among equals within the senate, and *as a result* accepting him as a god would have implied that the emperor was clearly superior to every other senator. [British Academic Written English Corpus (BAWE)]

Example (2)

To sum up, we share the one earth with animals and have a responsibility to maintain the balance of the earth's ecological system. [Written English Corpus of Chinese Learners (WECCL)]

Ethos mainly concerns linguistic devices appealing to the trustworthiness and credibility of the author. Such appeal can be realised by a wide range of linguistic devices, both explicit and implicit, in the course of developing argumentative writings. According to Afros and Schryer (2009) and Hyland (2001), personal credibility is mainly conveyed by self-citations, the writer's reputation, as well as by an alignment of the proposed analysis with the views accepted in the field. This type of rhetorical strategy, however, constitutes the 'hidden persuader', as suggested by Aristotle, as it is not as overt as the other two types (logos or pathos). A preliminary analysis shows that most ethos-related expressions concern the sources-given expressions in the corpora under scrutiny. So this study focused just on the linguistic devices denoting the sources, such as *reported by, or according to*, as shown in Example (3).

Example (3)

Similar findings have been *reported by* Brown et al (1975, as in Leonard, 2000: 120) who discovered that preschool children with SLI had more difficulty than age matched controls using objects in a pretend manner. [BAWE]

Pathos relates to the linguistic devices manifesting in writers' endeavours to elicit emotional responses in their readers. Common linguistic devices of this type include expressions such as *interestingly, it is surprising to,* and *fortunate,* etc. Such uses allow writers to create a connection with their expected audience, and to evoke an emotional resonance (Cao & Hu, 2014; Gillaerts & Van de Velde, 2010; Mur Dueñas, 2007). For example, in Example (4) the writer appeals to the emotion of *surprise* when expressing the statement *hear that these aspects of her care had not been discusse*d. According to Dong and Jiang (2019), the use of emotion-oriented expressions enhances the interaction with readers and provokes readers to participate in the dialogue initiated in the discourse construction. By explicitly conveying his/her emotion towards this statement, the writer is able to 'generate a sense of personal proximity' (Fog, 2004: 30) to the evaluated entities or action, thus raising the readers' attention, or even provoking an emotional reaction from the envisaged readers. Examples (4) and (5) show two cases where writers resort to the use of emotional devices as a means of appealing to a kind of special emotion in the two cases examined.

Example (4)

It was quite *surprising* to hear that these aspects of her care had not been discussed, especially given the uncertainty that she suffered when deciding whether to continue with her treatment. [BAWE]

Example (5)

Because the feeling of finger touch the paper is so *wonderful.* And I believe that a delicate book hold in both hands to appreciate is a kind of *enjoyment.* [WECCL]

Methods

Corpora

This study is based on argumentative essays selected from the following two corpora: WECCL (Written English Corpus of Chinese Learners) and BAWE (British Academic Written English Corpus). The texts in both corpora were written by undergraduates in an educational setting and were written to fulfil the course requirements. Both corpora have been generally accepted to represent the writing of Chinese and British students and have been used previously in addressing the writings of Chinese and British students (Gardner & Nesi, 2013; Jiang, 2015).

Given that the BAWE corpus consists of students' writing as homework or course papers, and in untimed situations, this study selected the untimed argumentative essays in WECCL to ensure that the corpora selected in the study were comparable. The selected native English student corpus consists of 75 argumentative essays written by British university students, with a total size of 82,329 words. The selected non-native Chinese student corpus is comprised of 181 untimed essays written by Chinese undergraduates majoring in English, containing 82,344 words in total.

Judging from the size of the corpora, we can see that the texts vary greatly in terms of the length of each text. As Halliday (1994) suggested, the text types falling under the same genre are seen to accomplish similar communicative purposes and thus can be characterised by some similar patterns. Underpinned by this premise, this study analysed the text types of argumentative essays by following the general practice in corpus linguistics and calculating the normalised frequency.

Procedures

The coding of the persuasion makers was carried out in the following steps. Firstly, a coding was carried out by following the classification scheme presented in Section 2, using the qualitative coding software MAXQDA (VERBI Software, 2012), to decide whether a linguistic marker is related to persuasive meaning. To ensure the reliability of the semantic coding, three months later the author randomly selected 30% of the sampled texts and conducted the coding using the same approach. The two codings were analysed using Cohen's kappa to determine the intra-rater reliability, and the result was found to be 0.95 (significance <0.01). This indicates a relatively high agreement between the two codings. In the second step, the author extracted the persuasive devices and carried out coding using the automatic search function of MAXQDA by referring to the persuasive linguistic devices obtained in the previous step. In addition, to include a more comprehensive picture of the coded samples, this study considered the various inflectional forms of the persuasion-oriented linguistic devices. For example, *results in, resulted in, resulting in,* were all coded as persuasion devices, under the category of logos.

In the specific analysis, this study compared the normalised frequency against the overall tokens in each corpus (the occurrence per million words) of the three types of persuasive strategy in the two corpora. Also, chi-square statistics was used to compare the differences in the two corpora. To measure the degree of the statistical difference, this study used effect size, a measurement of the scale of significance between variables. The scale of the significance was interpreted by following Cohen's (1988) magnitude guidelines. That is, 0.1 or below is regarded as a small effect, >0.1 and < 0.5 is a medium effect, while ≥0.5 is a large effect.

Results and Discussion

The first part of this section presents the general use of the persuasion devices shared by native and non-native students' argumentative essays. The second part of the section reports the results of comparing the persuasive strategies used in the WECCL and BAWE corpora.

Overall comparison of persuasion devices in the two corpora

Figure 7.1 illustrates the occurrence of the three types of persuasion device in the two corpora. The three pairs of columns in Figure 7.1 represent the normalised frequencies of the ethos, logos and pathos strategies. The left-hand column represents the normalised frequency in the Chinese students' corpus, while the right-hand column stands for the normalised frequency in the British students' argumentative writings. As can be seen, the overall frequency of logos is found to be overwhelmingly high in the student writings of both corpora. The high frequency of this type of persuasive strategy indicates that students in the two corpora tend to make more use of reason-oriented linguistic devices to construe

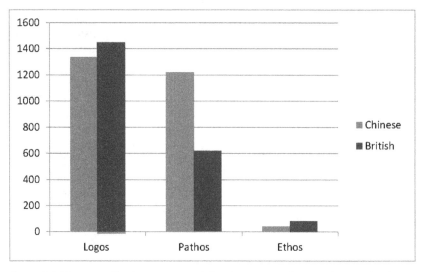

Figure 7.1 The normalised occurrence of the three types of persuasion marker in the two corpora

their logic-oriented presence. This predominant use of logos confirms Bazerman's (2010) findings that academic writing placed great emphasis on logos expressions. Examples (6) and (7) show two cases where Chinese and British students use a causal logic connective (*as a result*) and an additional logic connective (*in addition*) to construct their reason-oriented presence. By doing so, writers are able to achieve 'the social justification of belief' (Rorty, 1979: 170) in the course of developing their arguments and convincing the readers of the credibility of a statement.

Example (6)

Evidence suggests that crimes committed by boys are of a more serious nature, yet it is clear that what is judged to be acceptable behaviour for boys is not necessarily the case for girls. *As a result* what is perceived to be delinquent behaviour will vary considerably between boys and girls. [BAWE]

Example (7)

E-dictionary is one of the best assistants. *In addition*, people can enjoy other convenience it has such as calculation. [WECCL]

Pathos markers are seen to occur the second most frequently among the three strategies in the two corpora. As previously suggested, the suitable use of these attitude devices is able to not only embed writers' attitudes towards the statements, but to also show 'how they simultaneously engage their readers to share and endorse their value positions' (Cheng & Unsworth, 2016: 45). The use of emotion-oriented linguistic devices thus can help to promote the engagement of the audience in processing the text information. In Examples (8) and (9), we see two instances where the writer uses emotional appeals to establish solidarity with the expected readers by using *essential* and *extraordinarily important* and *useful* in British and Chinese argumentative writings respectively.

Example (8)

His personality and ideas, whether understood or not, initiated the Reformation and were *essential* in its early development. [BAWE]

Example (9)

Therefore, the books and the written word are *extraordinarily important* and *useful* for us. [WECCL]

Compared to the other two types of persuasive device, ethos-devices are used least frequently, particularly in Chinese students' argumentative writings. Such low preference for this kind of linguistic device is in sharp contrast with their high occurrence identified in Afros and Schryer (2009). This difference may be due to the differing rhetorical function and communicative purposes entailed in the students' argumentative writings and research articles examined in these two studies. In Examples (10) and (11), we see two cases where the writers appeal to the linguistic devices *described by* and *it has been found that* to point out the source as a way to win support for the statements made in the two sentences.

Example (10)

The Commission is certainly being endowed with stronger enforcement powers as can be clearly seen from its powers to obtain oral statements under Article 19. This has *been described by* Whish as being a 'novel provision', implying that it is a new, interesting and different kind of provision. [BAWE]

Example (11)

It has been found that patients aware of the nature of their illness usually are able to offer several distinct benefits to the physician in his provision of care. [WECCL]

To summarise, the two corpora are seen to share noticeable similar patterns in their use of persuasive strategies. That is, the linguistic devices conveying logos-oriented persuasion are predominately used in the two corpora; pathos is the second most frequent, followed by ethos expressions. This indicates that the argumentative writings in the two corpora may be underpinned by similar ideologies in constructing persuasion and in establishing a similar convincingness in the course of developing arguments. By the appropriate use of persuasive devices, writers are able to strengthen their argument to a greater extent (Lancaster, 2016; Lee & Deakin, 2016).

Cross-corpora comparison in the persuasion devices used in the two corpora

Table 7.2 shows a statistical comparison of the persuasive strategies used in English and Chinese students' argumentative writings. The comparison of the overall occurrence of persuasive strategies shows that Chinese students tend to draw upon significantly more persuasive linguistic devices in the course of argumentative text construction, with a normalised frequency of 2597.64 and 2149.91 in Chinese and English students' writing corpus respectively (significance = 0.00), but with a small effect size ($w = 0.09$).

To be more specific, the occurrence of logos expressions is found to be significantly higher in British students' argumentative writing

Table 7.2 The statistical comparison of persuasion devices in English and Chinese student corpora (per 100,000 words)

Strategies	Chinese		British		Chi-square	Sig.	Effect size w
	raw frequency	Normalised frequency	raw frequency	Normalised frequency			
Logos	1100	1335.86	1193	1449.06	3.84	0.05	0.04
Pathos	1005	1220.49	509	618.25	163.91	0.00	0.30
Ethos	34	41.29	68	82.60	11.35	0.00	0.30
Total	2139	2597.64	1770	2149.91	35.61	0.00	0.09

(significance = 0.05), with a small effect size (w = 0.04). The less frequent use of logic-oriented expressions indicates that Chinese students tend to draw on less reason-oriented resources when construing persuasion in comparison to native speakers. For example, we can see two instances of using the linguistic devices, *due to* and *in contrast* respectively, to construct and convey a rational argument in Examples (12) and (13).

Example (12)

The courts are often faced with understandably controversial cases in which an individual has been denied treatment *due to* a shortage of resources. [BAWE]

Example (13)

In contrast, some people never bow to age and memory's limitation; they keep studying at every period of their life. [WECCL]

The cross-corpora analysis shows that Chinese students utilised significantly more pathos devices, with a normalised frequency of 1220.49 and 618.25 respectively in the Chinese and British students' corpora, with a medium effect size (w = 0.30). This shows that Chinese students are more likely to put greater weight on emotion-oriented appeal in their persuasion construction in comparison to their British counterparts. This finding is in line with what has been identified in Liu and Thompson (2009) and Jiang (2015) regarding the high use of attitudinal expressions in Chinese students' writing. This variation indicates the diverging use of persuasive rhetoric practices in Western and traditional Chinese writing (Wu & Rubin, 2000). That is, Chinese students are more likely to make emotional appeals in comparison with their British counterparts. In terms of persuasive effectiveness, previous studies have suggested that attitude expressions can 'deviate from readers' expectation for argumentative essays' (Jiang, 2015: 99); The high use of these expressions thus can show less unappropriated practices in constructing persuasion.

Example (14) and (15) illustrate two cases where Chinese and British students employ emotional appeal (i.e. *interesting* and *wonderful*) to grab readers' attention in processing the text information.

Example (14)

Furthermore, it is *interesting* to note that this blog phenomenon is also propagating considerably in Latin America, particularly in Panama. [BAWE]

Example (15)

By building sports stadiums and theatres, we can rich our free life and have time to enjoy the *wonderful* world. [WECCL]

Aside from the significant differences identified in the use of pathos strategies, the analysis also shows that the native English-speaking students' writing consisted of a notable number of introductory *it* patterns (*it +be+ adjective + to*) in using the pathos strategies. This pattern has been suggested to be advantageous in initiating a 'dialogical exchange between the different instances of interaction' (Dressen, 2003: 274), thereby enabling writers to 'build an inclusive relationship with addressees in the conversations and forge a social collegiality towards what is being talked of' (Dong & Jiang, 2019: 43). The more frequent use of this pattern by British students indicates that they tend to be more skilful in packaging their assertion in a covert way through this pattern, as shown in Examples (16) and (17).

Example (16)

Clearly for this reason *it is highly desirable to* limit insider dealing as much as possible and protect market-makers and thereby investors from the low liquidity of assets. [BAWE]

Example (17)

Stringing up all the above issues discussed, *it is evident that* a food blogging discourse may illuminate as much as it may conceal important thematic issues in this field of study. [BAWE]

The occurrence of ethos strategies is significantly higher in the native British students' argumentative writing (significance = 0.00). The effect size analysis shows a medium scale of difference in using the ethos strategy (w = 0.30). According to Hyland (2001), reporting verbs serve as useful strategies in communicating the suitable voices to the readers, as well as in persuading them of the credibility of the argument developed in the texts. The lower occurrence of such expressions in Chinese students' writing suggests that Chinese students displayed an insufficiency in employing ethos-oriented expressions to construct source-supported and source-informed persuasiveness. The most common linguistic manifestations of the ethos-oriented persuasive expressions include *according to, reported by, as suggested by, it has been found*. By employing these examples, writers are able to support their statements by drawing upon the previous literature or an extra source.

It is also interesting to note that the cross-corpora analysis also reveals a notable variation in the source of the citation. Specifically, Chinese students tend to resort to the resource of media, as in Example (18), to win support for the statements or assertions to be made in their follow-up writings. In contrast, their British counterparts exhibited a strong preference for citing literature to support their views. This thus reveals a great variation in the sources that students often resort to when citing a source to support their arguments. Example (19) illustrates a case of using such expressions to win support for an upcoming statement concerning *children of this age*. By making explicit the source, writers are able to create logical proof for the statement to be made in the following statement.

Example (18)

A survey that *reported by the China National Environmental Association* shows that thousands tons of garages are produced by paper cards every year. [WECCL]

Example (19)

According to Piaget's theory, children of this age are not able to classify things into categories, but this was not the case in this experiment. [BAWE]

Conclusion

This study has adopted an approach of contrastive interlanguage analysis and investigated how some English and Chinese students constructed their persuasion in their argumentative writing. The analysis revealed certain common patterns in the rhetoric use of persuasive strategies by native and non-native students. The students tended to utilise logos and pathos devices predominantly; they used ethos devices to a lesser extent. However, the cross-corpora analysis indicated that the Chinese students tended to employ a pathos strategy more often to appeal to readers' emotional response, while the English students were more likely to resort to a logos strategy when constructing their persuasion. According to Hyland (2005), language practices are embedded in social cultures and can 'contribute to and connect with a communal ideology or value system' (2005: 175). Thus, the differing practices of persuasive strategies might reflect the latent conventionalised ideologies and sociocultural values underpinning the persuasion construction and possibly influence how writers establish their persuasion and convey their assertions. The results can provide insight into cross-cultural preferences for persuasion strategies in students' writing. The Chinese students displayed a stronger preference for pathos linguistic devices, while the English students displayed a more salient presence of reason-oriented linguistic devices and a more frequent use of ethos-directed expressions in developing their arguments.

Persuasion, however, is a complex concept, involving a wide range of linguistic items. Furthermore, the way writers construct persuasion may be embedded in some other linguistic devices and thus the findings from the present study may simply reveal the tip of the iceberg in persuasive strategies. Future endeavours may need to explore how persuasion is constructed by means of both explicit and implicit linguistic expressions. Also, this study treated all the argumentative texts as a whole and identified the similarities and differences from a cross-cultural perspective, while not considering the variation that may be caused by the length and the topic of the argumentative texts. Further studies may take these factors into account and examine the differences in the rhetorical appeals and persuasive strategies utilised in the argumentative texts of different lengths and with different topics.

Pedagogically, the findings from this study can be integrated into classroom instruction or workshop training to foster students' awareness of, and competence in, persuasion construction. In practice, the findings regarding linguistic devices can be operationalised as teaching materials and can be incorporated into class instruction and curriculum design for EFL argumentative writing, particularly to guide EFL/ESL students to express an appropriate tone in constructing persuasion in their argumentative writings.

References

Ädel, A. (2006) *Metadiscourse in L1 and L2 English*. Amsterdam: John Benjamins.

Ädel, A. and Erman, B. (2012) Recurrent word combinations in academic writing by native and non-native speakers of English: A lexical bundles approach. *English for Specific Purposes* 31 (2), 81–92. https://doi.org/10.1016/j.esp.2011.08.004.

Afros, E. and Schryer, C.F. (2009) Promotional (meta)discourse in research articles in language and literary studies. *English for Specific Purposes* 28 (1), 58–68. https://doi.org/10.1016/j.esp.2008.09.001.

Altenberg, B. and Tapper, M. (1998) The use of adverbial connectors in advanced Swedish learners' written English. In S. Granger (ed.) *Learner English on Computer* (pp. 80–93). Harlow: Longman.

Aristotle. (1954) *On Rhetoric*. Translated by W. Rhys Roberts. London: Random House.

Bazerman, C. (2010) *The Informed Writer: Using Sources in the Disciplines*. Fort Collins, CO: Houghton Mifflin.

Berkenkotter, C. and Huckin, T. (1995) *Genre Knowledge in Disciplinary Communication: Cognition, Culture, Power*. Hillsdale, NJ: Lawrence Erlbaum.

Bhatia, V.K. (1993) *Analysing Genre: Language Use in Professional Settings*. London: Longman.

Braet, A.C. (1992) Ethos, pathos, and logos in Aristotle's rhetoric: A reexamination. *Argumentation* 6 (3), pp. 307–320.

Çandarli, D., Bayyurt, Y. and Marti, L. (2015) Authorial presence in L1 and L2 novice academic writing: Cross-linguistic and cross-cultural perspectives. *Journal of English for Academic Purposes* 20, 192–202. https://doi.org/10.1016/j.jeap.2015.10.001.

Cao, F. and Hu, G. (2014) Interactive metadiscourse in research articles: A comparative study of paradigmatic and disciplinary influences. *Journal of Pragmatics* 66, 15–31. https://doi.org/10.1016/j.pragma.2014.02.007.

Cheng, F.W. and Unsworth, L. (2016) Stance-taking as negotiating academic conflict in applied linguistics research article discussion sections. *Journal of English for Academic Purposes* 24, 43–57. https://doi.org/10.1016/j.jeap.2016.09.001.

Cohen, J. (1988) *Statistical Power Analysis for the Behavioral Sciences* (2nd edn). Hillsdale, NJ: Erlbaum.

Crismore, A., Markkanen, R. and Steffensen, M.S. (1993) Metadiscourse in persuasive writing. *Written Communication* 10 (1), https://doi.org/0803973233.

Dong, J. and Buckingham, L. (2018) The textual colligation of stance phraseology in cross-disciplinary academic discourse: The timing of authors' self-projection. *International Journal of Corpus Linguistics* 23 (4), 409–437.

Dong, J. and Jiang, F. (2019) Construing evaluation through patterns: Register-specific variations of the introductory it pattern. *Australian Journal of Linguistics* 39 (1), 32–56.

Dressen, D. (2003) Geologists' implicit persuasive strategies and the construction of evaluative evidence. *Journal of English for Academic Purposes* 2 (4), 273–290. https://doi.org/10.1016/S1475–1585(03)00046–8.

Fog, A. (2004) The supposed and the real role of mass media in modern democracy. *Working Paper, 2004—05—20 (22)*, (1990), 1–49. Retrieved from http://www.comsci.uzulu.ac.za/Downloads/Main Campus/Media Studies ACOM232/2011/mediacrisis.pdf.

Gardner, S. and Nesi, H. (2013) A classification of genre families in university student writing. *Applied Linguistics* 34 (1), 25–52.

Gillaerts, P. and Van de Velde, F. (2010) Interactional metadiscourse in research article abstracts. *Journal of English for Academic Purposes* 9 (2), 128–139.

Grant, L. and Ginther, A. (2000) Using computer-tagged linguistic features to describe L2 writing differences. *Journal of Second Language Writing* 9, 123–145.

Halliday, M.A.K. (1978) *Language as a Social Semiotic: The Social Interpretation of Language and Meaning*. London: Edward Arnold.

Halliday, M.A.K. (1994) *Introduction to Functional Grammar*. London: Edward Arnold.

Ho, V. and Li, C. (2018) The use of metadiscourse and persuasion : An analysis of first year university students' timed argumentative essays. *Journal of English for Academic Purposes* 33, 53–68. https://doi.org/10.1016/j.jeap.2018.02.001.

Hyland, K. (1990) A genre description of the argumentative essay. *RELC Journal* 21 (1), 66–78.

Hyland, K. (1998) Persuasion and context: The pragmatics of academic metadiscourse. *Journal of Pragmatics* 30 (4), 437–455.

Hyland, K. (2001) Bringing in the reader: Addressee features in academic articles. *Written Communication* 18 (4), 549–574.

Hyland, K. (2005) Stance and engagement: A model of interaction in academic discourse. *Discourse Studies* 7 (2), 173–192.

Hyland, K. and Jiang, F. (Kevin) (2018) 'We believe that … ': Changes in an academic stance marker 1965–2015. *Australian Journal of Linguistics* 38 (2), 139–161. https://doi.org/1 0.1080/07268602.2018.1400498.

Jiang, F. (2015) Nominal stance construction in L1 and L2 students' writing. *Journal of English for Academic Purposes* 20, 90–102. https://doi.org/10.1016/j.jeap.2015.07.002.

Khedri, M., Heng, C.S. and Ebrahimi, S.F. (2013) An exploration of interactive metadiscourse markers in academic research article abstracts in two disciplines. *Discourse Studies* 15 (3), 319–331. https://doi.org/10.1177/1461445613480588.

Lancaster, Z. (2016) Expressing stance in undergraduate writing: Discipline-specific and general qualities. *Journal of English for Academic Purposes* 23, 16–30.

Lee, J. and Deakin, L. (2016) Interactions in L1 and L2 undergraduate student writing: Interactional metadiscourse in successful and less successful argumentative essays. *Journal of Second Language Writing* 33, 21–34.

Li, T. and Wharton, S. (2012) Journal of English for Academic Purposes metadiscourse repertoire of L1 Mandarin undergraduates writing in English: A cross-contextual, cross-disciplinary study. *Journal of English for Academic Purposes* 11 (4), 345–356. https://doi.org/10.1016/j.jeap.2012.07.004.

Liu, X. and Thompson, P. (2009) Attitude in students' argumentative writing: A contrastive perspective. *University of Reading Language Studies Working Papers* 1, 3–15.

Martín, P. and Pérez, I.K.L. (2014) Convincing peers of the value of one's research: A genre analysis of rhetorical promotion in academic texts. *English for Specific Purposes* 34 (1), 1–13.

Martin, J.R. and White, P.R. (2005) *The Language of Evaluation*. London: Palgrave Macmillan.

Mei, W.S. (2006) Creating a contrastive rhetorical stance: Investigating the strategy of problematization in students' argumentation. *RELC Journal* 37, 329–353.

Milagros del Saz Rubio, M. (2011) A pragmatic approach to the macro-structure and metadiscoursal features of research article introductions in the field of agricultural sciences. *English for Specific Purposes* 30 (4), 258–271. https://doi.org/10.1016/j.esp.2011.03.002.

Mu, C., Zhang, L.J., Ehrich, J. and Hong, H. (2015) The use of metadiscourse for knowledge construction in Chinese and English research articles. *Journal of English for Academic Purposes* 20, 135–148. https://doi.org/10.1016/j.jeap.2015.09.003.

Mur Dueñas, P. (2007) 'I/we focus on...': A cross-cultural analysis of self-mentions in business management research articles. *Journal of English for Academic Purposes* 6 (2), 143–162. https://doi.org/10.1016/j.jeap.2007.05.002.

Parkinson, J. (2011) The discussion section as argument: The language used to prove knowledge claims. *English for Specific Purposes* 30 (3), 164–175. https://doi.org/10.1016/j.esp.2011.03.001.

Perloff, R.M. (2003) *The Dynamics of Persuasion: Communication and Attitudes in the 21st Century* (2nd edn). New York: Lawrence Erlbaum Associates.

Rorty, R. (1979) *Philosophy and the Mirror of Nature*. Princeton, NJ: Princeton UP.

Swales, J.M. (1990) *Genre Analysis: English in Academic and Research Settings*. Cambridge: Cambridge University Press.

VERBI Software (2012) *MAXQDA* (Version 11) [Computer software]. Berlin: VERBI GmbH.

Wu, S.-Y. and Rubin, D.L. (2000) Evaluating the impact of collectivism and individualism on argumentative writing by Chinese and North American college students. *Research in the Teaching of English* 3, 148–178.

8 Crossing Literacy Borders through Writing: Transformational Apprenticeship and Repositioning of EAL Learners

Lawrence Jun Zhang
University of Auckland, New Zealand

Introduction

With an increasing interest in academic writing, or English for academic purposes (EAP), particularly writing in English as an additional language (EAL), the issue of meeting the expected norms in this additional language becomes evident and students find writing really challenging. With ever-increasing numbers of international students crossing borders to pursue various academic qualifications in English as the medium of instruction in institutions of higher learning in the West, it is important to put such interest in perspective. Indeed, it is common understanding that developing academic writing skills in English as a second/foreign language, or English for academic purposes, for that matter, is no easy task, irrespective of whether one is a native or nonnative speaker (Hyland, 2019; Shen *et al.,* 2019; Zhang, 2013, 2016). Hyland (1996, 2000) posits that EAP is no one's first language, highlighting the difficulties that native and non-native English-speaking writers face. Nonetheless, how differently each student experiences the learning process, and how teachers conduct their teaching, vary.

Golden *et al.* (2017) report that evaluations of texts in the new context often reveal greater difficulties in writing for some than for others. For example, writers from the global South and the global East seem to have greater challenges when they have to meet norms in the global North and the global West than do writers who move within these parts of the world. Students of English as a foreign language (EFL), in particular, oftentimes struggle to succeed in completing a research thesis or a dissertation (which ultimately needs to be evaluated as part of the graduation requirements) when they have to write it in English in order to earn their postgraduate qualifications. Conveying ideas appropriately in academic English has to be understood in the light of the changing sociocultural contexts in which these students work when completing their academic qualifications. Such a process needs to be understood with empathy, as and when these students go through the 'apprenticeship', whereby their border-crossing experience is, in fact, one of transformation and repositioning when they have to learn to write in accordance with Western norms.

In this chapter, I explore these issues from a sociocultural perspective in order to bring to the fore the real challenges that researchers, supervisors and teachers alike need to take into serious consideration if they are keen to show understanding of these students and are interested in offering the much-needed help. I conclude the chapter with a discussion of the possibilities of writing-teacher preparation that might be able to help facilitate the transition for these students (see Zhang, 2016).

Importance of Writing Skills for Border-crossing

For many students who are planning to study abroad, the idea of stepping out of their own home countries is already a border-crossing experience, or at least, mentally it is a significant leap forward towards realising their dreams. This process of planning for international travel after serious contemplations of what to study, and of what other academic preparations are required of them, has afforded them an opportunity of looking beyond their own shores. These students have already gone through the struggles of having to undertake the various chores of writing their letters of intent, or study plans, for example, and it is evident that the most useful skill that they can possess is that of written communication. Depending on the level of mastery attained in their writing skills in their first language as well as in their second or foreign language (e.g. English as a foreign language), the degree of difficulty for many international students with a Chinese background is exacerbated when they have to write in academic settings in a second or foreign language due to the sharp orthographic, syntactic and rhetorical differences in the way these two languages express meanings (Wei *et al.*, 2020).

Academic writing, particularly writing in English as an additional language (EAL), imposes tremendously high demands on such students when they matriculate and start their academic programmes in the institutions from which they once dreamed of getting an offer. They might have already experienced both anxiety and excitement along the way but they may not have encountered a real border-crossing in English as the medium of instruction in institutions of higher learning in the West. Therefore, putting these students' experiences in perspective will help illuminate why these international students quickly feel that developing academic writing skills in English as a second/foreign/ additional language (or EAP, for that matter) is no easy task. Such fact-checking also helps to confirm Hyland's (1996, 2000) claim that academic English is no one's first language, regardless of whether you are native or non-native speakers of English. Understandably, how differently each student goes through the learning process, and how teachers conduct their teaching, vary.

In their recent work, Golden *et al*. (2017) found that L2 writers from the East writing in the West do experience different types of challenges when writing in a new context. This might well explain how international students from a variety of first language backgrounds need to embrace these new challenges, which they might have anticipated but never personally experienced prior to their embarking on the real journey of academic study in a foreign country. Given the relative familiarity I have with particular groups of students who have to write in EFL, I next focus my discussion on their border-crossing experiences.

Journeying to the West: Multiple Pathways, Diverse Experiences

In my professional experience of working in Singapore and New Zealand, both of which utilise systems whose medium of instruction in academic institutions is English, from childcare centres to higher education establishments, writing in English is not always easy for students. For Singaporean students, who are schooled in English as the first language as stated in the national curriculum documents (see Silver & Bokhorst-Heng, 2016; Zhang *et al*., 2016), the challenges they face are very similar to those faced by other native English-speaker writers such as those in New Zealand. This is because they are native speakers of a different variety of what are now commonly known as 'New Englishes' (Brown *et al*., 2000; Kachru, 1992; Low & Brown, 2005). The only discernible difference is what contrastive rhetoric scholars typically refer to as rhetorical differences in argumentation by virtue of the different first languages in which they are fluent (when it comes to speaking, listening, reading and writing) in addition to English, which could be a factor that influences Singaporean students' writing in English for academic purposes in educational settings (Zhang, 2014, 2016). Understandably, the hurdle to academic success, and to professional success for that matter, for non-native English-speaking writers, especially EFL student writers, is evidently far greater (Zhang, 2013).

To make my point clearer, I describe the different requirements of a typical English-medium university in a traditionally English-dominant country: New Zealand. I intend to show how academic writing is compounded by factors beyond rhetorical differences.

The Faculty of Education and Social Work of the University of Auckland offers several postgraduate qualifications, which require a research component in order for the students to earn the prospective degree. The specific requirements for four main written assignments as part of the higher degree programmes in terms of the extent of work that is expected are as follows.

For the master's degree, candidates are given several options to satisfy the requirements for completion of the programme. They can earn the degree by taking the required number of compulsory and elective courses and satisfy their requirements by passing the courses. They can also complete the programme by including a small research component called 'Research Portfolio' of about 10,000 words, which is 25% of the total course load, or a dissertation that is in the range of 10,000–15,000 words in length, which is about 40% of the total course load.

The research-based master's degree is awarded based on the external examination of a full research thesis of about 25,000 words.

The Doctor of Philosophy (PhD) degree, which is the highest academic degree awarded by the University of Auckland, usually requires the submission of a research thesis of about 60,000–100,000 words. The award of the PhD degree is contingent upon the external examiners' independent examination or evaluation and the candidate's successful defence in an oral examination or viva. It needs to be pointed out that international students do not satisfy the Immigration New Zealand visa requirements for taking the professional doctorate, the Doctor of Education (EdD) programme, which is offered only to domestic candidates, who are either citizens or legal residents of New Zealand, studying as part-time students.

As is understood, regardless of the postgraduate programmes on which these international students pursue their studies, the ability to convey ideas appropriately in academic English, especially in relation to writing a portfolio, a thesis, or a dissertation, has to be understood in the light of the changing sociocultural contexts. For the majority of the postgraduate students, whose first language is not English, undertaking such a large written assignment is burdensome even while it is a worthwhile pursuit. As mentioned above, the experiences are not uniform for students of different levels of academic English proficiency. Zhang (2013) posits that writing provides an ideal platform for ESL/EFL learners not only to improve their language skills but also to experience cultural differences, a kind of border-crossing for these student writers. It is easy to discern that many English learners' personal written narratives are embodiments of their dreams and aspirations for studying and living in a developed country, where English is expected to be used as the dominant language for communication both in social and academic settings. Due to financial, political, and other reasons, the international mobility of many such learners is restricted. Thus, participating in online communities can fulfil their dreams and aspirations. They do so through 'imagined communities' (Anderson, 1991; Norton, 2000; Norton & Pavlenko, 2019; Pavlenko & Norton, 2007), with greatly increased probability of computer-mediated communication, such as various chat rooms, including but not limited to, for example, DingDing, QQ, WeChat, Line and WhatsApp, among many others.

Markus and Nurius (1986) think that learners anticipate possible selves as the link between motivation and behaviour. Norton's (2001) view on imagined communities is constructed through two complementary sources: Anderson's (1991) imagined communities and Wenger's (1998) view on imagination as one mode of engagement (see also Bao *et al.*, 2021). Pavlenko and Norton (2007) argue that the imagining process includes 'other meanings, other possibilities, other perspectives' in one's identities (2007: 670). The centrality of Norton's model of imagined communities rests on the idea that it presupposes an imagined identity – an identity that offers 'an enhanced range of possibilities for the future' (Pavlenko & Norton, 2007: 678; see also De Costa & Norton, 2017). Because of online censorship and restriction of Western social networking media platforms such as Facebook, Twitter, and so on, a large number of international students often use English or mix languages (code-mixing) to realise their dreams. This process can be compared to one that is reflected in a classical Chinese novel, *Journey to the West* (or *Xi You Ji*, in Chinese), which presents an analogy of how going to the West is a way of seeking spiritual wealth and knowledge. For some, it can be predicted, real border-crossing may never come to fruition, but for others their acquired language skills, including those they learned through their own writing practice or teachers' writing instruction, come into play and place them in good stead once they are in a country they have dreamt of, despite the fact that this is also a process that requires writing instructors, academic readers and dissertation/ thesis supervisors to show empathy. Meanwhile, the plight that these students are put in for realising their dreams is in fact a soul-searching effort to reconcile their learned discourse traditions with the new ones. Accordingly, readiness for repositioning is called for and this will be addressed later in this chapter.

Anderson (1991) argues that imagination is a social process, during which process, as Pavlenko and Norton posited, 'those in power oftentimes do the imagining for the rest of their fellow citizens, offering them certain identity options and leaving other options *unimaginable*' [italics mine] (2007: 670). This could be a reflection of how some international students feel about their sometimes reluctant attitude to the Western norms of discourse and argumentation, which is understandably a predicament facing them as well as their supervisors who are the immediate readers expected to offer feedback to them on their writing (e.g. Xu & Zhang, 2019).

The various topics on which presentations were given in the colloquium during SS22 in 2019 on learning new academic literacies as border-crossing illustrate many of the issues discussed in this chapter. The original presentations at this colloquium included 'Evaluation of L2 texts when errors have been corrected: What borders are left?' by Golden and Kulbrandstad, 'A contrastive analysis of stance construction in Engineering student and professional academic writing' by Dong, 'Doctoral candidates from the East learning to write in the West' by Morena Magalhães, 'Unbuilding the walls: Helping Pasifika students transition into diverse academic writing contexts' and 'Empathy, immersion and apprenticeship: Border-crossing as transformation and repositioning in academic practice: A Discussion' by Zhang. As is evident, a theme that cuts across the topics is the challenges international students meet in academic writing. Unfortunately, in the process of finalising the list of contributors, Matheson decided to withdraw from contributing to this volume due to unexpected circumstances. Our open call attracted three additional contributions by Fang and Li, Leskinen, and Rosmawati.

Border-crossing as Apprenticeship

In addressing the challenges facing international students, we need to ask ourselves important questions such as:

(1) What are the L1 sociocultural norms that these writers bring to their writing tasks in English as an additional language (EAL)?
(2) How do their writing skills in EAL emerge through their 'apprenticeship' in their academic study (border-crossing experience)?
(3) How can socioculturally-embedded thinking on academic writing instruction help us understand issues that frequently emerge from EAP writers' experiences?
(4) How do these students confront or 'combat' the challenges in EAP writing, especially those students who pursue their research degrees in English in an English-speaking country?

Important aspects of such socioculturally-unique practices, namely, the role of apprenticeship and empathy in shaping EAL students' development of EAP in the 'community of practices', of which they aspire to obtain membership, need to be given sufficient attention. How students have attained the success that they aspired to through such apprenticeship with their supervisor as the more 'capable peer' remains a worthwhile endeavour to explore to deepen our understanding of their border-crossing experiences, be they successes or failures.

In the existing literature, English for academic purposes oftentimes refers to research and practice in and outside the classroom that considers specific communicative needs and practices in broadly defined academic contexts (see, for example, Gillette, 1989). Such an understanding of EAP takes into account the cognitive, social and linguistic demands of specific academic disciplines and requires teachers' and researchers' attention in their research and practice. Hyland and Hamp-Lyons (2002: 2) argued that such thinking takes practitioners beyond preparing learners for study in English to developing new kinds of literacy: namely, they need to equip them with the communicative skills to participate in particular academic and cultural contexts (see also Ding & Bruce, 2017). Higher degree students undertaking their research for a Masters' or PhD degree are a typical group of the student population who are learning the 'kinds of new literacy'. As mentioned above – and I concur from my own experience as a research student as well as a research supervisor – EAP writing is no one's familiar territory, including native-speaker candidates. It is acquired from practice and apprenticeship when working with a more experienced writer or when reading other scholars' published works.

The work of these student can be used as an example to showcase the opportunities that the sociocultural contexts afforded them for developing such new academic literacy skills through apprenticeship in 'communities of practice' (Lave & Wenger, 1991). The concept of 'communities of practice' was first proposed by cognitive anthropologist Jean Lave and educational theorist Etienne Wenger in their 1991 book *Situated Learning* (Lave & Wenger, 1991). Wenger then significantly expanded the concept in his 1998 book *Communities of Practice* (Wenger, 1998). For Lave and Wenger (1991), a community of practice is a group of people who share a craft and/or a profession. We need to resort to various theoretical perspectives to scrutinise the phenomenon in order to tease out students' successes and failures in this apprenticeship experience (e.g. Bakhtin, 1981; Ivanič & Camps, 2001; Vygotsky, 1987). Evidently, the challenges facing these EAL students, who have to write their Master's or PhD theses in English are a reality (as seen in Dong, Chapter 7 of this volume).

EAL Writers as Biliterate/Multiliterate Users

Hornberger defines biliteracy as 'the conjunction of literacy and bilingualism' (2003: 3). In this sense, EFL writers are already biliterate to varying degrees. It is definitely the case for research students who have to write a research thesis as part of the requirement for being awarded their degree. By virtue of them being fluent users of their L1s, EFL writers are already well equipped with many of the knowledge sources that monolingual writers do not have the luxury of possessing. These EFL writers' understanding of various L1 resources, including repertoires of lexical choices induced by their L1s, formal knowledge, subject knowledge, reader schema, strategy or process knowledge, among many others, are what we may take to be the advantages they have (see Tardy, 2009, 2019).

Recent scholarship on L2 writing has provided us with multiple avenues to understanding the aims and purposes of L2 writing (Polio & Friedman, 2016). Provision of academic support through writing centres, as widely practised in the USA and Canada, is based on cumulative research evidence that shows the significance of teacher intervention on a relatively large scale using genre-based pedagogy (Hyland, 2018; Rose & Martin, 2012; Swales, 1990), process-genre pedagogy (Deng *et al.*, 2016; Huang & Zhang, 2019), or strategies-based instruction (Teng & Zhang, 2020; Zhang *et al.*, 2016). Scaffolding students towards successful completion in thesis writing by teaching them how to move forward step by step (Bitchener, 2009; Carter, 2011) is also a way of helping them cross literacy borders.

Border-crossing as Transformational Apprenticeship

Many EAL student writers with a background of strong Asian literacy practices may encounter serious challenges when they have to write in English in the West, where English is predominantly used as the language for academic and professional communication. The multiple challenges often resurface in relation to writer identity (Chen & Zhang, 2019; Matsuda, 2015; Xu & Zhang, 2019), different discourse structures (Chen & Zhang, 2017; Mu *et al.*, 2015; Qi & Zhang, 2017), features of sections of academic articles (Shen *et al.,* 2019), stance-taking (Zhang & Zhang, 2021), and intercultural rhetoric (Atkinson & Matsuda, 2013; Belcher, 2014; Connor, 1996, 2008). Understandably, the serious challenge that EAL students face in writing argumentation /exposition / persuasion texts is most evident. Such challenges remind us of Kaplan's (1966) formulation of his rhetorical model, as it is commonly known: different cultures were understood to practise different rhetorical strategies for presenting an argument (see also Grabe & Kaplan, 1989).

Increasingly, Toulmin's (1958/2003) argument model has been embraced in research studies into the ways student writers present their argument. If it were true that Chinese EFL writers' argumentative text takes the eight-legged structure, or, 起承转合[*qǐ chéng zhuǎn hé*], which means that the writer opens the topic, continues with it, takes a turn, and closes the essay, then the benefits to be had from taking stock of this already existing schematic genre knowledge about argumentative writing could have been foregrounded through teacher-led or student-initiated discussions on cross-cultural rhetoric for meeting the expected norms among members of a particular discourse community.

Embracing Challenges for Crossing Literacy-Borders

Learners from the East learning to write in academic English within the norms widely accepted and practised in the West, or even in diverse contexts in the West for that matter, necessarily face multiple challenges. There are multiple variables that affect their decision-making in the writing process, including their pre-writing planning. These factors include, but not exclusively, the following: linguistic challenges; differences in rhetorical traditions in argumentation; contrastive rhetoric/inter-cultural rhetoric; affordances and disadvantages of being bilingual and biliterate; interplay of multiple identities in L2 student texts; adoption of appropriate and useful writing strategies; and the role of writing teachers in helping these learners' border-crossing adventures be successful.

Most often, it is assumed that the most obvious challenge is related to learners' mastery of the English language for academic purposes, which is indeed true. The linguistic challenges have much to do with how they have developed high levels of English proficiency reflected in the way that they are able to manipulate the text for fluency, accuracy, and complexity (Ong & Zhang, 2010, 2013; Rahimi & Zhang, 2018, 2019; Skehan, 2009; Wang & Zhang, 2019). However, these linguistic challenges are never divorced from EAL writers' in-built or programmed rhetorical norms or traditions with which they have been writing in their L1s for at least 15 years before they embark on the study abroad adventures. In the early years, Kaplan (1966) posed a very interesting question that guided many scholars to understand why the writings of different cultural backgrounds are so different in terms of their discourse moves in argumentation. This is commonly known in the field as contrastive rhetoric. With the passage of time and greater cultural interaction in the context of globalisation, Kaplan's theoretical position has been further expanded and revised substantially. We all know that these differences used to be regarded as very obvious and are not so evident in student writings these days. Most students can follow the Western rhetorical patterns but what is really lacking in their arguments is the substance that is required or expected for advancing the argument. As Stapleton and Wu (2015) reported in their case study of 125 high school students in Hong Kong, their participants' argumentative essays were evaluated in accordance with a modified Toulmin model to check if these writings reflected elements such as claims, counterargument claims and rebuttals. They also chose exemplary essays to examine if the surface structure showed the standards of the modified Toulmin mode. These essays were assessed for their quality of reasoning by 46 doctoral students who rated the 20 most common reasons advanced in the 125 essays with reference to a questionnaire. They found patterns of inadequacies in the reasoning of these student writers, which was regarded as evidence that the quality of reasoning in students' persuasive writing needs to be given more attention when providing instruction. Such findings suggest that good argumentative writing is not only a matter of correct linguistic expression.

Qin and Karabacak (2010) collected and analysed 133 third-year undergraduate English-major students' argumentative texts written in English after they were asked to read two opinion pieces whose authors expressed divergent views on the same controversial topic. Their analysis focused on the argument structures of these English texts with reference to the adapted Toulmin (1958, 2003) model, which comprises six key elements of argumentation: claim, data, counterargument claim, counterargument data, rebuttal claim, and rebuttal data. The purpose of their analysis was to find out whether using these Toulmin elements had any relationships with the overall quality of the argumentative texts. They found that each text had at least one claim with four pieces of data as supporting evidence. Use of counterargument claim, counterargument data, rebuttal claim, and rebuttal data in these texts was far less often, despite the fact that use of these significantly predicted their overall quality of argumentative texts. These are interesting findings, as they show us that learning the discourse moves in argumentation can be achieved through learning to write the Western way, but that lack of evidence as substance in argumentation is something which is not as easy to learn as usually assumed.

As outlined above, language knowledge and language proficiency are foundational to the writers' production of a coherent text. Language proficiency alone is not a guarantee of successful argumentation. Different rhetorical traditions need to be borne in mind in order to understand students' literacy border-crossing experiences in producing argumentation, a written assignment that is expected of all students studying in university. Recent developments in contrastive rhetoric, or more relatedly, inter-cultural rhetoric studies show us new directions. Instead of taking a binary view of a particular group of students' writings, literacy educators and researchers should, instead, view these texts as a successful weaving of ideas through two or even more cultural lenses. Comprehending such texts demands that we adopt a view that the written text reflects the writers' sometime definitive and at other times changing or fluid cultural bondage. Given the fact that students from the East writing in the West are most often highly bilingual and biliterate, their bilingualism already provides them with affordances that enable them to explore the word and the world in at least two languages. This puts them in an advantageous position when they aspire to analyse issues facing them in completing a writing task, by virtue of their ability to read and understand the world around them in the two languages and synthesise the information thus obtained. Nonetheless, being bilingual and biliterate also means that the two languages and linguistic systems might automatically play a role that is regarded as interference by some scholars (e.g. Kaplan, 1966), which is a kind of disadvantage if not managed well. Texts are not produced purely as linguistic forms: rather, in each writing act and the very process of producing a text, writers negotiate who they are and how they prefer to be portrayed in their own text (Zhang, 2013; Xu & Zhang, 2019; Zhang & Zhang, 2021).

The interplay of multiple identities in L2 student texts demonstrates that border-crossing is also a process of identity formation and re-formation. Related issues also include our understanding of L2 writers' writing processes and strategies that they have used for successful text production. As Zhang (2016) points out, the whole enterprise of L2 writing instruction is a systematic project that starts from trainee-teachers' willingness to approach writing and the writing teachers' pedagogical designs. The teacher and the student in the whole learning process are in a mutually interactive relationship. What happens in the classroom as either an explicit or implicit pedagogy is inherited by the student (see e.g. Qin & Zhang, 2018; Zhang *et al.*, 2019). History has told us that the debate over the issue of whether writing skills are taught or caught is no longer relevant. Human endeavours are so complicated that one cannot distinguish one from the other. A binary decision is not helpful at all. History has also informed us that the success of how some learners are taught to acquire writing skills is as much a question of learners' efforts as of writing teachers' responsibility. Writing in EAL requires the writers to know how to write and the writing teachers in this case to assume a role even more important than ever before.

Supporting EAL Students Crossing Literacy Borders

Successful literacy border-crossing for EAL students requires concerted effort from learners, teachers, researchers, administrators, and all other stakeholders. Taking into consideration research findings and research-informed practices which show that enhancing EAL writers' metacognition can be one of the effective ways for improving their writing, students and teachers should work together to explore possibilities for positive learning outcomes.

As I have argued elsewhere (Zhang, 2016; Zhang & Cheng, 2021; Zhang & Zhang, 2019), students whose first language is not English need to be made aware of the multi-resources they themselves bring into the learning process, in particular with regard to three main dimensions: person knowledge, task knowledge, and strategy knowledge (Flavell, 1979). A learner's person knowledge is their understanding of themselves as a learner or simply as a human being, including their strengths and areas for further improvement, learning style preferences, motivation, and many other factors related to the learner's individual differences. The learner's task knowledge is their prior knowledge of things they are expected to do in writing, having been equipped with much of the information they have acquired through their first language. Such knowledge ranges from their schematic storage of various 'scripts' of what a narrative text typically reads like, what a typical argumentative text should be, and what a poem should be made up of, among other things. These collections of knowledge in the learners' long-term memory can be activated at the pre-writing or planning stage to facilitate their successful drafting of a text.

It needs to be highlighted that EAL learners' literacy practices are greatly influenced and supported by their already well-developed, high-proficiency literacy, which can be leveraged by the classroom teachers, particularly if we are faced with different groups of learners, including those pursuing their undergraduate studies whose ages range from 18 to 22. They are learning writing in EAL through a constructive negotiation process in meaning-making. This process is heavily dependent upon their strategy knowledge. Much research has been conducted to examine high-achieving and low-achieving language learners. Findings clearly show that the former are a group of learners who not only have a large repertoire of learning strategies but also know how, where, why, and when to use them, and use them flexibly for optimal learning outcomes (see Oxford, 2017; Zhang, 2003, 2010; Zhang & Qin, 2018; Zhang & Zhang, 2019).

A common myth facing many teachers of English needs to be demystified in the light of the difficulties that EAP student writers encounter. Many classroom teachers whose teaching duties do not necessarily involve teaching academic writing to EAL students mistakenly assume that native English-speakers are good writers, and non-native English speakers do not or cannot write well. Such demystification requires a total facelift among English teaching professionals. Both groups need to understand that academic English, or writing in English for academic purposes, is a challenge that both native and non-native English speakers face as a natural course of action, that has to be faced sooner or later. As mentioned earlier in this chapter, Hyland (1996: 62; see also Hyland, 2000) clearly points out that academic English is no one's first language. Such an understanding is important because it helps many teachers to realise that non-native English-speaking writers ought to develop confidence in themselves and overcome the inferiority complex. This idea is also crucial to boosting EAL students' morale and to helping them hone their writing skills for successfully crossing the literacy borders to earn their academic qualifications.

DePalma and Ringer (2011) posit that education is about transfer or how to capitalise on existing knowledge for learning new things.

EAL writers from other contexts are in such a situation and their existing knowledge is the asset they bring with them to new contexts. Unfortunately, 'transfer has not been fully interpreted' as it is defined as 'intact knowledge' (2011: 137). Numerous studies have shown positive effects of the transfer of L1 writing experience/training on L2 writing (e.g. Cumming, 1989; Kobayashi & Rinnert, 2008). Cumming (1989) found that professional French L1 writers, regardless of their L2 English proficiency, applied knowledge of L1 discourse organisation in their L2 writing and were able to exert greater control in the L2 writing process than writers without such L1 experience (see also Rinnert *et al.*, 2015). As discussed in an earlier section, Wenger's (1998) theory of 'communities of practice' would be a good locale where EAL learners/ writers can be better understood.

If EAL writing teachers are intrinsically interested in helping their students to successfully cross literacy borders, they need to start early and prepare these students to get ready to accept the 'new norm', as it were. As Hirvela (2013) notes, high-school students may become versed in supporting theses with evidence, but other aspects of academic writing can be elusive. Specifically, 'knowing how to use the specialised language and discourse features of specific disciplinary fields in rhetorically appropriate and authoritative ways eludes many students, especially those entering their first year of university study' (Thompson *et al.*, 2013: 101; see also Aull & Lancaster, 2014; Zhang & Zhang, 2021). A key element of any argumentative text – and what distinguishes it in many ways from other written genres – is the evidence that is used to establish or further a given argument. Writers need to 'refer to information from other texts,' 'establish an authorial command of the subject,' and may 'involve hearsay or attribution to a reliable source' (2013: 51). At the same time, as they support arguments, evidentials can also be used to fulfil disciplinary-specific (Hyland, 2000) and personal (Li, X. 2008; Li, Y. 2013) goals while establishing the writers' authority (Le, 2004). EAL writers from the East attempting to cross literacy borders for entry into the West fall squarely into a similar category, which means that, in learning argumentative writing, they are not only involved in a balancing act of how much each of these needs is to be woven into their argument but they also need to be provided with opportunities for developing a sense of ownership of the texts they produce.

Conclusion

If EAL students are given the opportunity to engage in sustained exercise of the strategies mentioned above in supportive environments (Crowell & Kuhn, 2014; Teng & Zhang, 2020), especially through much needed 'apprenticeship' and by allowing for their repositioning in transitioning geographically and interculturally, it will not be difficult for teachers to see that the students' argumentation strategies will improve in such a way that they will pay attention to both the form and the content, or the structure and the substance in producing their argumentative texts (Toulmin, 1958/2003). Prior posits that 'writing and disciplinarity [in academic settings] are locally situated, extensively mediated, deeply laminated, and highly heterogeneous' (1998: 275). Such a statement actually defies singular notions of argument even within specific disciplinary settings (see also Fang, 2021). EAL students' experience of learning, relearning, and unlearning various literacies and related literacy practices in different sociocultural contexts will be a significant step they make towards their successful border-crossing and this process is closely tied to the critical friendship they develop with their teachers and peers through constantly evolving feedback loops in which they learn how to write well as 'apprentices'. This process is definitely one that is ever-changing and is probably a non-stop journey of repositioning themselves in the very process of learning how to write to successfully cross the literacy borders for ultimately earning their academic qualifications.

References

Anderson, B.R. O'G. (1991) *Imagined Communities: Reflections on the Origin and Spread of Nationalism*. Revised and extended edition. London: Verso.

Atkinson, D. and Matsuda, P.K. (2013) Intercultural rhetoric: A conversation – the sequel. In D. Belcher and G. Nelson (eds) *Critical and Corpus–based Approaches to Intercultural Rhetoric* (pp. 227–242). Ann Abor, MI: University of Michigan Press.

Aull, L.L. and Lancaster, Z. (2014) Linguistic markers of stance in early and advanced academic writing: A corpus-based comparison. *Written Communication* 31, 151–183.

Bakhtin, M.M. (1981) *The Dialogic Imagination: Four Essays* (ed. by Michael Holquist; translated by Caryl Emerson and Michael Holquist). Houston, TX: University of Texas Press.

Bao, C.R., Zhang, L.J. and Dixon, H.R. (2021). Teacher engagement in language teaching: Investigating self-efficacy for teaching based on the project 'Sino-Greece Online Chinese Language Classroom'. *Frontiers in Psychology* 12, 710736, 1-11. https://doi.org/10.3389/fpsyg.2021.710736.

Belcher, D. (2014) What we need and don't need intercultural rhetoric for: A retrospective and prospective look at an evolving research area. *Journal of Second Language Writing* 25, 59–67.

Bitchener, J. (2009) *Writing an Applied Linguistics Thesis or Dissertation: A Guide to Presenting Empirical Research*. London: Macmillan.

Bitchener, J., Basturkmen, H. and East, M. (2010) The focus of supervisor written feedback to thesis/dissertation students. *International Journal of English Studies* 10 (2), 79–97.

Brown, A., Low, E.L. and Deterding, D. (eds) (2000) *The English Language in Singapore: Research on Pronunciation*. Singapore: Singapore Association for Applied Linguistics.

Carter, S. (2011) Doctorate as genre: Supporting thesis writing across campus. *Higher Education Research and Development* 30 (6), 725–736.

Chen, C.H. and Zhang, L.J. (2017) An intercultural analysis of the use of hedging by Chinese and Anglophone academic English writers. *Applied Linguistics Review* 8 (1), 1–34.

Chen, J. and Zhang, L.J. (2019) Assessing student-writers' self-efficacy beliefs about text revision in EFL writing. *Assessing Writing* 40, 27–41.

Connor, U.M. (1996) *Contrastive Rhetoric: Cross-cultural Aspects of Second Language Writing*. Cambridge: Cambridge University Press.

Connor, U. (2008) Mapping multidimensional aspects of research. In U. Connor, E. Nagelhout and W.V. Rozycki (eds) *Contrastive Rhetoric: Reaching to Intercultural Rhetoric* (Vol. 169, pp. 299–315). Amsterdam: John Benjamins Publishing.

Crowell, A. and Kuhn, D. (2014) Developing dialogic argumentation skills: A 3-year intervention study. *Journal of Cognition and Development* 15 (2), 363–381.

Cumming, A. (1989) Writing expertise and second-language proficiency. *Language Learning* 39 (1), 81–135.

De Costa, P.I. and Norton, B. (2017) Introduction: Identity, transdisciplinarity, and the good language teacher. *Modern Language Journal* 101 (S1), 3–14.

Deng, L., Chen, Q. and Zhang, Y. (2016) *Developing Chinese EFL Learners' Generic Competence*. Boston, MA: Springer.

DePalma, M.J. and Ringer, J.M. (2011) Toward a theory of adaptive transfer: Expanding disciplinary discussions of 'transfer' in second-language writing and composition studies. *Journal of Second Language Writing* 20 (2), 134–147.

Ding, A. and Bruce, I. (2017) *The English for Academic Purposes Practitioner: Operating on the Edge of Academia*. London: Palgrave.

Fang, Z.H. (2021) *Demystifying Academic Writing: Genres, Moves, Skills, and Strategies*. Abingdon: Routledge.

Flavell, J.H. (1979) Metacognition and cognitive monitoring: A new area of cognitive-developmental inquiry. *American Psychologist* 34, 906–911.

Gillett, A.J. (1989) Designing an EAP course: English language support for further and higher education. *Journal of Further and Higher Education* 13 (2), 92–104.

Golden, A., Jarvis, S. and Tenfjord, K. (eds) (2017) *Crosslinguistic Influence and Distinctive Patterns of Language Learning: Findings and Insights from a Learner Corpus*. Bristol: Multilingual Matters.

Grabe, W. and Kaplan, R.B. (1989) Writing in a second language: Contrastive rhetoric. In D.M. Johnson and D.H. Rohen (eds) *Richness in Writing: Empowering ESL Students* (pp. 263–283). White Plains, NY: Longman.

Hirvela, A. (2013) Preparing English language learners for argumentative writing. In T. Silva and L. Oliveira (eds) *Second Language Writing in the Secondary Classroom* (pp. 1–31). New York, NY: Routledge.

Hornberger, N.H. (2003) Multilingual language policies and the continua of biliteracy: An ecological approach. In N. Hornberger (ed) *Continua of Biliteracy: An Ecological Framework for Educational Policy, Research, and Practice in Multilingual Settings* (pp. 315–339). Clevendon, England: Multilingual Matters.

Huang, Y. and Zhang, L.J. (2020) Does a process-genre approach help improve students' argumentative writing in English as a foreign language? Findings from an intervention study. *Reading and Writing Quarterly* 36 (4), 339–364. online first 10.1080/10573569.2019.1649223.

Hyland, K. (1996) Academic publishing and the myth of linguistic injustice. *Journal of Second Language Writing* 31, 58–69.

Hyland, K. (2000) *Disciplinary Discourses: Social Interactions in Academic Writing*. London: Longman.

Hyland, K. (2002) Genre: Language, context, and literacy. *Annual Review of Applied Linguistics* 22 (1), 113–135.

Hyland, K. (2018) *Metadiscourse: Exploring Interaction in Writing*. London: Bloomsbury Publishing.

Hyland, K. (2019) *Second Language Writing*. Cambridge: Cambridge University Press.

Hyland, K. and Hamp-Lyons, L. (2002) EAP: issues and directions. *Journal of English for Academic Purposes* 1 (1), 1–12.

Ivanic, R. and Camps, D. (2001) I am how I sound: Voice as self-representation in L2 writing. *Journal of Second Language Writing* 10, 3–33.

Kachru, B.B. (1992) World Englishes: Approaches, issues and resources. *Language Teaching* 25 (1), 1–14.

Kaplan, R. (1966) Cultural thought patterns in inter-cultural education. *Language Learning* 16, 1–20.

Kobayashi, H. and Rinnert, C. (2008) Task response and text construction across L1 and L2 writing. *Journal of Second Language Writing* 17 (1), 7–29.

Lave, J. and Wenger, E. (1991) *Situated Learning: Legitimate Peripheral Participation*. Cambridge: Cambridge University Press.

Le, E. (2004) Active participation within written argumentation: Metadiscourse and editorialist's authority. *Journal of Pragmatics* 36, 687–714.

Li, X. (2008) From contrastive rhetoric to intercultural rhetoric: A search for collective identity. In U. Connor, E. Nagelhout and W. Rozycki (eds) *Contrastive Rhetoric: Reaching to Intercultural Rhetoric* (pp. 11–24). Amsterdam: John Benjamins.

Li, Y. (2013) Three ESL students writing a policy paper assignment: An activity-analytic perspective. *Journal of English for Academic Purposes* 12, 73–86.

Low, E.L. and Brown, A. (2005) *English in Singapore: An Introduction*. Singapore: McGraw-Hill.

Markus, H. and Nurius, P. (1986) Possible selves. *American Psychologist* 41 (9), 954.

Matsuda, P.K. (2015) Identity in written discourse. *Annual Review of Applied Linguistics* 35, 140–159.

Mu, C.J., Zhang, L.J., Ehrich, J. and Hong, H.Q. (2015) The use of metadiscourse for knowledge construction in Chinese and English research articles. *Journal of English for Academic Purposes* 20, 135–148.

Norton, B. (2000) *Identity and Language Learning: Gender, Ethnicity, and Educational Change*. London: Longman.

Norton, B. (2001) Non-participation, imagined communities, and the language classroom. In: M. Breen (ed.) *Learner Contributions to Language Learning: New Directions in Research* (pp. 159–71). Harlow: Pearson Education.

Norton, B. (2013) *Identity and Language Learning: Extending the Conversation* (2nd edn). Bristol: Multilingual Matters.

Norton, B. and Pavlenko, A. (2019) Imagined communities, identity, and English language learning in a multilingual world. In X. Gao (ed.) *Second Handbook of English Language Teaching* (pp. 1–12). Cham: Springer Nature.

Ong, J. and Zhang, L.J. (2010) Effects of task complexity on the fluency and lexical complexity in EFL students' argumentative writing. *Journal of Second Language Writing* 19 (4), 218–233.

Ong, J. and Zhang, L.J. (2013) Effects of the manipulation of cognitive processes on EFL writers' text quality. *TESOL Quarterly* 47 (2), 375–398.

Oxford, R.L. (2017) *Teaching and Researching Language Learning Strategies: Self-regulation in Context*. New York, NY: Routledge.

Pavlenko, A. and Norton, B. (2007) Imagined communities, identity, and English language learning. In J. Cummins (ed.) *International Handbook of English Language Teaching* (pp. 669–680). Boston, MA: Springer.

Polio, C. and Friedman, D.A. (2016) *Understanding, Evaluating, and Conducting Second Language Writing Research*. New York, NY: Routledge.

Prior, P. (1998) *Writing/Disciplinarity: A Sociohistoric Account of Literate Activity in the Academy*. Mahwah, NJ: Lawrence Erlbaum.

Qi, F. and Zhang, L.J. (2017) Reflections on macro-strategies and micro-techniques in English language teaching in the 'Postmethod' era in China. *Foreign Language Education* 38 (5), 54–59.

Qin, J.J. and Karabacak, E. (2010) The analysis of Toulmin elements in Chinese EFL university argumentative writing. *System* 38 (3), 444–456.

Rahimi, M. and Zhang, L.J. (2018) Effects of task complexity and planning conditions on L2 argumentative writing production. *Discourse Processes* 55 (8), 726–742.

Rahimi, M. and Zhang, L.J. (2019) Writing task complexity, students' motivational beliefs, anxiety and their writing production in English as a second language. *Reading and Writing* 32, 761–786.

Rinnert, C., Kobayashi, H. and Katayama, A. (2015) Argumentation text construction by Japanese-as-a-foreign-language writers: A dynamic view of transfer. *Modern Language Journal* 99 (2), 213–245.

Rose, D. and Martin, J.R. (2012) *Learning to Write, Reading to Learn: Genre, Knowledge and Pedagogy in the Sydney School*. Sheffield: Equinox.

Shen, L., Carter, S. and Zhang, L.J. (2019) EL1 and EL2 doctoral students' experience in writing the discussion section: A needs analysis. *Journal of English for Academic Purposes* 40, 74–86.

Silver, R.E. and Bokhorst-Heng, W.D. (2016) Overarching themes, bilingual dreams and multilingual landscapes: Quadrilingual education in Singapore. In R.E. Silver and W.D. Bokhorst-Heng (eds) *Quadrilingual Education in Singapore* (pp. 3–19). Singapore: Springer.

Skehan, P. (2009) Modelling second language performance: Integrating complexity, accuracy, fluency, and lexis. *Applied Linguistics* 30 (4), 510–532.

Stapleton, P. and Wu, Y.M.A. (2015) Assessing the quality of arguments in students' persuasive writing: A case study analyzing the relationship between surface structure and substance. *Journal of English for Academic Purposes* 17, 12–23.

Swales, J.M. (1990) *Genre Analysis: English in Academic and Research Settings*. Cambridge: Cambridge University Press.

Tardy, C.M. (2009) *Building Genre Knowledge*. West Lafayette, IN: Parlor Press.

Tardy, C.M. (2019) *Genre-based Writing: What Every ESL Teacher Needs to Know*. Ann Arbor, MI: University of Michigan Press.

Teng, L.S. and Zhang, L.J. (2020) Empowering learners in the second/foreign language classroom: Can self-regulated learning strategies-based writing instruction make a difference? *Journal of Second Language Writing* 48 (100701), 1–13.

Thompson, C., Morton, J. and Storch, N. (2013) Where from, who, why and how? A study of the use of sources by first year L2 university students. *Journal of English for Academic Purposes* 12 (2), 99–109.

Toulmin, S. (1958) *The Uses of Argument*. Cambridge: Cambridge University Press.

Toulmin, S. (2003) *The Uses of Argument*. Revised edition. Cambridge: Cambridge University Press.

Vygotsky, L.S. (1978) *Mind in Society: The Development of Higher Psychological Processes*. Cambridge, MA: Harvard University Press.

Vygotsky, L.S. (1987) Thinking and speech. In R.W. Rieber and A.S. Carton (eds) *The Collected Works of L.S. Vygotsky, Volume 1: Problems of General Psychology* (pp. 39–285). New York: Plenum Press. (Original work published 1934.)

Wang, L.P. and Zhang, L.J. (2019) Peter Skehan's influence in research on task difficulty: A bibliometric analysis using CiteSpace. In Z.E. Wen and M.J. Ahmadian (eds) *Researching L2 Task Performance and Pedagogy: In Honour of Peter Skehan* (pp. 183–196). Philadelphia, PA: John Benjamins.

Wei, X., Zhang, L.J. and Zhang, W.X. (2020) Associations of L1-to-L2 rhetorical transfer with L2 writers' perception of L2 writing difficulty and L2 writing proficiency. *Journal of English for Academic Purposes* 47(100907), 1–14. https://doi.org/10.1016/j.jeap.2020.100907.

Wenger, E. (1998) *Communities of Practice: Learning, Meaning, and Identity*. New York, NY: Cambridge University Press.

Xu, L.L. and Zhang, L.J. (2019) L2 doctoral students' experiences in thesis writing in an English-medium university in New Zealand. *Journal of English for Academic Purposes* 41 (100779), 1–13.

Zhang, D.L. and Zhang, L.J. (2019) Metacognition and self-regulated learning (SRL) in second foreign language teaching. In X. Gao (ed.) *Second Handbook of English Language Teaching* (pp. 883–897). Cham: Springer Nature.

Zhang, L. and Zhang, L.J. (2021) Fostering stance-taking as a sustainable goal in developing EFL students' academic writing skills: Exploring the effects of explicit instruction on academic writing skills and stance deployment. *Sustainability* 13 (4270), 1–20. https://doi.org/10.3390/su13084270.

Zhang, L.J. (2003) Research into Chinese EFL learner strategies: Methods, findings and instructional issues. *RELC Journal* 34 (3), 284-322.

Zhang, L.J. (2010) A dynamic metacognitive systems account of Chinese university students' knowledge about EFL reading. *TESOL Quarterly* 44 (2), 320–353.

Zhang, L.J. (2013) Making a difference in bilingual education: Biliteracy learning as curricular appropriation. In M. East and S. May (eds) *Making a Difference in Education and Social Policy* (pp. 173–189). Auckland, New Zealand: Pearson Education.

Zhang, L.J. (2014) A dynamic metacognitive systems perspective on developing academic writing skills: Writing across the genre and the curriculum. In H.P. Widodo and N.T. Zacharias (eds) *Recent Issues in English Language Education: Challenges and Directions* (pp. 161–179). Surakarta, Central Java, Indonesia: Sebelas Maret University Press.

Zhang, L.J. (2016) Reflections on the pedagogical imports of western practices for professionalizing ESL/EFL writing and writing-teacher education. *Australian Review of Applied Linguistics* 39 (3), 203–232.

Zhang, L.J. and Qin, L.T. (2018) Validating a questionnaire on EFL writers' metacognitive awareness of writing strategies in multimedia environments. In Haukås A, Bjørke, C. and M. Dypedahl (eds) *Metacognition in Language Learning and Teaching* (pp. 157–179). London & New York: Routledge.

Zhang, L.J. and Cheng, X.L. (2021) Examining the effects of comprehensive written corrective feedback on L2 EAP students' linguistic performance: A mixed-methods study. *Journal of English for Academic Purpose,* 49, 101043, 1–14.

Zhang, L.J., Aryadoust, V. and Zhang, D.L. (2016) Taking stock of the effects of strategies-based instruction on writing in Chinese and English in Singapore primary schools. In R.E. Silver and W. Bokhorst-Heng (eds) *Quadrilingual Education in Singapore: Pedagogical Innovation in Language Education* (pp. 103–126). New York, NY: Springer.

Zhang, L.J., Thomas, N. and Qin, T.L. (2019) Language learning strategy research in *System:* Looking back and looking forward. *System* 84, 87–93. 10.1016/j.system.2019.06.002.

Index

Academic writing 3, 4, 6, 8, 9, 10, 19, 38–41, 43, 56, 67, 85, 100, 101, 102, 131, 147, 149
  academic discourse 9, 93, 99, 100, 101
  academic identity 10, 87, 88, 102
  academic literacies 7, 10, 64, 65, 77, 84–85, 89, 107–110, 126–128
Accuracy 19, 20, 31, 154, 155
Agency 10, 79–80, 108, 109–112, 118, 122, 126–128
Anxiety 81, 149
Appeal, see *rhetoric*
Argument, see *rhetoric*
Assessment, see *language testing*

Beliefs 108, 111, 115–118, 126
Bias, see *language testing*
Biography, see *genre*
Border-crossing 33, 147, 149, 151, 152, 154, 155, 157, 159

CAF-triad 19
CEFR, see *Common European Framework of Reference for Languages*
Chinese 39, 40–41, 57, 131, 132, 133, 137, 138–144, 148, 154
Common European Framework of Reference for Languages (CEFR) 1, 18, 19, 20
Communities of practice 99, 152–153, 159
Complex Dynamic Systems Theory 44
Complexity 19, 20, 39, 41–45, 46–60, 155
  Complex Nominal 45, 50, 52, 55–57, 59
  Phrasal Complexity 43, 49, 51, 56–57, 59
  Syntactic complexity 41–42, 48, 53, 54, 55–57, 58, 59, 60
Content-related factors, see *language testing*
Criteria, scoring 22–23
  Answer to the prompt 28–30
  Content 28–30
  Formal correctness 32–33
  Operational criteria 31
  Structure and coherence 28–31
  Quality of language 28
Culture 2–4, 5, 9, 32, 66, 143, 154
  Cultural contexts 66, 148, 153
  Cultural transfer 10, 33
  Writing culture 6, 11, 33

Dialogical approach 108, 110
  Dialogical perspective 112, 115, 116, 118, 123
Disciplinary literacy 64, 66
Disciplines 2, 4–7, 9, 10, 39, 64–67, 77–81, 87–88, 100–102, 107, 153, 159

English, varieties 7, 8, 84, 85, 91, 159
  International English (IE) 7, 8
  World Englishes (WE) 7, 160
  Standard English 8
  English as additional language (EAL) 10, 64, 66, 73, 84–88, 102, 147, 148–149, 158
  English as a foreign language (EFL) 148, 153, 154, 163
English for academic purposes (EAP) 147, 152, 153, 160
Ethos, see *rhetoric*

Feedback 58, 60, 93, 95, 102, 152, 160
Finite Verb Token Ratio 47
Finnish 107, 110, 112, 113, 116
Fluency 19, 20, 22, 154, 155
Functional grammar 66

Gatekeeper 1, 2, 10, 18,33
Generic support 86, 93–95
Genre 4, 5–6, 9, 66, 67, 70, 72, 78–81, 109, 122, 133, 154
  Biography 66, 67, 70, 72, 73, 74
  Report 66, 67, 70, 72, 73, 74

Genre teaching-learning cycle 78–79, 81
Grammatical conventions 67, 70, 74–76, 77

Historical body 111, 112, 120, 122

Identity 107, 125, 151, 154, 157, 160
        See also *academic identity*
Idiosyncrasy 57
Imagined communities 151
Immigrants 108, 127

Language testing 1–2, 7, 18, 19
        Assessment 7, 18–22, 31–33, 88–89
        Bias 1–2, 7, 18
        Content-related factors 21, 22–23,
                28–31
        Test-takers 8–9, 23, 26, 30–32
        See also *rating*
Logos, see *rhetoric*

Mean Clause Length 42, 47
Mezzanine word 6
Monolingual ideology 9
Multilevel Synchrony Method 45

Narrative inquiry 89, 90
Nexus analysis 111–112, 121
Norwegian 4, 11, 19, 20, 24, 30

Pathos, see *rhetoric*
PELA (Post-entry language assessment)
        88–89, 102
Persuasion, see *rhetoric*
Phrasal Elaboration 40

Rater bias, see *bias*
Register 4, 5, 6, 39, 41, 66, 67, 70, 73–74,
        78, 81
        Academic registers 73 –75
        Everyday registers 73–75
Rhetoric 3–4, 5, 20, 41, 74, 78, 87, 131–135,
        140, 141, 143–144, 154
        Appeal 131, 134, 135, 140, 141, 143,
                144
        Argument 149, 155–156, 159, 160

Contrastive rhetoric 3, 4, 149, 155,
        156
Ethos 133–135, 138, 141, 142, 143, 144
Intercultural rhetoric 154
Logos 133–135, 13 8, 139, 140, 141,
        143
Pathos 133–135, 136, 138, 139, 140,
        141, 142, 143, 144
Persuasion 131–135, 1 37, 138, 140,
        143–144
Rhetorical differences 4, 144, 149,
        150, 155, 157 148, 157
Rating 7, 8, 11, 30, 31
        Rater bias 7, 18, 22
        Rater variability 7–8, 23, 24, 30
        Raters 9, 20–24, 31
Reading styles 21, 31
Reading-writing connection 78, 79, 107,
        108, 109, 117, 118, 122, 149
Report, see *genre*

Schema 158
Scientific language 6, 7
Science literacy 67
Sociocultural theory 152
Spanish 11, 19–21, 30–33, 31–33
Style 5, 9, 23, 24, 28, 31, 87
Subordination 40
Supervisors 87, 89, 93, 95–97, 98, 100
Swedish 6, 7
Systemic functional linguistics 6, 66

Test-takers, see *language testing*
Testing, see *language testing*
Transfer 3, 20, 159
        See also *cultural transfer*

Vietnamese 11, 19–21, 30–33

Writing development 43, 85, 86, 87, 93, 95,
        102, 110
Writing skills 40, 85, 95, 108, 115, 147,
        148–148, 152, 157, 158
Writing strategies 155, 157
Writing-teacher preparation 148

CPSIA information can be obtained
at www.ICGtesting.com
Printed in the USA
LVHW080144060322
712723LV00012B/738